Legal Scholars and Scholarship in the People's Republic of China

HARVARD EAST ASIAN MONOGRAPHS 448

Legal Scholars and Scholarship in the People's Republic of China

The First Generation (1949–1992)

Nongji Zhang

Published by the Harvard University Asia Center
Distributed by Harvard University Press
Cambridge (Massachusetts) and London 2022

© 2022 by The President and Fellows of Harvard College
Printed in the United States of America

The Harvard University Asia Center publishes a monograph series and, in coordination with the Fairbank Center for Chinese Studies, the Korea Institute, the Reischauer Institute of Japanese Studies, and other facilities and institutes, administers research projects designed to further scholarly understanding of China, Japan, Korea, Vietnam, and other Asian countries. The Center also sponsors projects addressing multidisciplinary, transnational, and regional issues in Asia.

Cataloging-in-Publication Data is on file at the Library of Congress.

ISBN 9780674267961 (hardcover; acid free paper)

Index by Alexander Trotter

♾ Printed on acid-free paper

Last figure below indicates year of this printing

31 30 29 28 27 26 25 24 23 22

Contents

Foreword

Harvard Law School's East Asian Legal Studies (EALS) program is honored to have facilitated the publication of Dr. Zhang Nongji's study entitled *Legal Scholars and Scholarship in the People's Republic of China: The First Generation (1949–1992)*.

Dr. Zhang is extraordinarily learned about Chinese law and legal history and, as such, has been a treasured and generous resource not only for generations of faculty and students at Harvard but for scholars throughout North America, East Asia, and beyond. She has built Harvard Law School's collection of materials pertinent to Chinese law into the Western academic world's best through a keen eye for quality and legendary ingenuity and determination. Additionally, she has created and maintained a bank of syllabi for all manner of courses on Chinese law and legal history that has proven of great value for both experienced hands in this field and younger scholars finding their own voice. And she always has time for anyone interested in advancing their knowledge of Chinese law. Indeed, I never begin a project regarding Chinese law without seeking her counsel.

Dr. Zhang earned her first degree (in law) at Beijing University, where her father has been a revered professor. Subsequently, she earned a master's in library science at Simmons College and a doctorate in law, policy, and society at Northeastern. To this day, she remains an avid student of law and life.

Dr. Zhang's book will add wonderfully to our understanding of law in the formative years of the People's Republic of China (PRC). The product of years of research, supported in part by a Douglas W. Bryant Fellowship, the book offers compact but enormously insightful accounts of a broad array of the first two generations of legal scholars in the PRC. I have read the work of many of them and been privileged to know many personally (including Gong Xiangrui, Jiang Ping, Li Buyun, Luo Haocai, and Wang Tieya), and I can attest that Dr. Zhang has done a marvelous job of capturing what is most important and telling about them. Scholars of Chinese law will find this work invaluable, but it also will be of interest and use to a much broader range of people interested in China's modern history and the challenges of trying to build respect for law in a one-party state.

Congratulations, Dr. Zhang, on your accomplishment, and on behalf of your many admirers, thank you.

William P. Alford

The Jerome A. and Joan L. Cohen
Professor of East Asian Legal Studies
Harvard Law School

Acknowledgments

I am grateful to the Harvard University Library Professional Development Committee and the Harvard East Asian Legal Studies Program for their financial support, which made my field research possible. My heartfelt gratitude goes out to Professor William P. Alford and Robert L. Buckwalter for their recommendations for me to obtain a Douglas W. Bryant Fellowship. Their encouragement has kept me going all these years. It has been my great fortune to work under Professor Alford's guidance. His rich knowledge of Chinese law and ample research experience make his many insights extremely valuable to the project.

My appreciation also goes out to the following individuals whose engagement and genuine support made my selection of featured scholars effective and relevant: Shen Zongling (沈宗灵), Zhu Suli (朱苏力), He Weifang (贺卫方), and Zhang Qi (张骐) from Peking University Law School; Zheng Chengsi (郑成思) from the Institute of Law, Chinese Academy of Social Science; Fang Liufang (方流芳) from the China University of Political Science and Law; Liang Zhiping (梁治平) from the Institute of Chinese Culture, Chinese Academy of Arts; Yu Jinsong (余劲松) and Wang Chunyan (王春燕) from Renmin University Law School; Zhang Mingkai (张明楷) from Tsinghua University Law School; Yuan Shuhong (袁曙宏) from the National Academy of Governance; and Yu Xingzhong (於兴中) from Cornell University Law School. In addition, I am especially grateful to Zang Dongsheng (臧东升) of the University of Washington School of Law and Long Weiqiu (龙卫球) of Beihang Law School for their advice and assistance in selecting and finalizing the entries of scholars for this project. It was a great pleasure to work with Professors Zang and Long.

My colleagues Lisa Junghahn and John Hostage, as well as Alonzo Emery, associate director of East Asian Legal Studies and lecturer on law at Harvard Law School, provided editorial assistance. John's patient and diligent efforts have helped to make the publication sound and polished. I learned a great deal from John, Lisa, and Alonzo during the process of editing and refining this manuscript and owe them a big thank you!

Under the guidance of Bob Graham, director of publications at Harvard University Asia Center, my manuscript went through the Center's publication process and a peer review process. Bob's advice and instructions were instrumental for the successful publication of the book. I am grateful for his guidance!

Abbreviations

CASS	Chinese Academy of Social Sciences
CLEEC	Committee on Legal Education Exchange with China
GATT	General Agreement on Tariffs and Trade
LSE	London School of Economics and Political Sciences
NPC	National People's Congress
PRC	People's Republic of China
ROC	Republic of China
TRIPS	Agreement on Trade-Related Aspects of Intellectual Property Rights
UN	United Nations
WIPO	World Intellectual Property Organization
WTO	World Trade Organization

Historical Events and Names

Anti-Rightist Movement: took place between 1957 and 1959 and consisted of a series of campaigns to purge alleged Rightists. The campaigns were instigated by Chairman Mao Zedong and saw the political persecution of some 550,000 individuals, mostly those intellectuals who appeared to favor capitalism or criticized the government.

Chinese Civil War: a war fought between the Kuomintang-led government and the Communist Party of China, which lasted intermittently between 1927 and 1949.

Cultural Revolution: called in full the Great Proletarian Cultural Revolution; launched by Chinese Communist Party chairman Mao Zedong during his last decade in power (1966–1976) in an attempt to renew the spirit of the Chinese Revolution. Fearing that China would develop along the lines of the Soviet model and concerned about his place in history, Mao threw China's cities into turmoil in a monumental effort to reverse the historic processes underway.

Great Leap Forward Campaign: took place between 1958 and early 1960 to organize China's vast population, especially in large-scale rural communes, to meet China's industrial and agricultural problems. It was a movement to combat the failure of the Soviet model of industrialization in China. However, it is widely considered to have caused the Great Chinese Famine between 1959 and 1961, with an estimated death toll due to starvation that ranged into the tens of millions.

Kuomintang: translated as the Nationalist Party of China; founded by Sun Yat-sen and led by Chiang Kai-shek. It was the ruling party of China until 1949 and is a major political party in Taiwan today. The Kuomintang-led government was named the Republic of China.

1911 Revolution: also known as the Chinese Revolution or Xinhai Revolution; a revolution led by Sun Yat-sen that overthrew China's last dynasty and established the Republic of China.

"One country, two systems": refers to the strategic situation that, as a nation, mainland China has a socialist system while Hong Kong, Macau, and Taiwan remain capitalist societies. This policy design was initiated by China's leader Deng Xiaoping in the early 1980s.

Peking University: Beijing University; Chinese name: Beijing Daxue (北京大学)

Second Sino-Japanese War: also known the War of Resistance against Japanese Aggression (1937–1945); a military conflict that mainly took place between the Republic of China and Japan.

Sino-American Indemnity Scholarship: known as the Boxer Indemnity Scholarship; funded by Boxer Indemnity and established by President Roosevelt; a scholarship program for Chinese students to receive education in the United States. The program, set up in 1909, funded the selection, preparatory training, transportation to the United States, and study for the scholarship beneficiaries.

Tsinghua University: Qinghua University; Chinese name: Qinghua Daxue (清华大学)

INTRODUCTION

In this book, I hope to introduce English-speaking researchers, students, and librarians to Chinese legal scholars and their scholarship. As a recipient of a Douglas W. Bryant Fellowship at Harvard University,[1] I started the project in 2003 and completed my first draft in 2006. I then took a break for other priorities and responsibilities. In 2016, after a ten-year hiatus, I came to realize that three things had since changed since I had started. First, some scholars who were alive in 2003 were no longer with us. I was very fortunate to have been able to meet and interview some of them previously. Second, more resources on Chinese legal scholarship and scholars had become available, including Evelyn Ma's article[2] and the three-volume set *Introduction to the Achievement of Famous Chinese Scientists*

---

1. Supported by a gift from the late Charles Tanenbaum (class of 1934), the scholarship is awarded to individual Harvard librarians in support of their independent scholarly research. The winners of the scholarship are chosen from competing applicants and their research proposals by a jury. For more information, see Harvard University (website), "Douglas W. Bryant Fellowship Program," https://beta.projects.iq.harvard.edu/launch/bryant (accessed Oct. 5, 2020).

2. Evelyn Ma, "Scholarly Chinese Legal Works in the Vernacular: A Selective Topical Treatise Finder (Part I)," *International Journal of Legal Information* 39, no. 3 (2011): 295–311; and "Scholarly Chinese Legal Works in the Vernacular: A Selective Topical Treatise Finder (Part II),"*International Journal of Legal Information* 41, no. 2 (2013): 162–178.

in the Twentieth Century: Law.[3] Finally, I had the opportunity to evaluate the relevance of the project in an evolved context. After all these years, I find that my selection of scholars has remained sound and that this book is unique, useful, and current. New materials, such as Ma's article, cover a different generation of scholars, offer a different focus, or are not available in English.

The most challenging part of this project was selecting the featured scholars. In 2003, when I began working on the project, existing materials in print or online offered little guidance in this task. The latest such work, *A Dictionary of Chinese Legal Scholars,*[4] was published in 1991, and its coverage was limited and outdated. China's Baidu Encyclopedia,[5] equivalent to Wikipedia, was about two years old and had hardly any articles on Chinese jurists. As U.S. interest in Chinese law and China's legal publications increased, there was a need for a research guide on Chinese legal scholars, not only for my own work in selecting legal publications for the Harvard Law School Library but also for students, researchers, and librarians at large. Therefore, I decided to select a group of featured scholars from scratch.

Initially, I had four criteria in choosing the scholars: they must be modern and/or contemporary scholars from the end of the nineteenth century to the present; they were pioneers or very influential in their fields; they have a robust record of scholarly publications; and their entire legal careers were based in mainland China. With these features in mind, I took the following steps in the selection process.

First, I conducted a survey to solicit recommendations from legal scholars in the United States and Hong Kong. Then, to make a preliminary list of featured scholars, I combined the names provided in the survey with names listed among the existing literature and reference tools. I

3. Jiang Ping, et al., eds. *20 Shiji Zhongguo Zhiming Kexuejia Xueshu Chengjiu Gailan: Faxuejuan* 20 世纪中国知名科学家学术成就概览: 法学卷 [Introduction to the Achievement of Famous Chinese Scientists in the Twentieth Century: Law Volumes] (Beijing: Kexue Chubanshe, 2014).

4. Wang Yuming 王玉明, ed., *Zhongguo Faxuejia Cidian* 中国法学家词典 [A Dictionary of Chinese Legal Scholars] (Beijing: Zhongguo Laodong Chubanshe, 1991).

5. Baidu Encyclopedia is an online open-source encyclopedia, compiled by experts in specialized fields, and developed by Baidu, Inc. The company was founded by Robin Li in 2000 in Beijing and provides the most popular internet search engine in China.

took this list to China in 2004 to consult with prominent legal scholars in various fields from several academic institutions. In the end, I finalized the selection based on the opinions collected from my interviews with the research community.

Of course, Chinese scholars have made many different types of contributions to the development of Chinese law. Scholars such as Pan Handian (潘汉典) spent most of their academic lives translating important works of foreign law. These works are stepping-stones and eye-opening materials for others to generate new ideas and theories. Other jurists like Dong Biwu (董必武) and Zhang Zhirang (张志让) held important political and judicial positions, inspiring a generation of scholars through their speeches and talks, but they produced few lengthy publications. For the purposes of a work of bibliographic reference, I did not include these scholars in this book. I apologize to these great jurists and to anyone else left out. I also acknowledge the paucity of female scholars in this publication. For historical reasons, influential female scholars were scarce in the field of legal studies during the period covered in this book. However, my original list of selected scholars featured more female scholars from recent generations. Perhaps a future project could introduce these younger scholars of Chinese legal studies.

The modern history of Chinese law started in the late Qing dynasty (or the mid-nineteenth century). Over the years, many accomplished legal scholars have emerged. As mentioned earlier, originally I intended to address all major jurists including such late Qing dynasty scholars as Shen Jiaben (沈家本) and Liang Qichao (梁启超), such Republican era scholars as Wu Jingxiong (吴经熊) and Yang Zhaolong (杨兆龙), and such contemporary scholars as Wang Liming (王利明) and Ji Weidong (季卫东). However, after I started writing the manuscript, I realized that my ambition to discuss all of the scholars on my prepared list was unrealistic. The work to study and address each scholar took me much more time than I originally expected. My slow pace of research and writing would have prevented me from completing the project in a timely fashion. Discussing all the scholars on my list at once would be an enormous task to undertake in my spare time. Therefore, I decided to narrow the scope of my writing and only focus on a specific group of scholars—namely, the first generation of legal scholars of the People's Republic of China from 1949 to 1992.

There is an instant advantage in presenting this group of scholars. As a law student in China in the 1980s, I studied under or have had knowledge of most of these scholars. I am more familiar with this generation of legal scholars than those from earlier and later generations. However, the most important reason I chose this group of legal scholars is their distinctive experience and features that deserve exploration and recognition.

To understand the uniqueness of this group of Chinese legal scholars, I should provide some background information on Chinese law and legal history. After all, the political, economic, social, and ideological changes in China in the second half of the twentieth century had a significant impact on the development of these scholars and their scholarship.

China has one of the oldest legal traditions in the world. Until the twentieth century, its legal system was based on the Confucian philosophy of social control through moral education and the legalist emphasis on codified law and criminal sanction.[6] The 1911 Revolution[7] led by Sun Yat-sen ended two thousand years of dynastic rule in China. The subsequent Republic of China adopted a largely Western-style legal code in the civil law tradition (specifically German influenced).[8]

Following the Civil War[9] and the subsequent Japanese occupation,[10] the Communist Party emerged victorious and overthrew the Kuomintang government.[11] Led by Mao Zedong and the Communist Party, the

6. For discussions about Confucianism and the legalist influence on Chinese law, see Albert Hung-yee Chen, *An Introduction to the Legal System of the People's Republic of China*, 4th ed. (LexisNexis, 2011), 12–16.

7. The 1911 Revolution, also known as the Chinese Revolution or Xinhai Revolution, was led by Sun Yat-sen. It overthrew China's last dynasty and established the Republic of China. For information, see Office of the Historian, "The Chinese Revolution of 1911," https://history.state.gov/milestones/1899-1913/chinese-rev (accessed Dec. 5, 2020).

8. This legal tradition continues in Taiwan today.

9. The Chinese Civil War, fought between the Kuomintang-led government and the Communist Party of China, lasted intermittently between 1927 and 1949.

10. The Japanese occupation of China lasted from 1937 to 1945.

11. Kuomintang, translated as the Nationalist Party of China, was founded by Sun Yat-sen and led by Chiang Kai-shek. It was the ruling party of China until 1949 and remains a major political party on Taiwan today. The Kuomintang-led government was named the Republic of China.

establishment of the People's Republic of China (PRC) in 1949 started a new legal regime. Today it is officially called "the socialist legal system with Chinese characteristics."[12] Nevertheless, earlier traditions from Chinese history have retained some influence.

The first thirty years of the People's Republic of China were a legal disaster. China's new political system based on Marxist-Leninist ideas was not compatible with the old legal system. The Communist Party abolished the old national codes. The new legal system relied heavily on the Soviet Russian legal system. By 1957, this system, a socialist version of a continental Western European legal system, proved a failure. Three major periods of ideological turmoil ensued: the Anti-Rightist Movement (1957–1959),[13] the Great Leap Forward Campaign (1958–1960),[14] and the Cultural Revolution (1966–1976).[15] Together they demolished the formal

12. In 1997, the report of the Fifteenth National Congress of the Communist Party of China included "Forming a Socialist Legal System with Chinese Characteristics by 2010." See Gao Minquan 高民权 and Wan Yi 万一, "The Proposal and Formation of the Socialist Legal System with Chinese Characteristics," http://www.npc.gov.cn/zgrdw /npc/xinwen/rdlt/fzjs/2010-12/29/content_1613444.htm (accessed July 11, 2021).

13. The Anti-Rightist Movement took place between 1957 and 1959. It consisted of a series of campaigns to purge alleged Rightists. The campaigns were instigated by Chairman Mao Zedong and saw the political persecution of 550,000 individuals, mostly those intellectuals who appeared to favor capitalism or criticized the government. For more information about the Anti-Rightist Movement, see Christine Vidal. *The 1957–1958 Anti-Rightist Campaign in China: History and Memory (1978–2014)*, https://halshs.archives -ouvertes.fr/halshs-01306892/ (accessed Dec. 5, 2020).

14. The Great Leap Forward Campaign took place between 1958 and early 1960 to organize China's vast population, especially in large-scale rural communes, to meet China's industrial and agricultural problems. It was a movement to combat the failure of the Soviet model of industrialization in China. However, it is widely considered to have caused the Great Chinese Famine between 1959 and 1961, with an estimated death toll due to starvation that ranged in the tens of millions. See *Encyclopedia Britannica Online*, s.v. "Great Leap Forward," https://www.britannica.com/event/Great-Leap-Forward (accessed Dec. 5, 2020).

15. "The Cultural Revolution, in full the Great Proletarian Cultural Revolution, was an upheaval launched by Chinese Communist Party Chairman Mao Zedong during his last decade in power (1966–1976) to renew the spirit of the Chinese Revolution. Fearing that China would develop along the lines of the Soviet model and concerned about his own place in history, Mao threw China's cities into turmoil in a monumental effort to reverse the historic processes underway." *Encyclopedia Britannica Online*, s.v. "Cultural Revolution," https://www.britannica.com/event/Cultural-Revolution (accessed Dec. 5, 2020).

legal systems, Soviet or otherwise.[16] The Communist Party of China believed that creating a legal system would restrict its power and create elites, which would ultimately harm the socialist revolution. At the same time, there was a perception that a formal legal system was largely unnecessary since the economy was centrally controlled and conflicts could thus be resolved through administrative means or mediation without reference to legal rights and obligations.[17] Until 1978, there was little effort within China to create a legal system.

After Mao's death in 1976, the party leader Deng Xiaoping decided to change the country's political and economic course. Deng's "Reform and Open Door" policy in the late 1970s began China's current rapid economic development. It initiated the ongoing transition to a market economy and has had enormous implications for the country's legal development. The 1980s and 1990s saw the massive and rapid enactment of laws. Since then, China has formed an increasingly sophisticated legal system and built up the institutions and the personnel necessary to apply this new body of legislation.[18]

For over one hundred years since 1911, Chinese legal scholars played various roles in the tumultuous and transforming political, economic, and legal landscape. Yet there are no clear divisions among different groups/generations in different historical periods. Some scholars may have lived in two or more historical periods but were most active, productive, or influential in one era. For example, Yang Zhaolong (1904–1979), an important scholar in private international law and jurisprudence, lived in both pre- and post-Communist China. Due to his tragic life during the political turmoil between 1957 and 1976, his most important works were published before the establishment of the PRC. For this reason, I put him into the earlier group of scholars and did not include him in this

16. Jerome A. Cohen, "A Looming Crisis for China's Legal System," *Foreign Policy*, Feb. 22, 2016, https://foreignpolicy.com/2016/02/22/a-looming-crisis-for-chinas-legal-system/ (accessed July 2, 2021).

17. Liu Jingjing "Overview of the Chinese Legal System," *ELR China Update*, January–March 2013, https://elr.info/sites/default/files/chinaupdate1.1.pdf (accessed July 2, 2021).

18. Volker Behr, "Development of a New Legal System in the People's Republic of China," *Louisiana Law Review* 67 (2007): 1163, https://digitalcommons.law.lsu.edu /lalrev/vol67/iss4/8.

book. The same treatment applies to other scholars of earlier and later generations.

The distinctive feature of the first generation of PRC legal scholars is resilience in the face of interruptions of their work, career, and research by political movements in China. This group of scholars received their education between the 1920s and 1960s, either in China or abroad. As young or new scholars, they should have had their most productive years from the 1950s to 1970s. Instead, they were purged and/or sent to the labor camps for reeducation during the Anti-Rightist Movement and the Cultural Revolution. These scholars were also forced to learn and accept Soviet legal doctrines and the Communist Party's policies and ideologies. They were denied all access to scholarship from the Western world between the 1950s and 1976 and published hardly anything academic between 1965 and 1977. When they reemerged, they were typically very active and productive in the academic world of the 1980s and 1990s. They became established, influential, and well known by 1992, when Deng Xiaoping gave his famous "Southern Tour Speech" to push forward the implementation of economic reform and the opening-up policy.[19] The speech marked the moment when China's socialist market economy was confirmed, and many new laws were in the works. To serve, address, and engage with the rapid development of China's economic reform alongside with law making and legal reform, these scholars became the explorers, creators, pioneers, and teachers of the new Communist legal regime. They were responsible for the full-scale recovery and reconstruction of legal studies, while simultaneously cultivating new disciplines and branches of learning. They separated Chinese law theories from political doctrines and defined legal studies as an independent field of social science.

The subsequent generations of Chinese legal scholars were their students and only received their education after China reopened college entrance exams in 1977. With uninterrupted education and research lives, they started to rise to prominence after 1992 when legal education and research entered a rapid growth period in China. Meanwhile, it was the ideas, philosophies, and experiences of the first generation of PRC scholars

19. Kerry Brown, "Deng Xiaoping's Southern Tour," in *Berkshire Encyclopedia of China*, vol. 5, edited by Linsun Cheng, 2667 (Great Barrington, MA: Berkshire, 2009).

that helped to shape the field of Chinese legal studies as we see it today. From their scholarship, we can see where it has come from, where it has been, and where it is going.

Because this is an English-language publication, I have provided English translations of the titles in the text and have given their original Chinese citations and references in the footnotes. Names of institutions are given in English in the form adopted by the institution, if any, such as Peking University. For the convenience of the readers, I provide bibliographies of English publications written by the scholars.[20] At the suggestion of one of my manuscript reviewers, I have arranged the chapters in ascending order of the scholars' birth years. Scholars born in the same year appear alphabetically.

I trust that this book will reveal to the English-speaking world the leading first-generation legal scholars of the PRC along with their educational backgrounds, major academic contributions, and important works. I hope to provide an essential tool and resource for the study of Chinese law, useful for faculty, students, scholars, librarians, and anyone who is interested in the field.

---

20. The bibliographies were generated from WorldCat (https://www.worldcat.org/). I apologize for any omissions of entries.

1. Zhang Youyu (张友渔)

(1899–1992)

Constitutional Law

A legal scholar, politician, and journalist, Zhang Youyu was an architect of China's legal system. He led China's mainstream ideology of legislation during the late 1970s and 1980s[1] and made major contributions to the creation of the Constitution of the People's Republic of China (1982).

Educational Background

Zhang was born in Lingshi (灵石) County of Shanxi Province. He graduated from the No. 1 Normal School of Shanxi Province[2] in 1923. In the same year, he entered the Law Department of National Beijing University of Law and Political Science.[3] In 1927, he graduated from the university and joined the Chinese Communist Party. He was sent to Japan three times, in 1930, 1932, and 1934, by the party to study and conduct political activities.[4]

---

1. See Zhou Wangsheng, "Zhang Youyu Lifa Sixiang Jishu Shang."
2. Shanxi Diyi Shifan Xuexiao 山西第一师范学校 [The No. 1 Normal School of Shanxi Province].
3. Beijing Fazheng Daxue 北京法政大学 [National Beijing University of Law and Political Science].
4. See "Zhang Youyu."

Career Highlights

After coming back from Japan, until 1949, Zhang worked as a journalist and a professor in many cities, including Tianjin, Beijing, Chongqing, and Hong Kong. His positions allowed him to make personal connections with people from the opposition party (the Nationalist Party) and enabled him to work undercover for the Communist Party. He was a prominent journalist and worked as an editor or chief editor for several important newspapers, including the *World Daily*, *Xinhua Daily*, and *China Commercial News*. He also created two magazines: *World Forum* and *Times Culture*. He taught at several universities including Yenching (燕京) University, China University, and Beiping (北平) University. The subjects he taught included constitutional law, labor law, journalism, and Japanese studies.

After 1949, Zhang was involved in legislation, politics, teaching, and management. In 1958, he was appointed director of the Law Institute of the Chinese Academy of Social Sciences (CASS). Among other responsibilities, he oversaw editorial work for the law journal *Political and Legal Research*.[5] During the Cultural Revolution, his academic and political positions were taken from him. He was forced to do physical labor until 1975. After that, he became the adviser to the Law Institute of CASS and associate director of the Editorial Board of the Encyclopedia. He also held the positions of executive director of the Law Committee of the Standing Committee of the National People's Congress, vice president of CASS, president of the China Law Society, and vice mayor of Beijing and Tianjin, among others. He taught at CASS and Peking University.

Research Areas and Publications

In both political and academic circles, Zhang had a reputation of daring to speak truth. He is often quoted as saying, "When I speak and write,

---

5. *Zhengfa Yanjiu* 政法研究 [Political and Legal Research] (Beijing: Zhongguo Zhengzhi Falü Xuehui, 1954–1964).

I always speak my own mind. I don't copy or follow blindly. I oppose dogmatism and don't cater to fashion. It's not like everyone said that, or any authoritative person said, so I followed. Rather, I thought about it, researched it, and thought it was right, so I said."[6] He stood at the forefront of legal research and engaged in the dissemination of Marxist legal and political views. He often had independent explanations of politically sensitive issues. For example, he pointed out: "The relationship between the Communist Party and the People's Congress is that the Party leads the Congress politically, rather than organizationally becoming a superior organ of the People's Congress. . . . The Party's leadership of the judiciary mainly refers to the leadership of the principles, lines, and policies, and refers to the supervision of the judiciary in dealing with cases and equipping cadres, which does not replace the specific business of political and legal institutions."[7]

According to his colleague Professor Wang Jiafu (王家福), Zhang's scholarship was based on the following principles: integration of theory with practice, guidance with Marxism, meticulous scholarship based on accurate and verified data, academic freedom, and equality before the truth.[8]

Zhang wrote a variety of articles and books on journalism, politics, international relations, and law. He also published poems, short stories, and movie reviews. He is best known for his works on journalism and law. In journalism, his major works include *Thirty Years of a Newsman* (1982)[9] and *Theory and Phenomenon of Journalism* (1936).[10] His views on journalism were based on the position of class control. He believed that

6. Zhang Youyu, "Wode Zhixue Jingyan" 我的治学经验 [My Research Experience], *Faxue Yanjiu* 法学研究 4 (1989).

7. Zhang Youyu, "Yige Bixu Renzhen Yanjiu He Tantao De Wenti" 一个必须认真研究和探讨的问题 [An Issue that Must Be Carefully Studied and Discussed], in *Zhang Youyu Xueshu Jinghualu* 张友渔学术精华录 [Best Academic Works of Zhang Youyu] (Beijing: Beijing Shifan Xueyuan Chubanshe, 1988), 148.

8. Wang Jiafu et al., "Gongye Changzai Fengfan Yongcun Jinian Zhuming Faxuejia Zhang Youyu Tongzhi."

9. *Baoren Shengya Sanshinian* 报人生涯三十年 [Thirty Years of a Newsman] (Chongqing: Chongqing Chubanshe, 1982).

10. *Xinwen Zhi Lilun Yu Xianxiang* 新聞之理論與現象 [Theory and Phenomenon of Journalism] (Taiyuan: Zhongwai Yuwen Xuehui, 1936).

the news media were an instrument of the ruling class. The ruling class used news media to control ideology. Therefore, it was very difficult to separate the news media from politics. It was impossible for newspapers to stay neutral and to have freedom of speech. As long as the government existed, the people would not enjoy absolute freedom of speech. Freedom of speech was only a part of the freedom of politics.

In law, Zhang's scholarship spanned the period from the 1930s to his death in 1992. His writings touched on constitutional law, legislation, criminal law, labor law, the rule of law, legal history, human rights, and other topics. Some of his representative works include *On Chinese Constitutionalism* (1944),[11] *A Study of the 1936 Constitutional Draft* (1944),[12] *A Few Issues Concerning Socialist Legal System* (1982),[13] *Discussions on Constitutionalism* (1986),[14] *Best Academic Works of Zhang Youyu* (1988),[15] *Forty Years of PRC's Legal Science* (1989),[16] *Self-Selected Academic Works of Zhang Youyu* (1992),[17] *On Establishment and Improvement of Socialist Democracy and Legal System* (1992),[18] and *A Collection of Theses on Constitutional Law* (2003).[19] As a practical jurist in the early years of China's reconstruction of the legal system, Zhang's scholarship reflected the social development during the 1980s and early 1990s. He proposed that legal studies must be

11. *Zhongguo Xianzheng Lun* 中国宪政论 [On Chinese Constitutionalism] (Chongqing: Shengsheng Chubanshe, 1944).

12. *Wuwu Xiancao Yanjiu* 五五宪草研究 [A Study of the 1936 Constitutional Draft] (Chongqing: Shenghuo Chubanshe, 1944).

13. *Guanyu Shehui Zhuyi Fazhi De Ruogan Wenti* 关于社会主义法制的若干问题 [A Few Issues Concerning Socialist Legal System] (Beijing: Falü Chubanshe, 1982).

14. *Xianzheng Luncong* 宪政论丛 [Discussions on Constitutionalism] (Beijing: Qunzhong Chubanshe, 1986).

15. *Zhang Youyu Xueshu Jinghualu* 张友渔学术精华录 [Best Academic Works of Zhang Youyu] (Beijing: Beijing Shifan Xueyuan Chubanshe, 1988).

16. Zhang Youyu 张友渔 and Wang Shuwen 王叔文, *Zhongguo Faxue Sishinian* 中国法学四十年 [Forty Years of PRC's Legal Science] (Shanghai: Shanghai Renmin Chubanshe, 1989).

17. *Zhang Youyu Xueshu Lunzhu Zixuanji* 张友渔学术论著自选集 [Self-Selected Academic Works of Zhang Youyu] (Beijing: Beijing Shifan Xueyuan Chubanshe, 1992).

18. *Jianli Jianquan Shehui Zhuyi Minzhu Yu Fazhi* 建立健全社会主义民主与法制 [On the Establishment and Improvement of Socialist Democracy and Legal System] (Beijing: Xiandai Chubanshe, 1992).

19. *Xianfa Lunwenji* 宪法论文集 [A Collection of Essays on Constitutional Law] (Beijing: Shehui Kexue Wenxian Chubanshe, 2003).

guided by Marxism, Leninism, and Mao Zedong's thought. Chinese legal studies must take into account China's reality and absorb any useful features of Chinese and foreign law. As a senior leader of both the government and academic institutions, Zhang was an influential figure who helped frame China's ideology of legislation, the rule of law, and its legal system after the Cultural Revolution. He participated in the drafting of China's first Constitution (1954). In the capacity of deputy secretary of the Constitutional Law Revision Committee, he led the creation of China's current Constitution (1982).[20]

References

Chen Hefu 陈荷夫, ed. *Zhang Youyu Huiyilu* 张友渔回忆录 [A Memoir of Zhang Youyu]. Beijing: Beijing Daxue Chubanshe, 1990.

He Lai 何来. "Faxue Jujiang Zhang Youyu" 法学巨匠张友渔 [The Master of Law: Zhang Youyu], *Zhongguo Renda* 中国人大 18 (2010).

Wang Jiafu 王家福, Wu Jianfan 吴建璠, Liu Hainian 刘海年, and Li Buyun 李步云. "Gongye Changzai Fengfan Yongcun Jinian Zhuming Faxuejia Zhang Youyu Tongzhi" 功业常在 风范永存 纪念著名法学家张友渔同志 [Forever Merits and Example: In Memory of the Famous Jurist Comrade Zhang Youyu]. *Faxue Yanjiu* 法学研究 2 (1992).

Zhang Youyu 张友渔. *Zhang Youyu Wenxuan* 张友渔文选 [Selected Works of Zhang Youyu]. Beijing: Falü Chubanshe, 1997.

"Zhang Youyu" 张友渔 [Zhang Youyu]. http://baike.baidu.com/view/111913.htm (accessed June 5, 2016).

Zhou Wangsheng 周旺生. "Zhang Youyu Lifa Sixiang Jishu, Shang, Zhong, Xia" 张友渔立法思想记述, 上中下 [Descriptions of Zhang Youyu's Legislation Ideology, Parts 1, 2, 3]. http://www.gov.cn/guoqing/2018-03/22/content_5276318.htm (accessed Dec. 12, 2020).

20. Zhonghua Renmin Gongheguo Xianfa 中华人民共和国宪法 [The Constitution of the People's Republic of China] (promulgated by the National People's Congress, Dec. 4, 1982, effective Dec. 4, 1982, amended in 1988, 1993, 1999, 2004, and 2018).

2. Chen Shouyi (陈守一)

(1906–1995)

Jurisprudence and Legal Philosophy

Professor of Law at Peking University, Chen Shouyi was a respected educator and an influential scholar. A major cultivator of China's Marxist legal theory, Professor Chen was the chief editor of China's first legal theory book that replaced the Soviet-influenced mainstream textbook.

Educational Background

Chen was born in Pi (邳) County of Jiangsu Province. In 1925, he entered Chaoyang (朝阳) University[1] in Beijing. He graduated from the Department of Politics and Economics in 1929.

Career Highlights

While a student at Chaoyang University, Chen joined the Communist Party and worked undercover for the organization. After graduating from college, he returned to his hometown and taught at a local high school.

---

1. Chaoyang (朝阳) University was a famous law school established in 1912. Its name was changed to China University of Political Science and Law in 1949 (no relation to the current China University of Political Science and Law). It was merged into Renmin University in 1950.

At the recommendation of a friend, he was hired as a clerk in the Justice Department of the Shandong Government. In 1938, he went to work for the Communist Party again and held a position in the Justice Department of the Northern China People's Government. He later held various positions, including director of civil affairs and director of justice. By the time the Communist Party took power in 1949, Chen was the director of the Legal Education Bureau of the national government. In 1954, he was assigned to establish the Law Department of Peking University. He also participated in the establishment of the China University of Political Science and Law. He held the position of director of the Law Department of Peking University until 1981, except during the Cultural Revolution. Because of his refusal to sign the first *dazibao* (big-character poster),[2] which officially launched the Cultural Revolution at Peking University, he became a frequent target of criticism and a victim of those purges. He experienced humiliation and banishment to a labor camp. When the Cultural Revolution ended, he regained his position in 1978. Besides teaching at Peking University, Chen also served as vice president of the China Law Society, president of the Beijing Law Society, president of the Beijing Lawyers Association, and a member of the Law Committee of the Standing Committee of the People's Congress.

Research Areas and Publications

When he came back to the Law Department of Peking University at the age of seventy-two, Chen felt the urgency to achieve certain things. He changed the course name from the Struggles of State Affairs and Policies to the Theory of State and Law, which acted as a first step in separating legal studies from politics. He then founded the Beijing Law Society— an academic organization of legal scholars. He attended various law con-

---

2. *Dazibao* (big-character poster) are handwritten posters displayed in a prominent place, such as a university bulletin board or a city wall, and contain complaints about government officials or policies. *Dazibao* often consist of large Chinese characters created with ink and brush. *Encyclopedia Britannica Online*, s.v. "dazibao," https://www.britannica.com/topic/dazibao (accessed Dec. 5, 2018).

ferences. In 1980, Chen created the *Journal of Legal Studies*,[3] a core legal journal[4] sponsored by the Beijing Law Society. He was the first chief editor of the magazine.

Chen's works appeared mostly after 1978. He emphasized the approach of starting legal research based on China's reality and then going beyond the boundaries of old theories and methodologies. He was a leader in the ideological reform of legal theory in China during the early 1980s. He and his colleagues were the first to move away from the dominant legal theory of the Soviet Union. Instead of "class struggle," as suggested in the old textbooks for over thirty years, his 1981 book[5] defined "law" as the subject of legal studies. He also encouraged scholars and students to study law from an interdisciplinary perspective and urged them to be open to broader and different views, knowledge, and methodologies from economics, sociology, history, and political science.

Chen wrote and coauthored a few influential essays on law, including "Thirty Years of Legal Construction in China" (1979),[6] "Thirty Years of Legal Studies in China" (1980),[7] "On Enhancement of the Legal System" (1981),[8] and "On the Construction and Reform of the Legal System in the Primary Stage of Socialism" (1988).[9] His 1984 book is a collection

3. *Faxue Zazhi* 法学杂志 [Journal of Legal Studies] (Beijing: Faxue Zazhishe, 1980–).

4. Since 2009, the China Law Society has evaluated and created a list of the most important legal journals in China. The journals that made the list are called "core legal journals" and included in the China Legal Science Citation Index (CLSCI). Currently there are twenty-two titles on the CLSCI. For more information, see http://www.zgfxqk.org.cn/WKA3/WebPublication/wkTextContent.aspx?contentID=183bb26f-60b4-4867-8da2-bce73a6809a4 (accessed Dec. 12, 2020).

5. Chen Shouyi 陈守一 and Zhang Hongsheng 张宏生, eds., *Faxue Jichu Lilun* 法学基础理论 [On Basic Theories of Law] (Beijing: Beijing Daxue Chubanshe, 1981).

6. Chen Shouyi 陈守一, Liu Shengping 刘升平, and Zhao Zhenjiang 赵震江, "Woguo Fazhi Jianshe Sanshinian" 我国法制建设三十年 [Thirty Years of Legal Construction in China], *Faxue Yanjiu* 法学研究 1 (1979).

7. "Zhongguo Faxue Sanshinian" 中国法学三十年 [Thirty Years of Legal Studies in China], *Faxue Yanjiu* 法学研究 1 (1980).

8. "Shishi Qiushi Di Jiaqiang Fazhi Jianshe" 实事求是地加强法制建设 [On the Enhancement of the Legal System], *Faxue Zazhi* 法学杂志 1 (1981).

9. "Lun Shehuizhuyi Chuji Jieduan De Fazhi Jianshe Jiqi Gaige" 论社会主义初级阶段的法制建设及其改革 [On the Construction of the Legal System in the Primary Stage of Socialism], *Xiandai Faxue* 现代法学 1 (1988).

of his essays published over the course of the preceding twenty-eight years.[10]

Chen's works explored many important issues in socialist legal studies, including legal education, democracy, and legal construction; the method of legal studies; the origins, nature, and functions of law; rule of law and rule by man; policy and law; reform and law; the law's cultural heritage; and other topics. He believed that a socialist constitution is the general charter for ruling and governing the country. The constitution is an expression of the will of the people and a confirmation of the people's achievements during socialist construction. Class struggle is not the subject of legal study, but law itself serves the needs of the ruling class. Law and policy are similar in terms of their ruling function; they are different in terms of their origin, the degree of authority, and the procedure of creation. Both law and policy are needed for the governance of the country. A pure rule of law or rule by man has never existed in the history of the world. No law is implemented without man. In different historical periods, people view or emphasize rule of law or rule by man differently. Therefore, scholars should avoid addressing the two complicated concepts from an absolute perspective.

References

Chen Shouyi 陈守一. *Faxue Yanjiu Yu Faxue Jiaoyulun* 法学研究与法学教育论 [On Legal Research and Legal Education]. Beijing: Beijing Daxue Chubanshe, 1996.

Chen Yi 陈颐. "Chen Shouyi: Jiechu De Makesi Zhuyi Fali Xuejia, Faxue Jiaoyujia" 陈守一: 杰出的马克思主义法理学家, 法学教育家 [Chen Shouyi: Excellent Marxist Jurist and Legal Educator]. *Xinmin Wanbao* 新民晚报, May 31, 2010.

"Guanyu Faxue Lilun Gengxin De Jige Wenti: Ji Chen Shouyi He Zhang Zonghou De Yixitan" 关于法学理论更新的几个问题: 记陈守一和张宗厚的一夕谈 [On Issues Concerning Updating Legal Theories: Conversations between Chen Shouyi and Zhang Zonghou]. *Faxue Zazhi* 法学杂志 4 (1986).

Liu Longheng 刘隆亨 and Wu Zhipan 吴志攀. *Chen Shouyi Jinian Wenji* (v. 2) 陈守一纪念文集 [A Collection of Essays in Memory of Chen Shouyi (v. 2)]. Beijing: Beijing Daxue Chubanshe, 2004.

10. *Faxue Lunwenji* 法学论文集 [A Collection of Legal Essays] (Beijing: Beijing Daxue Chubanshe, 1984).

Xue Qian 薛谦. "Chen Shouyi" 陈守一 [Chen Shouyi], in *20 Shiji Zhongguo Zhiming Kexuejia Xueshu Chengjiu Gailan: Faxuejuan* 20 世纪中国知名科学家学术成就概览: 法学卷 [Introduction to the Achievements of Famous Chinese Scientists in the Twentieth Century: Law Volumes], edited by Jiang Ping 江平, et al. Beijing: Kexue Chubanshe, 2014.

Wang Yashan 王亚山 and Fu Zitang 付子堂. "Chen Shouyi Jiaoshou Faxue Sixiang He Faxue Jiaoyu Sixiang Yantaohui Jishi" 陈守一教授法学思想和法学教育思想研讨会纪实 [Recording of the Seminar on Professor Chen Shouyi's Legal Theory and Legal Education Ideas]. *Zhongwai Faxue* 中外法学 1 (1996).

Zhou Enhui 周恩惠. "Fayuan Tuwo Songzhumao Yanyuan Chunshen Jidashi" (法苑土沃松竹茂, 燕园春深祭大师) [The Fertile Legal Land Mourns the Loss of Our Master Professor]. *Faxue Zazhi* 法学杂志 6 (2007).

3. Li Haopei (李浩培)

(1906–1997)

Public and Private International Law

Legal adviser of the Ministry of Foreign Affairs, Li Haopei was a prominent scholar and practitioner of international law. He served as an appeals court judge of the United Nations International Criminal Tribunal for the former Yugoslavia. As Antonio Cassese, the former president of the tribunal put it: "Judge Li was the model of an international judge. He is truly independent, had absolute integrity, and, of course, deep knowledge of international law."[1]

Educational Background

Li was born in the Hongkou (虹口) District of Shanghai. He graduated from the Comparative Law School of Soochow University with an LLB degree in 1928. He attended a one-year training program for judges in 1935. He then passed the study abroad exam sponsored by the British and Chinese governments and was admitted to the London School of Economics and Political Science (LSE) in 1936. In three years at the LSE, he studied public international law under Sir Hersch Lauterpacht and private international law, as well as comparative civil and commercial law,

---

1. Antonio Cassese, "A Eulogy for Judge Li Haopei," in *International Law in the Post-Cold War World: Essays in Memory of Li Haopei*, ed. Sienho Yee and Wang Tieya (London: Routledge, 2001).

under Sir Otto Kahn-Freund. Due to the start of World War II, Li returned to China without finishing his study in 1939.

Career Highlights

After graduating from college, Li created a high school in Shanghai with his friends. He was the principal and teacher of the high school and, at the same time, practiced law between 1928 and 1936. At the invitation of Professor Zhou Gengsheng (周鲠生), he went on to teach at Wuhan University after returning from London in 1939. He taught private international law, jurisprudence, Anglo-American law, and civil law. He became director of the Law Faculty in 1941 and worked at Wuhan University until 1945.

Li was then invited by Zhu Kezhen (竺可桢), president of Zhejiang University, to establish a law school. From 1946 to 1949, Li was professor of law and dean of the College of Law at Zhejiang University. When the law school was closed in 1949, he went to Beijing and was first appointed special member of the Committee of Foreign Affairs Regulation in the Government Administration Council. He later worked at the Bureau of Legislative Affairs of the State Council. In the late 1950s, Li worked as a researcher at the Institute of International Relations (now the China Institute of International Relations) and as a professor at the China Foreign Affairs College. In 1963, he became legal adviser of the Ministry of Foreign Affairs, a position he held for more than thirty years. Between 1969 and 1971, he was sent to labor camps in Hunan and Jiangxi. In 1985, Li was elected academician of the Institute of International Law in Helsinki and became a chief editor of the *Chinese Yearbook of International Law*.[2] He lectured on private international law at The Hague Academy of International Law in 1990 and was elected judge of the United Nations International Criminal Tribunal for the former Yugoslavia in 1993. He also held other academic and expert positions.

---

2. *Zhongguo Guojifa Niankan* 中国国际法年刊 [Chinese Yearbook of International Law] (Beijing: Zhongguo Duiwai Fanyi Chuban Gongsi, 1982).

Research Areas and Publications

According to Ling Yan (凌岩), Li's daughter, he wrote and published more than the public is aware of today. Many of his works were unknown or lost during the Cultural Revolution.[3] Many of his early works, either theoretical or experimental, focused on private international law. Many of his later works dealt with public international law and real-life cases. As a practitioner of international law, his publications are uniquely practical and precise. Most of his works have been included in the following two publications: *Selected Works of Li Haopei* (2000)[4] and *A Collection of Li Haopei's Works on Law* (2006).[5]

Li's major works include his early publication *Introduction to Private International Law* (1945).[6] His best-known book, *The Law of Treaties*,[7] is a thorough and systematic discussion of the topic. From writing preparation in 1974 to publication in 1987, *The Law of Treaties* was thirteen years in the making. In this book, Li addressed the Vienna Convention on the Law of Treaties; explored related issues, practices, and cases; and established his views on the field. With the ability to read Latin, he provided unique perspectives in this book. In 1993, *The Law of Treaties* earned him China's first national book award and has been regarded as a masterpiece of international law in China.

Li was an expert in comparative study. In the article "Jus Cogens and International Law,"[8] he examined the civil law of foreign countries, including France, Germany, Austria, Portugal, Spain, Italy, and Russia, and concluded that *jus cogens* was a common principle in these countries. In

---

3. Ling Yan 凌岩, "Houji" 后记 [Postscript], in Li Haopei, *Li Haopei Wenxuan* 李浩培文选 [Selected Works of Li Haopei] (Beijing: Falü Chubanshe, 2000), xxi.

4. Li Haopei, *Li Haopei Wenxuan*.

5. Li Haopei 李浩培, *Li Haopei Faxue Wenji* 李浩培法学文集 [A Collection of Li Haopei's Works on Law] (Beijing: Falü Chubanshe, 2006).

6. *Guoji Sifa Zonglun* 国际私法总论 [Introduction to Private International Law] (Wuhan: Wuhan Daxue Chubanshe, 1945).

7. *Tiaoyuefa Gailun* 条约法概论 [The Law of Treaties] (Beijing: Falü Chubanshe, 1987).

8. "Qiangxingfa Yu Guojifa" 强行法与国际法 [Jus Cogens and International Law], *Zhongguo Guojifa Niankan* 中国国际法年刊 62 (1982).

the article "On Jurisdictional Immunity of State,"[9] he used publications from the United Nations and discovered that only 28 out of the 150 nations featured in the publication adopted limited immunity, and 20 countries continued the practice of absolute immunity. His 1979 book, *The Law of Nationality: A Comparative Study*,[10] promoted an approach of systematic comparison among nations and looking beyond China's law of nationality. He compared nationality laws and regulations from 99 countries and explored relevant cases and varied theories on such issues as freedom of denaturalization, choice of nationality, forced naturalization, women's marriage and nationality, and so on. An early work in the field, his monograph *Introduction to International Civil Procedure Law* (1996)[11] addressed domestic and international civil procedure legislation of multiple countries, including Switzerland, Germany, France, England, and the United States. He also examined China's work in the field and provided detailed explanations of related bilateral and multilateral treaties of civil procedure.

In addition, Li was a pioneer in discussing other important issues in international law, including enforcement of international law, retention and conflict in treaties, sources of international law, and so on. Professor Wang Tieya wrote, "He was unique in present-day China in that he was a learned jurist in both public and private international law."[12] Li also wrote articles on the rule of law, jurisprudence, labor law, and other legal topics. As coeditor in chief, Li made great contributions to improve the quality of the *Chinese Yearbook of International Law*, which was first published in 1982. According to Wang, Li "had a fine command of English. He also read and wrote French, Russian, German, and Latin. He translated various classics from English, French, and German into Chinese. It is rare in China that a person can use materials and references in English,

9. "Lun Guojia Guanxia Huomian" 论国家管辖豁免 [On Jurisdictional Immunity of State], *Zhongguo Guojifa Niankan* 中国国际法年刊 301 (1986).

10. *Guoji Wenti De Bijiao Yanjiu* 国籍问题的比较研究 [The Law of Nationality: A Comparative Study] (Beijing: Shangwu Yinshuguan, 1979).

11. *Guoji Minshi Chengxufa Gailun* 国际民事程序法概论 [Introduction to International Civil Procedure Law] (Beijing: Falü Chubanshe, 1996).

12. Wang Tieya 王铁崖, "My Friend Li Haopei," in *International Law in the Post-Cold War World: Essays in Memory of Li Haopei*, edited by Sienho Yee and Wang Tieya (London: Routledge, 2001), xxiii.

German, and other languages to do research on international law issues as he could."[13]

Bibliography of English Publications by Professor Li Haopei

Li Haopei. "'Jus Cogens' and International Law." In *International Law in the Post–Cold War World: Essays in Memory of Li Haopei*, edited by Sienho Yee and Tieya Wang, 499–522. London: Routledge, 2001.

———. "Some Recent Developments in the Conflict of Laws of Succession," In *Collected Courses of the Hague Academy of International Law*, vol. 224, http://dx.doi.org/10.1163/1875 -8096_pplrdc_A9780792323174_01 (accessed July 3, 2021). First published online: 1990.

References

He Qisheng 何其生. "Li Haopei" 李浩培 [Li Haopei]. In *Luojia Guojifa Xueren Yu Xuewen* 珞珈国际法学人与学问 [Luojia International Law: Scholars and Their Scholarship], edited by He Qisheng 何其生, 122–55. Wuhan: Wuhan Daxue Chubanshe, 2011.

Li Haopei 李浩培. *Li Haopei Faxue Wenji* 李浩培法学文集 [A Collection of Li Haopei's Works on Law]. Beijing: Falü Chubanshe, 2006.

———. *Li Haopei Wenxuan* 李浩培文选 [Selected Works of Li Haopei]. Beijing: Falü Chubanshe, 2000.

"Li Haopei Shengping Jianjie" 李浩培生平简介 [An Introductory Biography of Li Haopei]. https://www.fichl.org/cn/li-haopei-lecture-series/life-and-service-of-li-haopei/ (accessed Dec. 12, 2020).

Li Xiuping 李秀平. "Li Haopei Xiansheng Zhuiyilu Zhiyi" 李浩培先生追忆录之一 [In Memory of Mr. Li Haopei (Part One)]. http://pilzt.bokee.com/4409756.html (accessed April 30, 2016).

Ling Yan 凌岩. "Li Haobei" 李浩培 [Li Haopei]. In *20 Shiji Zhongguo Zhiming Kexuejia Xueshu Chengjiu Gailan: Faxuejuan* 20 世纪中国知名科学家学术成就概览: 法学卷二 [Introduction to the Achievements of Famous Chinese Scientists in the Twentieth Century: Law Volume II], edited by Jiang Ping, et al., 45–58. Beijing: Kexue Chubanshe, 2014.

Liu Surong 刘素荣. "*Tiaoyuefa Gailun* Shuping" 《条约法概论》书评 [On Li Haopei's *The Law of Treaties*]. http://service.law-star.com/cacnew/201005/365058118.htm (accessed Dec. 12, 2020).

13. Wang Tieya, "My Friend Li Haopei."

4. Ni Zhengyu (倪征噢)

(1906–2003)

International Law and the Law of the Sea

Ni Zhengyu was a judge, a prosecutor, an educator, and a government legal adviser to the Chinese Ministry of Foreign Affairs. He was a prominent practitioner of international law and an important scholar of the law of the sea.

Educational Background

Ni was born in Wujiang (吴江) County of Jiangsu Province. He started college at Hujiang (沪江) University in Shanghai in 1923. During his sophomore year, Ni transferred to Dongwu (东吴) University in Shanghai and studied under well-known legal scholars, including Wu Jingxiong (吴经熊) and He Shizhen (何世桢). In his senior year, Ni also took liberal arts classes at Chizhi (持志) University.[1] He graduated with an LLB degree from Dongwu University and a BA in literature from Chizhi University in 1928. In the same year, he was accepted by Stanford Law School and became the first Chinese student there. In 1929, he

---

1. Chizhi Daxue 持志大学 [Chizhi University] was established in 1924 in Shanghai. It is the predecessor of Shanghai International Studies University. For more information, see https://baike.baidu.com/item/%E6%8C%81%E5%BF%97%E5%A4%A7%E5%AD%A6 (accessed Aug. 17, 2020).

obtained a JD degree with a thesis titled "The Progress of Law from Chance to Choice."[2]

Career Highlights

Upon graduation from Stanford, Ni was offered a position as an honorary research fellow at the Law School of Johns Hopkins University for the year 1930–1931. He returned to China in 1931 and taught at Dongwu University and three other universities until 1945. He also practiced law and was a judge at the Regional Court of Shanghai Special District in 1933, and he was assigned to the Jiangsu High Court for two years. In 1943, Ni was appointed president of the Chongqing Regional Court. There, he tried the court's first case involving an American defendant. After a year at the Chongqing Regional Court, Ni requested to change his job and became an adviser to the Ministry of Justice Administration. In 1945 and 1946, he took a research trip across Asia, Africa, England, and the United States, after which he participated in the Tokyo War Crimes Trials as China's chief prosecution counsel, 1947–1948. During the trials, his contributions to evidence presentation and cross-examination were instrumental for the success of the case. In 1949, he returned to teach at his alma mater Dongwu University, later becoming dean of the law school. In 1952, Dongwu University merged with other law schools to become East China University of Political Science and Law. Ni was appointed library director of Tongji University. At the same time, he learned and taught Russian there.

In 1956, Premier Zhou Enlai invited Ni to Beijing and appointed him to the Treaty Committee of the Ministry of Foreign Affairs, where he became legal counsel to the Ministry of Foreign Affairs. From 1972 to the 1980s, Ni attended every United Nations Conference on the Law of the Sea. In 1981, he became coordinator of the Law of the Sea Treaty and was elected to be a member of the International Law Commission of the United Nations. In 1984, Ni was elected judge of the International Court

---

2. Nyi, Tsung Yuh, "The Progress of Law from Chance to Choice" (JD thesis, Stanford University, 1929).

of Justice (ICJ) and became the first person in China to hold this position. He completed his mission at the court in 1994. The following year he was elected first president of the Chinese Association of the Law of the Sea. In 2000, he was made honorary president of the Chinese Association of International Law and the Chinese Association of the Law of the Sea. He was a member of the Third, Fourth, Fifth, and Sixth National Committees of the Chinese People's Political Consultative Conference (CPPCC).

Research Areas and Publications

Besides his significant contributions in the Tokyo War Crimes Trials, Ni is known for his work in the law of the sea and international jurisdiction. Representing the People's Republic of China, Ni participated in the creation of the United Nations Convention on the Law of the Sea. As a practitioner, his scholarship is reflected in opinions of the International Court of Justice. As a government legal adviser, his scholarship is shown in speeches, reports, and government documents. His law school thesis, articles, and other writings are also important sources of his legal thought. All these materials have been compiled in a publication titled *A Collection of Ni Zhengyu's Legal Writings*.[3] Notable works include "The Legal Systems of the United States and England" (1947),[4] "Jurisdictional Issues in International Law" (1964),[5] and "The Theory and Practice in State Immunity" (1983).[6]

After his overseas visit in 1945 and 1946, Ni wrote his report "The Legal Systems of the United States and England." This was a useful introduction for the Chinese lawyers working in the Tokyo trials, which had procedures similar to the U.S. and UK systems. It became required

3. Ni Zhenyu, *Ni Zhengyu Faxue Wenji*.

4. "Meiguo He Yingguo De Sifa Zhidu" 美国和英国的司法制度 [The Legal Systems of the United States and England].

5. "Guojifazhong De Sifa Guanxia Wenli" 国际法中的司法管辖问题 [Jurisdictional Issues in International Law].

6. "Guanyu Guojia Huomian De Lilun He Shijian" 关于国家豁免的理论和实践 [The Theory and Practice in State Immunity].

reading for Chinese diplomats in the early years of the People's Republic. His 1964 publication, *Jurisdictional Issues in International Law*,[7] discussed the concept of jurisdiction, criminal jurisdiction, civil jurisdiction, and various cases and their jurisdictions. It became one of the classics in the field. Based on his experience of five years' involvement in the China Bondholder Suit,[8] Ni published "The Theory and Practice in State Immunity"[9] to explain the theoretical grounds for the practice of the case. He also published several articles on territorial sea and waters,[10] as well as an article on outer space.[11]

Ni pointed out that the jurisdiction of foreign-related cases was a practical and important issue in international law. In public international law, the enforcement of jurisdiction was to practice national sovereignty. Jurisdiction in international law dealt with disputes and cooperation between and among countries. He disagreed with the traditional doctrines of absolute territorialism and absolute nationality in international criminal jurisdiction and believed that the combination of the two was practical. He had comprehensive discussions on the issues in international civil jurisdiction, which would vary from contract cases to tort cases to property cases and so on.

Ni was a leading scholar of the law of the sea. As early as in 1958, he was one of the experts invited by Chairman Mao Zedong and Premier Zhou Enlai to give advice on territorial water issues. In his opinion, the reason that developed countries claimed territorial waters within three nautical miles of the coast was because they wanted to exploit the ma-

---

7. *Guojifazhong De Sifa Guanxia Wenli* 国际法中的司法管辖问题 [Jurisdictional Issues in International Law] (Beijing: Shijie Zhishi Chubanshe, 1964).

8. Jackson v. People's Republic of China, 550 F. Supp. 869 (N.D. Ala. 1982).

9. "Guanyu Guojia Huomian De Lilun He Shijian" 关于国家豁免的理论和实践 [The Theory and Practice in State Immunity], *Zhongguo Guojifa Niankan* 中国国际法年刊 (1983): 3–30.

10. These include the unpublished essays "Issues in Restrict Areas of the Sea" (1965), "History and Reality of the Width of Territorial Waters" (1971), "The Legal Issues of International Seabed" (1972), "The Legal Status of the Sky over the Territorial Waters" (1976), and so on, which are included in the monograph Ni Zhengyu, *Collection of Ni Zhengyu's Legal Writings*.

11. "Guanyu Waiceng Kongjian De Guojifa Wenti" 关于外层空间的国际法问题 [Some Problems of International Law Concerning Outer Space], *Zhongguo Guojifa Niankan* 中国国际法年刊 (1982): 64–84.

rine resources of developing countries. He believed that it was in China's best interests to stand with developing countries and promote a claim of twelve nautical miles as territorial seas. This idea was presented in the Statement of the People's Republic of China on Territorial Waters.[12] He pointed out that in ocean boundaries, "equal distance" had no absolute standard. The "fairness principle" should be applied effectively. The measurement of population and economic conditions should not be a permanent and immutable standard but rather applied on a case-by-case basis. Sometimes, historical rights were applicable in cases of special circumstances. It is possible to apply proportionality of the coastlines of both parties in drawing ocean boundaries.[13]

In addition, Ni's scholarship is seen in the theory of state immunity in international law, the general principles of international law, and judicial systems. He also published a memoir[14] in 1999.

Bibliography of English Publications by Ni Zhengyu

Ni Zhengyu. "A Legal Luminary from the Orient: Judge Nagendra Singh's Concept of Human Rights, Peace and Development." *Indian Journal of International Law.* 28 (3/4) (1988): 337–47.

———. "Memories of the Tokyo Trial." In *Tokyo Trial: Recollections and Perspectives from China*, 209–25. Cambridge: Cambridge University Press, 2016.

———. "Some Problems of International Law Concerning Outer Space." In *Selected Articles from Chinese Yearbook of International Law*, edited by the Chinese Society of International Law, 76–105. Beijing: Zhongguo Duiwai Fanyi Chuban Gongsi, 1983.

12. Ministry of Foreign Affairs, "Zhonghua Renmin Gongheguo Guanyu Linghai De Shengming" 中华人民共和国关于领海的声明 [Statement of the People's Republic of China on Territorial Waters], Sept. 4, 1958, https://www.fmprc.gov.cn/diaoyudao/chn/flfg/zcfg/t1304542.htm.

13. See Shi Juehuai 施觉怀, "Daodu: Dongwu Mingjia Guoji Faguan—Mianhuai Ni Zhengyu Xiansheng" 导读: 东吴名家 国际法官—缅怀倪征燠先生 [Preface: Dongwu's Famous Expert, International Court Judge—in Memory of Mr. Ni Zhengyu], in Ni Zhengyu, *Collection of Ni Zhengyu's Legal Writings*, 10.

14. "Danbo Congrong Li Haiya" 淡泊从容莅海牙 [Neutrally and Calmly Entering The Hague] (Beijing: Falü Chubanshe, 1999).

References

Li Lingling 李伶伶. *Fajie Jubo: Ni Zhengyu Zhuang* 法界巨擘: 倪征㠄传 [An Authority in the Field of Law: A Biography of Ni Zhengyu]. Nanjing: Jiangsu Renmin Chubanshe, 2009.

Ni Zhengyu 倪征㠄. *Ni Zhengyu Faxue Wenji* 倪征㠄法学文集 [A Collection of Ni Zhengyu's Legal Writings]. Beijing: Falü Chubanshe, 2006.

"Ni Zhengyu" 倪正征㠄 [Ni Zhengyu]. http://baike.baidu.com/view/476499.htm?fromtitle=%E5%80%AA%E5%BE%81%E5%A5%A5&fromid=120761&type=search (accessed Feb. 20, 2017).

Shen Weidong 沈伟东. "XinZhongguo Diyiwei Guoji Dafaguan Ni Zhengyu: Qingqing 'Haiyangfa Gongyue'" 新中国第一位国际大法官倪征㠄: 倾情《海洋法公约》 [The First International Court Judge of the New China: Ni Zhengyu on *The Law of the Sea Treaty*]. *China News*, Dec. 16, 2010. http://www.chinanews.com/cul/2010/12-16/2727669.shtml.

5. Zhou Nan (周枏)

(1908–2004)

Roman Law and Historical Studies of Foreign Law

Professor of law at Anhui University, Zhou Nan was trained as a jurist in Belgium. With expertise in Roman law, he was celebrated as a "living dictionary of Roman law" in China. His book *On Roman Law*[1] is an authority in the field.

Educational Background

Zhou was born in Liyang (溧阳) City of Jiangsu Province. In 1926, he entered Zhongguo Gongxue University[2] and finished the coursework for a business major in 1928. He then entered Katholieke Universiteit Leuven in Belgium. There he studied Roman law and became interested in its rich and extensive legal system. He earned a master's degree in political diplomacy in 1931 and a doctoral degree in law in 1934. He returned to China upon graduation.

---

1. *Luomafa Yuanlun* 罗马法原论 [On Roman Law] (Beijing: Shangwu Yinshuguan, 1994).

2. Zhongguo Gongxue Daxue 中国公学大学 [Zhongguo Gongxue University] was founded in 1906 in Shanghai. For more information, see https://baike.baidu.com/item /%E4%B8%AD%E5%9B%BD%E5%85%AC%E5%AD%A6 (accessed Aug. 17, 2020).

Career Highlights

Zhou started his teaching career at Chizhi (持志) University in Shanghai
in 1935. He taught Roman law and wrote a textbook on the subject, but
due to the interruption of World War II, the book didn't get published.
From 1937 to 1949, he moved around and taught civil law, commercial
law, and Roman law at National Central University, Hunan University,
Jiangsu College, Xiamen University, Jinan University, and the Shanghai
College of Political Science and Law. He had influential discussions with
other important Roman law scholars, including Qiu Hanping (丘汉平)
and Chen Chaobi (陈朝璧). During the political movements from the
1950s to the 1970s, Zhou was forced to give up teaching and research. He
was sent to a labor camp and later settled in the library of Qinghai Normal College. In 1980, Zhou was invited to teach civil law at Anhui University. He became one of the founders of the Law Department of Anhui
University. He retired from this position in 1990. At age eighty-six, Zhou
was invited to speak at the first International Conference of Roman Law,
Chinese Law, and the Civil Law Codification in Beijing in 1994.

Research Areas and Publications

Zhou's publications include *An Introduction to Civil Law* (1936),[3] *An Introduction to Law*,[4] and other books and articles. His research career
eventually flourished when he was in his seventies. His most important
work is *On Roman Law*, a two-volume set that has been published and
reprinted seven times since 1994 and won provincial and national research
awards. According to Professor Shi Jichun (史际春) of Renmin University, this book is so far "the most accurate and most original work on Ro-

3. *Minfa Gailun* 民法概论 [An Introduction to Civil Law] (Fujian: Suwan Zhengzhi Xueyuan, 1936).

4. *Faxue Xulun* 法学绪论 [An Introduction to Law] (Fujian: Jiangsu Xueyuan,
1941).

man law in China."[5] Professor Xu Guodong (徐国栋) of Xiamen University has stated that this book represents a more accurate understanding of Roman law and that it might be one of the most cited works in China since 1994.[6]

However, in the same article, Xu also points out some mistakes in this book. He notes that certain factors—such as Zhou's advanced age, the assistance he received from people with varied academic backgrounds, his incomplete Roman law training, and his outdated knowledge—contributed to these mistakes. Nevertheless, *On Roman Law* is still the most important work in the field of Roman law study in China since 1994.

Zhou made many contributions in the field of Roman law study. He proposed a suitable Chinese translation for the name of the Law of the Twelve Tables. He provided new explanations for many concepts in the Law of the Twelve Tables, which include torts, private wrongs, and property. His scholarship on Roman law was instrumental in the following: (1) Zhou outlined the fundamental features of Roman law; (2) on value objectives, Zhou pointed out that Roman jurists defined law as justice; (3) in terms of methodology, Zhou emphasized the implications of Roman law for today's circumstances.[7]

Besides Roman law, Zhou's works explored legal systems of foreign countries and modern civil and commercial law. These foreign jurisdictions include Belgium and Spain.

Zhou also took part in other important research projects. In the early 1980s, he participated in the editing of *A Law Dictionary*[8] and the *Law Volume of the Encyclopedia of China*.[9] In 1985, as one of five experts, Zhou participated in the final review of the General Principles of Civil Law.[10] After his retirement, he published an article titled "A Study on the

5. See Chen Xiahong, "Zhongguo 'Luomafa De Huozidian.'"

6. Xu Guodong, "Zhou Nan Xiansheng De."

7. See Gao Shang, "Zhou Nan Xiansheng Yu."

8. *Faxue Cidian* 法学词典 [A Law Dictionary] (Shanghai: Shanghai Cishu Chubanshe, 1980).

9. *Zhongguo Dabaike Quanshu, Faxue* 中国大百科全书, 法学 [The Law Volume of the Encyclopedia of China] (Beijing: Zhongguo Dabaike Quanshu Chubanshe, 1984).

10. *Zhonghua Renmin Gongheguo Minfa Tongze* 中华人民共和国民法通则 [The General Principles of Civil Law] (promulgated by the National People's Congress, Apr. 12, 1986, effective Jan. 1, 1987).

Provisions of 'Private Offenders' in the Law of the Twelve Tables."[11] In 1997, at age eighty-nine, he participated in proofreading the *Yuanzhao Dictionary of English and American Law*.[12]

References

Chen Xiahong 陈夏红. "Zhongguo 'Luomafa De Huozidian'" 中国 "罗马法的活字典" [China's "Living Dictionary of Roman Law"]. In Chen Xiahong 陈夏红, *Bainian Zhongguo Falüren Jianying* 百年中国法律人剪影 [Profiles of Chinese Jurists in a Hundred Years]. Beijing: Zhongguo Fazhi Chubanshe, 2006.

Gao Shang 高尚. "Zhou Nan Xiansheng Yu Zhongguo De Luomafa Yanjiu" 周枏先生与中国的罗马法研究 [Mr. Zhou Nan and the Study of Roman Law in China]. In *Guji De Huihuang* 孤寂的辉煌 [The Brilliance of Loneliness], edited by He Qinhua 何勤华. Beijing: Shangwu Yinshuguan, 2017.

Mi Jian 米健. "Daizou Yige Shidai De Luoma Faxuejia—Daoyi Zhou Nan Xiansheng" 带走一个时代的罗马法学家—悼忆周枏先生 [A Gong Roman Law Scholar Who Took Away the Decade with Him—in Memory of Mr. Zhou Nan]. http://www.nmql.com/wenji/zhuanjia/mj/2513.html (accessed Mar. 28, 2017).

Xu Guodong 徐国栋. "Zhongguo De Luomafa Jiaoyu" 中国的罗马法教育 [Roman Law Education in China]. http://www.romanlaw.cn/sub2-54.htm (accessed Aug. 16, 2006).

———. "Zhou Nan Xiansheng De *Luomafa Yuanlun* Cuowu Juyao—Yi Shangce Wei Zhongxin" 周枏先生的《罗马法原论》错误举要—以上册为中心 [Examples of Mistakes in Mr. Zhou Nan's *On Roman Law*]. http://www.romanlaw.cn/sub2-128.htm (accessed Mar. 28, 2017).

Zhou Nan 周枏. "Wo Yu Luomafa" 我与罗马法 [Roman Law and Me]. In *Luomafa Yu Xiandai Minfa* 罗马法与现代民法 [Roman Law and Modern Civil Law], edited by Xu Guodong 徐国栋. Beijing: Zhongguo Fazhi Chubanshe, 2001.

———. *Zhou Nan Yu Luomafa Yanjiu* 周枏与罗马法研究 [Zhou Nan and the Study of Roman Law]. Hefei: Anhui Renmin Chubanshe, 2010.

"Zhou Nan" 周枏 [Zhou Nan]. http://baike.baidu.com/item/%E5%91%A8%E6%9E%8F (accessed Mar. 28, 2017).

11. "Shier Biaofa Zhong 'Sifan' Guiding De Yanjiu" 十二表法中 "私犯" 规定的研究 [A Study on the Provisions of "Private Offenders" in the Law of the Twelve Tables]. *Anhui Daxue Xuebao* 安徽大学学报 1 (1992).

12. *Yuanzhao Ying Meifa Cidian* (元照英美法词典) [Yuanzhao Dictionary of English and American Law] (Beijing: Falü Chubanshe, 2003).

6. Rui Mu (芮沐)

(1908–2011)

Civil Law and Economic Law

Professor of Law at Peking University, Rui Mu was a distinguished scholar of civil law and economic law. Trained in Paris and Frankfurt, Rui became a multilingual jurist. He was the founder of the study of Chinese economic law and international economic law. He was the first person to propose the concept of economic law in China. With a lifespan of 103 years, Rui was a witness to modern Chinese history from the late Qing dynasty, through the Republic era, to the People's Republic of China.

Educational Background

Rui was born in Shanghai. He received his primary and secondary education in the British and French concessions of Shanghai, where he learned English and French. He then went to Aurora University[1] and graduated

---

1. Aurora University, 震旦學院 (Zhendan Xueyuan) in Chinese, was a preeminent Catholic university in Shanghai from 1903 to 1952. The founder was Fr. Joseph Ma Xiangbo, SJ (1840–1939), and the French Jesuits. Due to disagreements over the school's governance between Fr. Ma and the French Jesuits, Fr. Ma resigned from Aurora to establish Fudan University. Meanwhile, Aurora was run by French Jesuits until the Communist Revolution. In 1952, Aurora University was merged into Fudan University and East China Normal University. Its medical school has been a part of Shanghai Second Medical College since 1952.

in 1930. The following year, he went to the University of Paris and received his master's degree in law in 1933. He continued his education at the Goethe University Frankfurt and studied civil law, civil procedure, law of obligations, and legal theory under Professor Fritz von Hippel and others. He earned a doctoral degree in law in 1935. Between 1945 and 1947, Rui was a visiting scholar at Columbia University.

Career Highlights

In 1938, Rui concluded his study overseas and returned to China. He first taught at the Law Department of the National Central University (now Nanjing University) in Chongqing. He also practiced law on the side. Between 1941 and 1945, he taught at the Law Department of the National Southwest Associated University[2] in Kunming. From 1945 to 1947, he was a visiting scholar at Columbia Law School. Upon returning to China, he began teaching at Peking University. This job lasted the rest of his life except for a short period from 1952 to 1954 when he taught briefly at the Beijing College of Political Science and Law (now the China University of Political Science and Law).

After the Communist Party came to power in China, it modeled its legal and educational systems on the Soviet Union. To learn and adapt to the new system and knowledge, Rui visited the Soviet Union and Eastern Europe a few times, which allowed him to become fluent in Russian. His language skills gave him the opportunity to serve as a personal interpreter for Zhang Zhirang (张志让), then vice president of the Supreme People's Court, during his overseas constitutional law research trips in 1954.

Like most Chinese scholars, Rui's teaching career was interrupted during the Cultural Revolution. He was sent to a labor camp in Jiangxi Province. Upon returning to his job, Rui became one of the first doc-

---

2. The National Southwest Associated University (Guoli Xinan Lianhe Daxue 国立西南联合大学) was a combination of Peking University, Tsinghua University, and Nankai University, which emerged in Changsha in 1937 and was moved to Kunming in 1938, to escape the Japanese invasion. It was dissolved in 1946.

toral dissertation advisers in China in 1977. His last batch of doctoral students graduated in 1999 when he was ninety-one years old. Many of his students have become prominent in their fields today. Chen Guangzhong (陈光中), former president of the China University of Political Science and Law, and Shen Sibao (沈四宝), dean of Shanghai University Law School, are among them.

Rui was the director of the Civil Law Department, later associate dean of the Peking University Law School. He founded and became the first director of the Economic Law Institute and the International Economic Law Institute at Peking University. Among many academic and political appointments, Rui was a member of the Academic Degree Review Committee of the State Council, vice president of the Chinese Society of International Law, member of the Legal Work Committee of the Standing Committee of the National People's Congress, and member of the Drafting Committee of the Basic Law of the Hong Kong Special Administrative Region.

He was a visiting professor at John Jay College of Criminal Justice in New York City and the University of Minnesota Law School between 1985 and 1987. He taught at the University of London in 1986 and other academic institutions around the world.

Research Areas and Publications

Rui is known as "a jurist who is famous for having no published books."[3] He demonstrated his serious scholarship mostly with articles. However, he did write a seminal publication titled *The Complete Theory of Legal Act in Civil Law: Debt*,[4] which was first published in 1948 and revised and

---

3. In 1998, Rui was featured in *Oriental Son*, a China Central TV program to celebrate the centennial anniversary of Peking University. He was called "a jurist who is famous for having no published books." See Shang Wei, "Renduan Jinxiaoyao Mufa Dezhenyi."

4. *Minfa Falü Xingwei Lilun Zhi Quanbu (Min Zongzhai Hebian)* 民法法律行为理论 之全部 (民总债合编) [The Complete Theory of Legal Act in Civil Law: Debt] (Beijing: Zhongguo Zhengfa Daxue Chubanshe, 2003). The 1948 edition was printed by Hebei First Prison.

republished in 2003. From the continental civil law perspective, this book discussed the general provisions of civil law and debt and has been influential for its methodology, structure, language, and concepts.[5] At a time when most Chinese civil law books were derived from Japanese works, this original publication with easy-to-read language was hard to come by.

His other publications include *The Method and Cases of Comparative Legal Studies* (1948),[6] "The Development of Civil Law Legislation since the Establishment of the People's Republic of China" (1955),[7] *Foreign Civil and Commercial Law* (1962),[8] and *A Collection of International Economic Treaties and Conventions* (1994 and 1997).[9] He also published a few essays in English.

Rui believed that legal studies were applied science and practical science. Whoever does legal studies should start out from the study of realities. The mission of legal professionals was to assist legislators in building a socialist legal system with Chinese characteristics.[10]

With this mission in mind, Rui pointed out that civil law was a basic law that regulated the relationship between property and personality. In the early years of Communist China, the old civil law was abolished. The government seized enterprises, real property, and other personal property. In the absence of a working civil code, it was difficult to carry out economic development activities. Therefore, the call for economic law was practical and necessary. According to Rui, economic law was an independent discipline that dealt with complicated social relations. Economic

5. See Zhang Gu 张谷, "Rui Mu Xiansheng Minfa Xueshu Sixiang Jianshuo" 芮沐先生民法学术思想简说 [An Introduction to Mr. Rui Mu's Civil Law Theory], http://news.sina.com.cn/o/2007-09-14/032412567507s.shtml (accessed Nov. 20, 2016).

6. *Faxue Bijiao Fangfalun Ji Anli* 法学比较方法论及案例 [The Method and Cases of Comparative Legal Studies] (Beijing: Beijing Daxue Chubanshe, 1948).

7. "Zhonghua Renmin Gongheguo Chengli Yilai Woguo Minshi Lifa De Fazhan Qingkuang" 中华人民共和国成立以来我国民事立法的发展情况 [The Development of Civil Law Legislation since the Establishment of the People's Republic of China], *Zhengfa Yanjiu* 政法研究 5 (1955): 14–20.

8. *Waiguo Minshangfa* 外国民商法 [Foreign Civil and Commercial Law] (Beijing: Beijing Daxue Chubanshe, 1962).

9. *Guoji Jingji Tiaoyue Gongyue Jicheng* 国际经济条约公约集成 [A Collection of International Economic Treaties and Conventions] (Beijing: Renmin Fayuan Chubanshe, 1994). A supplement to this book was published by the same publisher in 1997.

10. Shang Wei, "Renduan Jinxiaoyao Mufa Dezhenyi."

law was a mechanism that combined instruments of public law and private law.

Shifting from civil law to economic law, Rui's scholarship is a reflection of his legal ideology, summarized as law serving reality. With the permission of the Ministry of Education, Rui founded the Economic Law Institute at Peking University and served as the director. To support the program, he published (with Mark A. Cohen) "New Developments in China's Economic Legislation" (1983),[11] *Lecture on Economic Law* (1984),[12] and other works.

Rui's research interests also expanded into international economic law. Like Professor Yao Meizhen (姚梅镇), he was instrumental in separating the study of public international law and the study of international economic law. As a result of his effort, the study of international economic law in China evolved from merely a chapter of public international law to an independent field of legal study. He proposed the whole package of theories and ideas for the study of international economic law. His argument was that international economic law not only covered the issues in public international law but also dealt with the economic relations between transnational business organizations and businesspeople. Therefore, international economic law could serve directly both institutions and businesspeople. As a contrast, public international law mainly dealt with the relations between and among countries and international organizations.[13] To solve a dispute in international economic law, we should use both domestic and international law. He published *Introduction to International Economic Law* (1983)[14] and other works on this topic.

As a multilingual jurist, Rui was fluent in German, English, French, and Japanese. Latin was the best among his languages. He could also read

11. Rui Mu and Cohen, "New Developments," 61–76.

12. Rui Mu et al., eds., Jingjifa Jiangyi 经济法讲义 [Lecture on Economic Law] (Beijing: Falü Chubanshe, 1984).

13. See Shen Sibao 沈四宝, "Jinghe Enshi Rui Mu Xiansheng Baisui Huadan" 敬贺恩师芮沐先生百岁华诞 [Congratulations with Respect on the One Hundredth Birthday of My Mentor, Mr. Rui Mu], *Beijing Daxue Xuebao* 北京大学学报 [Journal of Peking University] 4 (2008).

14. Guoji Jingjifa Gailun 国际经济法概论 [Introduction to International Economic Law] (Beijing: Shiyou Gongyebu Jijianju Zhongguo Shiyou Gongcheng Jianshe Gongsi, 1983).

Russian. It was said that at Peking University, faculty members from the Foreign Language Department often sought help from Rui whenever they could not find a phrase in the dictionaries.[15]

Bibliography of English Publications by Professor Rui Mu

Rui Mu. "Chinese View on the Future Possibilities of International Law and the World Economic Order." In *Public International Law and the Future World Order: Liber Amicorum in Honor of A. J. Thomas, Jr.*, edited by Joseph J. Norton. Littleton, CO: F.B. Rothman, 1987.
———. *New Period China: Foreign Economic Law in the Service of Peaceful Development*. Washington, DC: World Peace through Law Center, 1990.
Rui Mu and Mark A. Cohen. "New Developments in China's Economic Legislation." *Columbia Journal of Transnational Law* 22 (1983): 61–76.
Rui Mu and Guiguo Wang. *Chinese Foreign Economic Law: Analysis and Commentary*. Washington, DC: International Law Institute, 1990.

References

Chen Xiahong 陈夏红 and Li Yunshu 李云舒. "Rui Mu Zishu: Wo De Xuesheng Shidai" 芮沐自述：我的学生时代 [Rui Mu's Self Statement: My Student Time]. http://www .pkulaw.cn/fulltext_form.aspx?Gid=335572883&Db=art (accessed Feb. 20, 2017).
Li Meng 李蒙. "Shiji Laoren Rui Mu De Wuge Shunjian" 世纪老人芮沐的五个瞬间 [Five Moments of a Century Old Man: Rui Mu]. *Minzhu Yu Fazhi* 民主与法制 21 (2006).
Shang Wei 商伟. "Renrui Jinxiaoyao Mufa Dezhenyi: Ji Beida Faxueyuan Zishen Jiaoshou Rui Mu" 人瑞尽逍遥 牧法得真义：记北大法学院资深教授芮沐 [On Senior Professor of Peking University Law School: Rui Mu]. http://pkunews.pku.edu.cn/xwzh /2011-03/25/content_196034.htm (accessed Feb. 20, 2017).

15. See Hou Lei 侯磊, "Rui Mu" 芮沐 [Rui Mu], in *20 Shiji Zhongguo Zhiming Kexuejia Xueshu Chengjiu Gailan: Faxuejuan* 20 世纪中国知名科学家学术成就概览：法学卷 [Introduction to the Achievements of Famous Chinese Scientists in the Twentieth Century: Law Volumes], vol. 2, ed. Jiang Ping et al. (Beijing: Kexue Chubanshe, 2014), 117.

Wu Zhipan 吴志攀 and Shen Sibao 沈四宝. "Zhijing Baisui Faxuejia Rui Mu Xiansheng" 致敬百岁法学家芮沐先生 [A Tribute to a Century Old Jurist: Mr. Rui Mu]. *Zhongguo Falü* 中国法律 5 (2008).

Yang Zihui 杨紫烜. "Zhongguo Jingji Faxue De Kaituozhe He Dianjiren: Rui Mu Laoshi Dui Jingjifa Xueke Jianshe De Juda Gongxian" 中国经济法学的开拓者和奠基人——芮沐老师对经济法学科建设的巨大贡献 [The Cultivator and Founder of China's Economic Law Study: The Great Contribution of Professor Rui Mu]. *Journal of Peking University (Philosophy and Social Science)* 5 (2008).

7. Gong Xiangrui (龚祥瑞)

(1911–1996)

Constitutional Law and Administrative Law

Professor of law at Peking University, Gong Xiangrui was a prominent scholar in the fields of constitutional law, administrative law, and comparative law. He was an expert in Western civil service systems and a strong believer in political democracy and the rule of law.

Educational Background

Gong was born in Ningbo (宁波) City of Zhejiang Province. He received his primary and secondary educations from British and American missionary schools. In 1930, he was admitted to the Biology Department of the University of Shanghai,[1] a school sponsored by the Baptist church. The next year he transferred to the Political Science Department of Tsinghua University and studied under Professor Qian Duansheng (钱端升). In 1935, Gong graduated from Tsinghua and won a scholarship to study abroad. A year later, he was assigned to study at the London School of Economics and Political Science (LSE), where he focused on the study of constitutionalism and was a student of Professor Harold Laski and Professor Ivor Jennings. He earned a master's degree in political science in

---

1. Jianghu Daxue 江沪大学 [University of Shanghai], established in 1906, now Shanghai Ligong Daxue 上海理工大学 [University of Shanghai for Science and Technology (USST)].

1938. The title of his master's thesis was "Civil Service Discipline in Modern Democracies: An Essay on Code of Official Conduct in England, U.S.A., and France."[2]

He spent the next year researching administrative law at the Paris Institute of Comparative Law, now affiliated with Panthéon-Assas University. There he obtained a senior research certificate. In 1939, Gong returned to China.

Career Highlights

Gong started his teaching career in the Political Science Department of the National Southwest Associated University[3] in 1939. From 1945 to 1946, he was a professor of political science at the Central University in Chungqing. In 1947, Gong led a study tour to the United States, England, France, and other countries. During this period, he twice left his teaching positions and worked for the Nationalist government. Between 1948 and 1952, he taught political science at Peking University and Yenching University. He also worked at the Central Cadres School of Politics and Law[4] in 1951. After that, he went on to teach at Peking University and was director of the State and Law Department.

During the 1950s and 1960s, caught up in the political ideology in that era, Gong participated in the Anti-Rightist Movement. He wrote articles attacking his teacher and mentor Professor Qian Duansheng, his colleague Professor Wang Tieya (王铁崖), and other intellectuals,[5] which

2. H. J. Kung (Hsing-Jien), "Civil Service Discipline in Modern Democracies: An Essay on Code of Official Conduct in England, U.S.A., and France" (master's thesis, LSE, 1938).

3. See footnote 2 in chapter 6 on Rui Mu.

4. Zhongyang Zhengfa Guanli Ganbu Xuexiao 中央政法管理干部学校 [The Central Cadres School of Politics and Law] was established in 1951, dissolved, and merged into the China University of Political Science and Law in 2000. The school's mission was to provide political and legal training to cadres and leaders. For more information, see http://www.zfdxxyh.com/html/xszl/dsj/ (accessed Dec. 19, 2020).

5. In his autobiography, Gong admitted the selfishness of his actions during the political movements of this period. See Gong Xiangrui, *Mangren Aoliweng*, 269–316.

became a shameful memory in academic circles. In the last years of his life, Gong expressed regrets and admitted that this was a tragedy in his personal history.

In 1968, Gong himself became a victim of the Cultural Revolution. He was sent to the university's labor camp for reeducation. Between 1971 and 1981, he did translation work at the Law Department of Peking University. He was finally allowed to teach again in 1980 and started to recruit graduate students in 1982. China's Premier Li Keqiang (李克强) was one of his.favorite students. Gong also held a few academic positions, including adviser to the Administrative Law Section of the China Law Society.

Research Areas and Publications

Gong enjoyed a peak period in his academic life in the 1980s. He launched the first comparative administrative law class in China and teamed up with Professors Han Depei and Luo Haocai to attend an International Law Association conference in Amsterdam in 1980. He published several books, including *The Judicial Systems of Western Countries* (1980),[6] *The Administrative Organizations and Civil Service System in England* (1983),[7] *Comparative Constitutional Law of Foreign Countries* (1981),[8] and *The Civil Service System* (1985).[9] These books provided introductions to the political, judicial, and constitutional systems of the Western world and attracted broad attention in China.

6. Gong Xiangrui 龚祥瑞, Luo Haocai 罗豪才, and Wu Jiying 吴撷英, *Xifang Guojia De Sifa Zhidu* 西方国家的司法制度 [The Judicial Systems of Western Countries] (Beijing: Beijing Daxue Chubanshe, 1980).

7. *Yingguo Xingzheng Jigou He Wenguan Zhidu* 英国行政机构和文官制度 [The Administrative Organizations and Civil Service System in England] (Beijing: Renmin Chubanshe, 1983).

8. *Waiguo Bijiao Xianfa* (外国比较宪法) [Comparative Constitutional Law of Foreign Countries] (Beijing: Falü Chubanshe, 1981).

9. *Wenguan Zhidu* 文官制度 [The Civil Service System] (Beijing: Renmin Chubanshe, 1985).

His most influential publication in this period was *Comparative Constitutional Law and Administrative Law* (1985),[10] which won the prestigious Impact China Rule of Law Book Award.[11] From a comparative perspective, Gong examined the relationship between constitutional law and administrative law. He pointed out that constitutional law was the foundation of administrative law, which was the enforcement of constitutional law. Administrative law was the changing part of constitutional law. This textbook became widely used back then and is still influential years later. The legal scholar Liang Zhiping (梁治平) once put it this way: Gong's *Comparative Constitutional Law and Administrative Law* was rather special because Gong was trained in England. He was able to read the original texts and had personal experience with Western culture and political systems. The spirit of this book "cannot be found in ordinary textbooks."[12] Likewise, his book *The Civil Service System* (1985) is also recognized as a classic work in the field.

In the 1990s, Gong turned his attention to the rule of law and constitutionalism. He published *Recent Discussions on Law and Constitutional Law* (1992),[13] *The Ideals and Realities of Constitutionalism* (1995),[14] *On the Authority of Constitutional Law* (1995),[15] and other books and articles. He believed that constitutionalism had three components: (1) a constitutional

10. *Bijiao Xianfa Yu Xingzhengfa* 比较宪法与行政法 [Comparative Constitutional Law and Administrative Law] (Beijing: Falü chubanshe, 1985).

11. The 1978–2014 Yingxiang Zhongguo Fazhi Tushujiang 1978–2014 影响中国法治图书奖 [1978–2014 Impact China Rule of Law Book Award] was given to ten legal publications that had a significant impact on China's development of the rule of law. They were selected by a group of twenty-five prominent legal scholars. See http://www.cssn.cn/fx/fx_yzyw/201412/t20141205_1430151.shtml (accessed Dec. 18, 2020).

12. "Fa, Falü, Fazhi–Du Gong Xiangrui *Bijiao Xianfa Yu Xingzhengfa*" 法，法律，法治—读龚祥瑞《比较宪法与行政法》 [Law, Rule, the Rule of Law—on Gong Xiangrui's Comparative Constitutional Law and Administrative Law], http://www.aisixiang.com/data/18268.html (accessed Feb. 29, 2016).

13. *Fa Yu Xianfa Jinlun* 法与宪法近论 [Recent Discussions on Law and Constitutional Law]. (Beijing: Beijing Daxue Falüxi, 1992).

14. *Xianzheng De Lixiang Yu Xianshi* 宪政的理想与现实 [The Ideals and Realities of Constitutionalism] (Beijing: Zhongguo Renshi Chubanshe, 1995).

15. *Lun Xianfa De Quanweixing* 论宪法的权威性 [On the Authority of Constitutional Law] (Beijing: Shenghuo, Dushu, Xinzhi Sanlian Shudian, 1995).

government, (2) a constitution to confirm the rule of law rather than rule by man, and (3) a political democracy. According to him, constitutional law was not equal to constitutionalism, whose core theory was to restrict government's power and protect citizens' rights. Constitutional law could exist without constitutionalism.

Gong was interested not only in theory but also in reality. He led his students on several field trips and conducted surveys in many cities and provinces. They investigated the status of administrative litigation and completed two research projects. They published *The Ideals and Realities of the Rule of Law: A Survey Report on the Application and Developmental Directions of the Administrative Procedure Law of the People's Republic of China.*[16] This was the first field research on the implementation of a law since 1949 and represented a turning point of empirical legal studies as a research method in China.

Beyond his own research, Gong worked alone or with others to translate several important publications into Chinese. These works were instrumental in legal education and the study of comparative law.

Bibliography of English Publications by Professor Gong Xiangrui

Gong Xiangrui. "Political and Constitutional Change in China." *Asian Thought and Society* 14, no. 40 (1989): 3.

———. "The World-View and the Natural Law Thought of the Taoist School in Ancient China." In *Das Naturrechtsdenken Heute Und Morgen: Gedächtnisschrift Für René Marcic*, edited by Dorothea Mayer-Maly and Peter M. Simons, 255–62. Berlin: Duncker und Humblot, 1983.

---

16. Gong Xiangrui 龔祥瑞 et al., *Fazhi De Lixiang Yu Xianshi: "Zhonghua Renmin Gongheguo Xingzheng Susongfa" Shishi Xianzhuang Yu Fazhan Fangxiang Diaocha Yanjiu Baogao* 法治的理想与现实 《中华人民共和国行政诉讼法》实施现状与发展方向调查研究报告 [The Ideals and Realities of the Rule of Law: A Survey Report on the Application and Developmental Directions of the Administrative Procedure Law of the People's Republic of China] (Beijing: Zhongguo Zhengfa Daxue Chubanshe, 1993).

References

Chu Chenge 褚宸舸. "Gong Xiangrui Xianzheng Sixiang Yanjiu" 龚祥瑞宪政思想研究 [A Study on Gong Xiangrui's Theory of Constitutionalism]. http://www.aisixiang.com /data/62749.html (accessed Dec. 18, 2020).

Dou Bingle 豆饼乐. "Jinian Gong Xiangrui Xiansheng" 纪念龚祥瑞先生 [In Memory of Mr. Gong Xiangrui]. http://www.gongfa.com/gongxiangruixianshenganxi.htm (accessed Feb. 29, 2016).

Gong Xiangrui 龚祥瑞. "Gong Xiangrui Zishu" 龚祥瑞自述 [A Self Statement of Gong Xiangrui]. In *Shiji Xueren Zishu* 世纪学人自述 第四卷 [Statements of the Century's Scholars], vol. 4, edited by Ji Xianlin 季羡林, 214. Beijing: Beijing Shiyue Wenyi Chubanshe, 2000.

———. *Mangren Aoliweng: Gong Xiangrui Zizhuan* 盲人奥里翁: 龚祥瑞自传 [Blind Orion: An Autobiography of Gong Xiangrui]. Beijing: Beijing Daxue Chubanshe, 2011.

———. "Wo De Zhuanye De Huiyi" 我的专业的回忆 [A Recount of My Study Major]. In *Zhongguo Dangdai Shehui Kexuejia* 中国当代社会科学家 [Modern Social Scientists of China], vol. 6, edited by Beijing Tushuguan "Wenxian" Congkan Bianjibu 北京图书馆《文献》丛刊编辑部, 318–26. Beijing: Shumu Wenxian Chubanshe, 1984.

"Gong Xiangrui" 龚祥瑞 [Gong Xiangrui]. In *Dangdai Zhongguo Shehui Kexue Xuezhe Dacedian* 当代中国社会科学学者大辞典 [A Dictionary of Modern Chinese Scholars of the Social Sciences], edited by Chen Rongfu 陈荣富 and Hong Yongshan 洪永珊, 186. Hangzhou: Zhejiang Dexue Chubanshe, 1990.

Ma, Evelyn. "Gong Xiangrui." In "Scholarly Chinese Legal Works in the Vernacular: A Selective Topical Treatise Finder." *International Journal of Legal Information* 39 (2011): 297–99.

Yan Jiaqi 严家祺. "Li Keqiang De Daoshi Gong Xiangrui" 李克强的导师龚祥瑞 [Li Keqiang's Professor Gong Xiangrui]. https://2newcenturynet.blogspot.com/2013/09/blog -post_2907.html (accessed Dec. 18, 2020).

8. Han Depei (韩德培)

(1911–2009)

Private International Law

Professor of law at Wuhan University, Han Depei was a distinguished scholar in multiple fields of public international law, private international law, environmental law, and legal education. He was trained in Canada and the United States and became one of the leading authorities in international law in modern China. He is regarded as a National Treasure by the Chinese government.

Educational Background

Han was born in Rugao (如皋) County of Jiangsu Province. In 1930, he entered the Department of History and Political Science of Zhejiang University. A year later, the department was merged with Central University in Nanjing. Influenced by Xie Guansheng (谢冠生), the former head of the department, he switched to the Law Department and received his LLB degree from Central University in 1934. He read many books on international law and legal philosophy in English and French during his college years. In 1939, he passed the study abroad exam sponsored by the British and Chinese governments and was admitted by Cambridge University. In the following year, he went to study in Canada instead of England due to the start of World War II. As a student at the University of Toronto, he studied private international law under Professor Moffatt Hancock and wrote a thesis titled "Substance and Procedure in Anglo-American

Conflict of Laws."[1] He received his LLM degree in 1942. He then went to Harvard Law School and became a research fellow. At Harvard, Han audited the classes of Professors Erwin N. Griswold, Manley O. Hudson, and Roscoe Pound and collected research materials. He was a frequent user of the Harvard Law School Library. In 1945, he returned to China.

Career Highlights

After graduating from Central University, Han worked as an editor of school publications and as a lecturer between 1934 and 1939; he earned his LLM degree in Canada before moving to the United States to pursue his research and studies. In 1945, at the invitation of Zhou Gengsheng (周鲠生), president of Wuhan University, Han returned to China and went to teach at Wuhan University. In 1947, he became the head of the Law Department and was elected faculty chair. Between 1957 and 1977, Han was sent to work in a labor camp in the Hubei countryside due to the Anti-Rightist Movement and the Cultural Revolution. During this period, he was assigned briefly to teach English from 1961 to 1966 at Wuhan University. In 1978, Han was recalled to the university. A year later, he took the job of overseeing the reestablishment of the Law Department, of which he was director from 1979 to 1983. He also started China's International Law Research Institute in 1980 and the Environmental Law Research Institute in 1981. He was the first director of both institutes between 1980 and 1991. In 1986, Han was named honorary dean of Wuhan University Law School when it was upgraded from the Law Department. He was active in the academic world of international law and environmental law. He was a member of the Chinese People's Political Consultative Conference from 1978 to 1988 and a council member of several international environmental protection organizations.

1. Han, Du-Pei, "Substance and Procedure in Anglo-American Conflict of Laws" (master's thesis, University of Toronto, 1942).

Han attended and gave speeches at many international law and environmental law conferences overseas. He taught at the University of Missouri–Kansas City in 1982.

Research Areas and Publications

Han was fluent in English, French, and Russian. His research fields included private international law, public international law, international economic law, environmental law, jurisprudence, and legal education. His major works include *Private International Law* (1984)[2] (which took a first prize as a National Excellent Textbook of National Colleges and Universities[3]), *Modern International Law* (1992),[4] and *A New Exploration on Private International Law* (1997).[5]

His scholarship is best known in several areas of international law. In his book *Private International Law*, he expanded the research scope of private international law from merely conflict of laws to include foreign civil legal relationships. *A New Exploration on Private International Law* developed the theoretical system of modern private international law and defined the features and functions of conflict of laws. His article "On Current Developmental Trends of Private International Law"[6] predicted the future of private international law study. He published several articles to address the legal disputes in the area of mainland China, Hong Kong, Macau, and Taiwan and proposed theoretical and legislative frameworks

2. Han Depei 韩德培 et al., *Guoji Sifa* 国际私法 [Private International Law] (Wuhan: Wuhan Daxue Chubanshe, 1984).

3. See "Han Depei."

4. Han Depei 韩德培, *Xiandai Guojifa* 现代国际法 [Modern International Law] (Wuhan: Wuhan Daxue Chubanshe, 1992).

5. Han Depei 韩德培, Huang Jin 黄进, et al., *Guoji Sifa Xinlun* 国际私法新论 [A New Exploration on Private International Law] (Wuhan: Wuhan Daxue Chubanshe, 1997).

6. "Guoji Sifa De Wanjin Fazhan Qushi" 国际司法的晚近发展趋势 [On Current and Future Developmental Trends of Private International Law]. *Zhongguo Guojifa Niankan* 中国国际法年刊 (1988): 3–23.

to solve the problems. In the article "The Establishment of a Market Economy and the Re-creation of China's Private International Law,"[7] he discussed the legislative system of China's conflict of laws. He led the creation and revision of the Chinese model law of conflict of laws, which was translated into English. He encouraged comparative studies of international conflict of laws, which became theoretical foundations for the improvement of China's conflict of laws. He also carried out in-depth research on U.S. and European Union conflict of laws and published *Introduction to American Private International Law (Conflict of Laws)* (1994)[8] with coauthor Han Jian (韩健). Citing many court cases, this book was the first in China to systematically examine U.S. conflict of laws. He participated in an international conflict of laws conference in The Hague.

Besides private international law, Han was also an important scholar in public international law and international economic law. Much of his scholarship in international law focused on China and the General Agreement on Tariffs and Trade (GATT). He was the chief editor of *Modern International Law*.[9]

His interest in jurisprudence was seen in his writings on Roscoe Pound, Hans Kelsen, and Leon Duguit, published across five decades from the 1940s to the 1990s. He discussed the relationship between democracy and the rule of law, constitutional authority, supervision of political power, legal mechanisms of environmental protection, and the improvement of the rule of law environment. He was especially insightful in the discussion of a scientific and logical division of legal studies.

In international economic law, Han's interest was centered on the theories and practice in the field. He clarified the boundaries between

7. "Shichang Jingji De Jianli Yu Zhongguo Guoji Sifa Lifa De Chonggou" 市场经济的建立与中国国际私法的重构 [The Establishment of a Market Economy and the Re-creation of China's Private International Law]. *Faxue Pinglun* 法学评论 5 (1994): 1–18.

8. Han Depei 韩德培 and Han Jian 韩健, *Meiguo Guoji Sifa (Chongtufa) Daolun* 美国国际私法冲突法导论 [Introduction to American Private International Law (Conflict of Laws)] (Beijing: Falü Chubanshe, 1994).

9. *Xiandai Guojifa* 现代国际法 [Modern International Law] (Wuhan: Wuhan Daxue Chubanshe, 1992).

international economic law and other neighboring disciplines. He explored China's relationship with GATT and presented the opportunities and challenges China would face when returning to GATT. He provided academic supports for China's entry into the World Trade Organization (WTO) and proposed ideas and principles for the improvement of GATT.

Han was an author of China's first comprehensive environmental law textbook (1986).[10] His book *The Theory and Practice of China's Environmental Law* (1990)[11] received the Globe Award.[12] The fundamental ideas of his environmental law theory include the following: (1) environmental issues are problems dealing with the relationship between human beings and nature; science alone can't solve these problems; an environmental rule of law will be an effective mechanism; (2) environmental issues are not only a domestic problem but also a global problem; to comply and implement international environmental treaties, it is necessary to study international environmental law; (3) to protect and improve the environment and achieve the harmonious coexistence between human beings and nature, it is important to elevate people's, especially leaders' and senior intellectuals', awareness of the environment and environmental rule of law; (4) international cooperation of environmental studies must be enhanced. As a promoter and founder of environmental law study in China, Han's research provided guidance for legislation, practice, and the study of environmental law.

10. Han Depei 韩德培, Chen Hanguang 陈汉光, and Peng Shouyue 彭守约, *Huanjing Baohufa Jiaocheng* 环境保护法教程 [A Textbook of Environmental Protection Law] (Beijing: Falü Chubanshe, 1986).

11. Han Depei 韩德培, ed., *Zhongguo Huanjingfa De Lilun Yu Shijian* 中国环境法的理论与实践 [The Theory and Practice of China's Environmental Law] (Beijing: Zhongguo Huanjing Kexue Chubanshe, 1990).

12. Diqiu Jiang 地球奖 [The Globe Award] was created by the China Forum of Environmental Journalists and Friends of the Earth (Hong Kong) in 1997. It rewards organizations and individuals for their outstanding contributions to promote environmental awareness in Chinese society. See http://baike.baidu.com/view/293209.htm (accessed Feb. 9, 2017).

Bibliography of English Publications by Professor Han Depei

Han Depei. "The Harmonization of Law in China: How to Resolve the Problem of Regional Conflict of Laws." In *Law, Legal Culture and Politics in the Twenty First Century: Essays in Honour of Alice Erh-Soon Tay*, edited by Guenther Doeker-Mach and Klaus A. Ziegert, 386–88. Stuttgart: F. Steiner, 2004.

Han Depei and Huang Jin. "A Look at Regional Conflict of Laws in China." *Social Sciences in China* 11, no. 2 (1990): 150–69.

Han Depei and Stephen Kanter. "Legal Education in China." *American Journal of Comparative Law: A Quarterly* 32 (1984): 543–82.

References

Guo Yujun 郭玉军, ed. *Yige Faxuejia De Shiji Zhuimeng: Han Depei Sixiang Yanjiu 一个法学家的世纪追梦: 韩德培思想研究* [A Century of Chasing Dreams by a Legal Scholar: A Study of Han Depei's Thoughts]. Wuhan: Wuhan Daxue Chubanshe, 2015.

"Han Depei" 韩德培 [Han Depei]. http://baike.baidu.com/view/135629.htm (accessed Feb. 9, 2017).

Han Depei 韩德培. "Yi Faxue Weiye" 以法学为业 [Legal Study as a Career]. In *Fayi Lanshanchu–20 Shiji Zhongguo Falüren Zishu 法意阑珊处: 20 世纪中国法律人自述* [Law's Meaning in the Dim Light: Self Accounts of Twentieth-Century Legal Persons] edited by Chen Xiahong 陈夏红. Beijing: Qinghua Daxue Chubanshe, 2009.

Huang Jin 黄进 and Liu Weixiang 刘卫翔. *Han Depei Wenxuan 韩德培文选* [Selected Works of Han Depei]. Wuhan: Wuhan Daxue Chubanshe, 1996.

Huang Jin 黄进, Xiao Yongping 肖永平, and Han Jian 韩建. *Faxue Dajia Han Depei 法学大家韩德培* [Jurist Master Han Depei]. Wuhan: Hubei Meishu Chubanshe, 2011.

Xiao Yongping 肖永平. "Han Depei" 韩德培 [Han Depei]. In *Luojia Guojifa: Xueren Yu Xuewen 珞珈国际法: 学人与学问* [Luojia International Law: Scholars and Their Scholarship], edited by He Qisheng 何其生, 157–94. Wuhan: Wuhan Daxue Chubanshe, 2011.

———. "Han Depei Xiansheng De Xueshu Jingshen He Faxue Sixiang" 韩德培先生的学术精神和法学思想 [The Spirit of Mr. Han Depei's Research and His Legal Thought]. In *Wuhan Daxue Guojifa Yanjiusuo 武汉大学国际法研究所* [Wuhan University Institute of International Law]. http://translaw.whu.edu.cn/index.php/index-view-aid-250 .html (accessed Dec. 18, 2020).

Yu Minyou 余敏友. "Han Depei Xiansheng Fangtanlu" 韩德培先生访谈录 [Notes from an Interview with Mr. Han Depei]. In *Wuhan Daxue Guojifa Yanjiusuo (武汉大学国际法研究所)* [Wuhan University Institute of International Law], *Huanqiu Falü Pinglun 环球法律评论* 1 (2002).

9. Wang Tieya (王铁崖)

(1913–2003)

International Law

Professor of law at Peking University, Wang Tieya was an outstanding and respected international law scholar in the People's Republic of China. In addition to his teaching and admirable efforts to publicize international law throughout China, Wang authored well-known textbooks and reference materials on general international law and on the law of the sea in particular.[1] He was the longest serving full-time teacher of international law in recent Chinese history. He was also China's representative to the United Nations and the international community. He brought Western ideas on international law to China, as well as Chinese ideas about international law to the international community at large. He "has combined a life-long scholarly and professional interest in international law with a vision of a world community spanning continents and cultures and working towards peace, equality, and justice for all humankind."[2]

---

1. Zhang Haiwen 张海文, "Professor Wang Tieya and the Law of the Sea," *Journal of History of International Law* 4 (2002): 204.

2. Macdonald, Ronald St. J., "Wang Tieya: Persevering in Adversity and Shaping the Future of Public International Law in China," in *Essays in Honour of Wang Tieya*, edited by Ronald St. John Macdonald, 2 (Dordrecht, Netherlands: Maritnus Nijhott, 1994).

Educational Background

Wang was born in Fuzhou (福州) City of Fujian Province. His father, Wang Shouchang, was educated at the University of Paris, where he studied law. Upon returning to China, Wang Shouchang held a diplomatic position and was the translator of *The Lady of the Camellias*.[3] Wang Tieya also had a cousin who served as ambassador to Belgium. The work of his father and cousin gave him his first exposure to the world outside China, which contributed to his interest in international law at a young age.

When Wang was a child, he studied Chinese classical literature with a private teacher until he was twelve years old. After the death of his father, Wang was sent to a modern missionary school and then a government-run middle school.

In 1929, Wang entered Fudan University in Shanghai. At Fudan, he majored in English first and then political science. In 1931, he transferred to Tsinghua University in Beijing and graduated with a bachelor of laws degree in 1933. He then entered the Graduate School of Tsinghua University and obtained his master's degree in international law in 1936. He passed the exams to obtain a Sino-American Indemnity Scholarship.[4] Before he went overseas with the scholarship, he spent a year studying under Zhou Gengsheng (周鲠生), one of China's best-known international lawyers at the time. During this time, he read Sir Hersch Lauterpacht's *The Function of Law in the International Law Community*.[5] Inspired by this English scholar, he chose England over the United States for his overseas education. He entered the London School of Economics (LSE) and studied under Lauterpacht. After Lauterpacht's appointment as the

---

3. Alexandre Dumas, *Bali Chahuanü Yishi* 巴黎茶花女遗事 [La Dame aux Camélias (in French), The Lady of the Camellias (in English)] (Alexandre Dumas *fils*, 1848), translated by Wang Shouchang 王寿昌 and Lin Shu 林纾 (published in 1899).

4. The Sino-American Indemnity Scholarship, known as the Boxer Indemnity Scholarship, funded by Boxer Indemnity and established by President Roosevelt, was a scholarship program for Chinese students to receive education in the United States. The program was set up in 1909 and funded the selection, preparatory training, transportation to the United States, and study for the scholarship beneficiaries.

5. Hersch Lauterpacht, *The Function of Law in the International Community*. (Oxford: Clarendon, 1923).

Whewell Professor of International Law at Cambridge University, Wang remained at the LSE for two years. The start of the Second World War in Europe interrupted Wang's doctoral studies in England, and he returned to China in 1939.

Career Highlights

In 1940, with the recommendation of his former teacher, Zhou Gengsheng, Wang landed his first teaching job at Wuhan University, which was then situated in Leshan, Sichuan Province. He taught international law, Chinese history of diplomacy, European history of diplomacy, and international law cases. From 1942 to 1945, he taught at the Central University in Chongqing. In 1946, he accepted a position at Peking University and spent the rest of his teaching career there.

At Peking University, Wang first taught international law, history of diplomacy, and treaty law in the Department of Political Science. In 1947, he was appointed director of the department. In 1952, due to a university-wide departmental reorganization, Wang became a professor in the History Department. In 1954, the Law Department of Peking University, which had merged with Beijing College of Political Science and Law, resumed independent operation. Wang was appointed professor of law at the university in 1956. A year later, he was classified as a Rightist and was forced to leave his teaching position. Like other professors in China, Wang's teaching and research were again interrupted during the Cultural Revolution.

The end of the Cultural Revolution and the resumption of student admissions at Peking University brought new life to Wang's academic career. In 1979, he created China's first international law study program at the university. In 1983, he became the founding director of the International Law Institute at Peking University. He assisted in the establishment of China's first Association of International Law in 1980 and was elected vice president of the association. With the assistance of Professor Chen Tiqiang (陈体强), Wang edited and published the association's first publication, the *Chinese Yearbook of International Law*.[6]

6. See footnote 2 in chapter 3 on Li Haopei.

Wang was very active in both academic and political arenas inside and outside China. He was appointed adviser for international affairs by the Chinese government and represented China at many international conferences and law-making conferences. He was a member of the Drafting Committee of the Basic Law of the Hong Kong Special Administrative Region.

During the 1980s, he attended many conferences in the United States, Canada, and other countries. He was a visiting scholar at Columbia Law School and at the Max Planck Institute and a visiting professor at The Hague Academy of International Law. He gave lectures at the University of British Columbia, Harvard University, the University of Michigan, and the University of California, Los Angeles. He was appointed editor or adviser to multiple international journals, including *Ocean Development and International Law* and *Asian Yearbook of International Law*. In 1981, he became the first Chinese scholar elected as associate—and later, in 1987, full member—of the Institut de Droit International. He was a member of the Permanent Court of Arbitration (PCA) in The Hague and was appointed judge at the International Criminal Court in 1997.

Research Areas and Publications

Wang's scholarship is best known for the following areas: Chinese views on international law, analysis of international relations and world order, and the establishment of China's international law heritage. All of his important essays were published in a collection titled *Selected Essays by Wang Tieya* in 2003.[7]

From 1932 to 1948, as a student and later a young teacher, Wang focused on issues in treaty theory. He published several works on the topic, including *An Explanation on Clauses of the Most-Favored-Nation* (1933),[8]

---

7. Deng Zhenglai, *Wang Tieya Wenxuan*.

8. "Zuihuiguo Tiaokuan De Jieshi" 最惠国条款的解释 [An Explanation on Clauses of the Most Favored Nation], *Qinghua Zhoukan* 清华周刊 11 (1932).

A Study of New Treaties (1943),[9] and *The War and Treaties* (1944).[10] He also wrote an English essay titled "The Status of Aliens and Foreign Enterprise in China" (1945).[11]

During this period, the most pressing issue facing Chinese international law scholars was to address the abolishment of the unequal treaties imposed by foreign powers. A starting point for the mission was to collect, compile, and study all treaties signed between China and foreign countries. Wang realized the importance of the project and devoted over ten years to gathering more than one thousand pieces of such treaties from the late Qing dynasty to the beginning of the People's Republic of China. This labor-intensive work yielded a grand publication, in three volumes, titled *The Old Treaties and Agreements between China and Foreign Powers*. The three volumes were published between 1957 and 1962[12] and have been recognized as a great achievement in the field. The historical value and practical significance of this publication make it an important resource for the study of treaty law and Chinese diplomatic history.

Wang denounced unfair international relations created by unequal treaties. He pointed out that China, as a sovereign state, was one of the builders of the international order rather than a subject of adjustment. He proposed his ideas on an equal and just international order. His articles published between 1946 and 1949 seemed to have been more political in nature. They were aimed at defending the Chinese government and condemning foreign invasions and wars.[13]

His most important academic works emerged after 1978, when the Cultural Revolution ended and economic reform started. His speech at The Hague Academy of International Law titled "International Law in China: Historical and Contemporary Perspectives"[14] and his last book,

9. *Xinyue Yanjiu* 新約研究 [A Study of New Treaties] (Chongqing: Qingnian Shudian, 1943).

10. *Zhanzheng Yu Tiaoyue* 戰爭與條約 [The War and Treaties] (Chongqing: Zhongguo Wenhua Fuwushe, 1944).

11. Wang Tieya, *Status of Aliens.*

12. *Zhongwei Jiuyuezhang Huibian* 中外旧约章汇编 [The Old Treaties and Agreements between China and Foreign Powers] (Beijing: Sanlian Shudian, 1957, 1959, 1962).

13. See "Wang Tieya," 233.

14. "International Law in China: Historical and Contemporary Perspectives, Collected Courses," *The Hague Academy of International Law* 221 (1990): 195.

titled *Introduction to International Law*,[15] represent the height of his scholarship. The former addresses the development of international law, theories of international law, and China and international law. The latter concludes his scholarship in international law[16] and explores such topics as the authority and effectiveness of international law, the origins and evidence of international law, and the relationship between international law and international relations.

Since the study of international law originated in the West, it is very important for Chinese scholars to access reference works and classic textbooks, as well as primary sources from the Western world. Wang made a major contribution in this regard. Together with Professor Chen Tiqiang, he translated the two-volume publication *Oppenheim's International Law*.[17] He was also an editor of the dictionary *English, French, and Chinese International Law Terms*.[18] His scholarship has helped the development of international law study in China. The field of international law is forever linked with the name Wang Tieya.

Bibliography of English Publications by Professor Wang Tieya

McWhinney, Edward, Lev N. Orlov, and Wang Tieya. *Judicial Settlement of Disputes Jurisdiction and Justiciability*. Dordrecht, Netherlands: Martinus Nijhoff, 1990.
McWhinney, Edward, Wang Tieya, and Lev N. Orlov. *Judicial Settlement of Disputes: Jurisdiction and Justiciability*. Recueil Des Cours—Académie De Droit International De La Haye. Dordrecht, Netherlands: Martinus Nijhoff, 1991.
Wang Tieya. "Grotius' Works in China." *International Law and the Grotian Heritage: A Commemorative Colloquium Held at The Hague on 8 April 1983 on the Occasion of the*

---

15. *Guojifa Yinlun* 国际法引论 [Introduction to International Law] (Beijing: Beijing Daxue Chubanshe, 1998).

16. See Li Zhaojie, "Teaching, Research, and Dissemination of International Law in China: The Contribution of Wang Tieya," *Canadian Yearbook of International Law* 31 (1993): 209.

17. L. Oppenheim, *Aobenhai Guojifa* 奥本海国际法 [Oppenheim's International Law] (Beijing: Shangwu Yinshuguan, 1981).

18. Wang Tieya, *Ying Fa Han Guojifa*.

Fourth Centenary of the Birth of Hugo Grotius, edited by T. M. C. Asser Instituut, 265–72. The Hague: T. M. C. Asser Instituut, 1985.

———. *International Law in China: Historical and Contemporary Perspectives*. Leiden, Netherlands: Martinus Nijhoff, 1990.

———. "International Law in China: Historical and Contemporary Perspectives." *Recueil Des Cours* 221 (1991): 195–369.

———. "My Friend Li Haopei." In *International Law in the Post-Cold War World: Essays in Memory of Li Haopei*, edited by Sienho Yee and Wang Tieya, xxii–xxiv. London: Routledge, 2001.

———. *The Status of Aliens and Foreign Enterprise in China*. Chongqing: China Institute of Pacific Relations, 1945.

———. "The Third World and International Law." In *Structure and Process of International Law: Essays in Legal Philosophy, Doctrine and Theory*, edited by R. St. J. Macdonald and Douglas M Johnston, 955–76. The Hague: Martinus Nijhoff, 1983.

———. "Universal Approach to the Teaching of International Law." In *International Law as a Language for International Relations—Le Droit International Comme Langage Des Relations Internationales*, edited by United Nations. The Hague; Boston: Kluwer Law International, 1996.

———. *Ying Fa Han Guojifa Cihui* 英法汉国际法词汇 [English-French Chinese Dictionary of International Law]. Beijing: China Translation, 1984.

Wang Tieya and Mark A. Cohen "Teaching and Research of International Law in Present Day China." *Columbia Journal of Transnational Law* 22 (1983) 77–82.

Wang Tieya and Jia Bingbing. "Is Defective Composition a Matter of Lack of Jurisdiction Within the Meaning of Rule Seventy-Two?" In *Essays on ICTY Procedure and Evidence in Honour of Gabrielle Kirk McDonald*, edited by Richard May, David Tolbert, John Hocking, Ken Roberts, Bingbing Jia, Daryl Mundis and Gabriël Oosthuizen. The Hague; Boston: Kluwer Law International, 2001.

References

Deng Zhenglai 邓正来, ed. *Wang Tieya Wenxuan* 王铁崖文选 [Selected Essays by Wang Tieya]. Beijing: Zhongguo Zhengfa Daxue Chubanshe, 2003.

———, ed. *Wang Tieya Xueshu Wenhua Suibi* 王铁崖学术文化随笔 [Wang Tieya's Cultural and Academic Writings]. Beijing: Zhongguo Qingnian Chubanshe, 1999.

Heuser, Robert. "China and Development in International Law: Wang Tieya as a Contemporary." *Journal of the History of International Law* 4 (2002): 142–58.

Jennings, R. "Wang Tieya: Our Dear Friend and Colleague." *Journal of the History of International Law* 4 (2002): 139–41.

Jia Bingbing 贾兵兵. "Judge Wang Tieya: The Yugoslav Tribunal Experience." *Journal of the History of International Law* 4 (2002): 209–15.

Ko Swan Sik. "Wang Tieya and International Law in Asia." *Journal of the History of International Law* 4 (2002): 159–66.

Sampayo, Dorothee de. "Judge Wang: Citizen of the World." *Journal of the History of International Law* 4 (2002): 238–41.

Van Dijk, Pieter. "My Visits with Professor Wang Tieya." *Journal of the History of International Law* 4 (2002): 236–37.

"Wang Tieya" 王铁崖 [Wang Tieya]. In *Luojia Guojifa Xueren Yu Xuewen* 珞珈国际法: 学人与学问 [Luojia International Law: Scholars and Scholarship], edited by He Qisheng 何其生. Wuhan: Wuhan Daxue Chubanshe, 2011.

Yee Sienho. "Professor Wang Tieya: My Friend, Critic, Colleague and Example." *Journal of the History of International Law* 4 (2002): 230–35.

Ying Song. "Wang Tieya and His Students." *Journal of the History of International Law* 4 (2002): 223–29.

Zhang Haiwen 张海文. "Professor Wang Tieya and the Law of the Sea." *Journal of the History of International Law* 4 (2002): 204–8.

Zhao Baoxu. "Professor Wang Tieya as I Knew Him." *Journal of the History of International Law* 4 (2002): 216–22.

Zheng D. "He Is Worthy of His Fame." *Journal of the History of International Law* 4 (2002): 242–46.

10. Yao Meizhen (姚梅镇)

(1915–1993)

International Economic Law

Professor of law at Wuhan University, Yao Meizhen was a pioneer in the study of international economic law in China. As an outstanding teacher, he was also an expert and founder of the study of international investment law in China.

Educational Background

Yao was born in Yiyang (益阳) City of Hunan Province. He entered the Law Department of Wuhan University on a scholarship in 1936 and graduated with an LLB degree four years later. His senior thesis, titled "The Theory and Practice on Compensation for Damage without Negligence," was awarded the first prize in the first national college senior thesis competition. After the People's Republic of China was established in 1949, he spent a year at the Central Cadres School of Politics and Law in Beijing.[1]

---

1. See footnote 4 in chapter 7 on Gong Xiangrui.

Career Highlights

Yao started working at Wuhan University in 1941. He first taught introduction to law between 1941 and 1943 and later civil law and property in 1946. During that period, he was also invited to teach at the National Business College[2] and Guizhou University. In 1957, he was classified as a Rightist and sent to a labor camp. He was allowed to come back to the city and work on the university farm in 1960. However, the Cultural Revolution brought him to another labor camp in Hubei. He worked as a farmer, a barber, and a cook during this period. He finally got his teaching job back at Wuhan University in 1976.

In 1979, Yao became associate director of the Law Department and a part-time associate director of the International Law Institute at Wuhan University. He was a member of the Standing Committee of the Wuhan People's Political Consultative Congress. Wuhan University named him a Model Teacher in 1985 and an Outstanding Teacher in 1987. Wuhan City gave him the honor of Model Teacher in 1986.

Research Areas and Publications

Yao's most important articles and shorter works have been assembled in a publication titled *A Collection of Yao Meizhen's Works* (2010),[3] which includes a portion of his work "On Compensation Liability for Damage without Negligence."[4] This was his first major work, a combination of a 1943 article published in the *Quarterly of Social Sciences of National Wu-*

---

2. Guoli Shangxueyuan 国立商学院 [The National Business College] was in operation between 1942 and 1946. For more information, see https://baike.baidu.com/item/%E5%9B%BD%E7%AB%8B%E5%95%86%E5%AD%A6%E9%99%A2 (accessed Aug. 14, 2020).

3. Yao Meizhen, *Yao Meizhen Wenji*.

4. "Wuguoshi Sunhai Peichang Zerenlun" 无过失损害赔偿责任论 [On Compensation Liability for Damage without Negligence], unpublished manuscript in five volumes.

han University[5] and his further in-depth research. However, four volumes of this five-volume manuscript were lost due to the chaos of the wars and political movements from the 1940s to the 1970s in China.[6] Early in his teaching career, he also translated Munroe Smith's *The Development of European Law* (1943),[7] which became a major source for the study of European law. Because of the interruption of the Cultural Revolution, there was a long pause in his academic career. He was able to be productive again starting in 1979. His other notable works include *International Investment Law* (1985),[8] *Introduction to International Investment Law* (1988),[9] *Introduction to International Economic Law* (1989),[10] and *Comparative Foreign Investment Law* (1993).[11] In addition, he published eight textbooks and some translations from English and Japanese to Chinese.

Yao pioneered the study of international economic law in China. As early as 1980, Yao claimed that international economic law was not a part of international public law or a branch of international law of economics. In his article "A Few Issues Concerning the Concept of International Economic Law,"[12] he pointed out that the study of international economic law included not only public international law but also domestic law and not only public law but also private law. He believed that in addition to the state and international organizations, the objectives of

---

5. "Wuguoshi Sunhai Peichang Zeren Zhi Lishi Fazhan" 无过失损害赔偿责任之历史发展 [The Historical Development of Compensation Liability for Damage without Negligence], *Quarterly of Social Sciences of National Wuhan University* 8, no. 1 (1943).

6. See Yu Jinsong 余劲松, "Zhongguo Guoji Jingji Faxue De Dianjiren—Yao Meizhen" 中国国际经济法学的奠基人—姚梅镇 [The Founder of International Economic Law in China—Yao Meizhen], in Yao Meizhen, *Yao Meizhen Wenji*, 4.

7. Munroe Smith, *Oulu Falü Fadashi* 欧陆法律发达史 [The Development of European Law], trans. Yao Meizhen 姚梅镇 (Chongqing: Shangwu Yinshuguan, 1943).

8. *Guoji Touzifa* 国际投资法 [International Investment Law] (Wuhan: Wuhan Daxue Chubanshe, 1985).

9. *Guoji Touzifa Rumen* 国际投资法入门 [Introduction to International Investment Law] (Beijing: Falü Chubanshe, 1988).

10. *Guoji Jingjifa Gailun* 国际经济法概论 [Introduction to International Economic Law] (Wuhan: Wuhan Daxue Chubanshe, 1989).

11. *Bijiao Waizifa* 比较外资法 [Comparative Foreign Investment Law] (Wuhan: Wuhan Daxue Chubanshe, 1993).

12. "Guanyu Guoji Jingjifa Gainian De Jige Wenti" 关于国际经济法概念的几个问题 [A Few Issues concerning the Concept of International Economic Law], *Faxue Yanjiu Ziliao* 法学研究资料 6 (1981).

international economic law also included individuals, legal persons, and other organizations. International economic law regulated the legal relationship in commercial production, financial transactions, capital and technology transfer, and taxation during international economic exchange. International economic law was a combination of studies of domestic and international legal doctrines that dealt with the transaction of international business. Based on this definition, Yao founded China's study of international economic law.

According to Yao, international investment law was a branch of the study of international economic law. From a comparative approach of domestic and international theories and practice, he divided the study of international investment law into three legal regimes: capital import country, capital export country, and bilateral and multilateral treaties. He was influential in discussions of the following topics: the treatment standard for international investors, concessions, and nationalization.

As for the treatment standard for international investors, he identified three mechanisms: the standard of national treatment, the standard of most favored nation treatment, and the international standards. The combination of the first two treatments was often applied in international investment. In the debate on national treatment and international standards, he suggested that national treatment meant the equality of legal status and prohibition of discrimination to foreign investors. It was not equal to granting a special status to foreign investors. Foreign investors did not have the same political and economic rights as domestic investors.

In discussing concessions, Yao believed that a concession was not an international treaty because one party of a concession was private individuals or a company rather than another national organization. Therefore, concessions belonged to domestic law regime and had no authority over the state or its international responsibilities.

In addressing nationalization, he stressed the attribute of sovereignty and rejected the theory of private property as a sacred and inviolable right. According to him, nationalization was the result of a state applying its sovereign right. For the sake of public security and common interests, a state had the right to nationalize domestic private property, whether it belonged to its citizens or foreigners. Government compensation was a remedy to nationalization, not a precondition of the action.

Bibliography of English Publications by Professor Yao Meizhen

Yao Meizhen. "Legal Protection of International Investments." In *Selected Articles from Chinese Yearbook of International Law*, edited by Wang Tieya and Chen Tiqiang, 147–88. Beijing: Zhongguo Duiwai Fanyi Chuban Gongsi, 1983.

References

Dangdai Zhongguo Shehui Kexue Xuezhe Dacidian 当代中国社会科学学者大辞典 [A Dictionary of Contemporary Chinese Social Science Scholars]. Hangzhou: Zhejiang Daxue Chubanshe, 1990.

Guo Zhongxiao 呙中校 and Wu Xiao 吴骁. "Wuda Hafo 'Sanjianke' Manji" 武大 "哈佛三剑客"漫记 [On the "Three Harvard Swordsmen" of Wuhan University]. http://canada-china-corp.org/home/node/232 (accessed Dec. 19, 2020).

Wang Yuming 王玉明 and Yu Xiaoguang 于晓光, eds. *Zhongguo Faxuejia Cidian* 中国法学家辞典 [A Dictionary of Chinese Legal Scholars]. Beijing: Zhongguo Laodong Chubanshe, 1991.

Xie Xiufen 解秀芬, Yao Ping 姚萍, and Cao Yuanlin 曹远林, eds. *Zhongguo Dangdai Jiaoyu Mingren Zhuanlue* 中国当代教育名人传略 [Biographies of Famous Contemporary Chinese Educators]. Hong Kong: Xianggang Weilai Zhongguo Chubanshe, 1997.

Yao Meizhen 姚梅镇. *Yao Meizhen Wenji* 姚梅镇文集 [A Collection of Yao Meizhen's Works]. Wuhan: Wuhan Daxue Chubanshe, 2010.

"Yao Meizhen" 姚梅镇 [Yao Meizhen]. http://baike.baidu.com/view/316182.htm (accessed Mar. 25, 2017).

Yu Jinsong 余劲松. "Guoji Jingji Faxue De Dianjiren" 国际经济法学的奠基人 [The Founder of the Study of International Economic Law]. *Zhongguo Shenpan* 中国审判 9 (2008): 22–27.

11. Zhao Lihai (赵理海)

(1916–2000)

Public International Law and the Law of the Sea

Professor of law at Peking University, Zhao Lihai received his legal education at the University of Chicago and Harvard University. As an expert in public international law and the law of the sea, he became a judge of the first International Tribunal for the Law of the Sea and was a founding member of the Chinese Association of Law of the Sea.

Educational Background

Zhao was born in Wenxi (闻喜) County of Shanxi Province. In 1935, he entered Yenching University in Beijing. Four years later, he earned a bachelor's degree in liberal arts and set forth to the United States. He enrolled in the University of Chicago in 1940 and graduated with a master's degree in international law in 1941. Then he went on to pursue a doctoral degree in international law at Harvard University and graduated in 1944.

Career Highlights

In 1945, Zhao returned to China and started teaching at Wuhan University. During his two years at Wuhan University, he taught international treaties and three other courses. From 1947 to 1952, he taught at the National Central University and Nanjing University. Then his career was interrupted by a nationwide university reorganization. In 1957, he obtained a teaching position at Peking University and spent the rest of his academic life there. He served as director of the International Law Department of the Law Faculty until 1966. His teaching career once again came to a halt due to the Cultural Revolution. During this time, he was assigned to a labor camp in Jiangxi Province and worked in a cowshed. Having no access to research materials, he collected newspaper clippings that reported information and developments in the field of the law of the sea. It was in this period that Zhao found his direction for future research. He decided to concentrate on the study of the law of the sea and accumulated knowledge and materials in the field. When his teaching position resumed in 1978, he was able to kick-start his teaching and research on this subject. In 1983, he became a visiting professor at New York University. In 1996, Zhao was elected as a judge of the International Tribunal for the Law of the Sea. He was the first Chinese person to hold this position.

Zhao participated in many law-drafting discussions including the Law of the People's Republic of China on the Territorial Sea and the Contiguous Zone[1] and the Civil Aviation Law of the People's Republic of China.[2] He was a member of the Seventh Chinese People's Political Consultative Conference, director of the China Law Society, and director of the China National Association for International Studies.

---

1. "Zhonghua Renmin Gongheguo Linghai Ji Pilianqufa" 中华人民共和国领海及毗连区法 [Law of the People's Republic of China on the Territorial Sea and the Contiguous Zone] (promulgated by the Standing Committee of the National People's Congress, Feb. 25, 1992, effective Feb. 25, 1992), *Falü Huibian* 3 (1992): 2, 5.

2. "Zhonghua Renmin Gongheguo Minyong Hangkongfa" 中华人民共和国民用航空法 [Civil Aviation Law of the People's Republic of China] (promulgated by the Standing Committee of the National People's Congress, Oct. 30, 1995, effective Mar. 1, 1996, amended in 2009 and 2015), *Falü Huibian* 4 (1995): 1, 50.

Research Areas and Publications

At the University of Chicago, Zhao wrote his master's thesis, titled "A Study of Commercial Treaties between China and the United States."[3] At Harvard University, he wrote his PhD dissertation, titled "International Law as Applied to the Sino-American Treaties."[4] His academic idol was Professor Manley Ottmer Hudson (1886–1960), an expert in public international law and a judge at the Permanent International Court of Justice. Zhao was a frequent visitor to the Harvard Law School Library. He read more than one thousand books in the library's collection and cited over three hundred books in his dissertation.[5]

While teaching at Wuhan University, he published his first book, *Public International Law*,[6] in 1947. Because public international law was an advanced and unfamiliar subject at the time, this quickly became a standard textbook across universities. In 1982, he published *On the Revision of the Charter of the United Nations*,[7] the first book on the United Nations in China. In 1984, he published another pioneering book: *The New Development of the Law of the Sea*.[8] This book came out a little more than a year after the adoption of the United Nations Convention on the Law of the Sea (1982). Being the first book in the field, it filled a research gap and was well received. It also became a classic in China. The period between 1986 and 1996 was the most productive time of Zhao's career. He published a few dozen articles and several books, including *On the*

3. Zhao, Lihai, "A Study of Commercial Treaties between China and the United States" (master's thesis, University of Chicago, 1941, held by Mansueto Library).

4. Zhao, Lihai, "International Law as Applied to the Sino-American Treaties" (PhD diss., Harvard University, 1944, held by Harvard University Archives, http://id .lib.harvard.edu/alma/990037995990203941/catalog).

5. See Yang Qinyun, "Zhao Lihai," 278.

6. *Guoji Gongfa* 国际公法 [Public International Law] (Beijing: Shangwu Yinshuguan, 1947).

7. *Lianheguo Xianzhang De Xiugai Wenti* 联合国宪章的修改问题 [On the Revision of the Charter of the United Nations] (Beijing: Beijing Daxue Chubanshe, 1982).

8. *Haiyangfa De Xinfazhan* 海洋法的新发展 [The New Development of the Law of the Sea] (Beijing: Beijing Daxue Chubanshe, 1984).

Theory and Practice of the Law of the Sea (1987),[9] *The Fundamental Theories of International Law* (1990),[10] *Issues in Contemporary International Law* (1993),[11] and *A Study on Issues of the Law of the Sea* (1996).[12] Because the original sources of international law are mostly in languages other than Chinese, Chinese scholars face an obstacle to publishing in the field. Zhao was one of the few scholars who had overcome this hurdle. Even after becoming a judge of the International Tribunal for the Law of the Sea, Zhao published five articles to discuss important cases of the court. The last article he published was in 2000, the same year he passed away. In addition, he was chief editor of the *Chinese Yearbook of International Law*.

Zhao's works often addressed China's pressing issues in the international arena. With the mission to protect China's rights and serve justice, his scholarship is a representation of China's position and practice in international law. His major contribution is the exploration of the fundamental concepts of international law with a socialist Chinese perspective.

The research areas he focused on included theories of international law, the law of the sea, and the reform of the United Nations. In theories of international law, his works are notable in the following dimensions: (1) the authority of international law, on which he disproved the nihilism[13] of international law; (2) foreign interference in domestic affairs in the name of human rights, on which he emphasized the rule of domestic jurisdiction in the Charter of the United Nations (also known as the UN

---

9. *Haiyangfa De Lilun Yu Shijian* 海洋法的理论与实践 [On the Theory and Practice of the Law of the Sea] (Beijing: Falü Chubanshe, 1987).

10. *Guojifa Jiben Lilun* 国际法基本理论 [The Fundamental Theories of International Law] (Beijing: Beijing Daxue Chubanshe, 1990).

11. *Dangdai Guojifa Wenti* 当代国际法问题 [Issues in Contemporary International Law] (Beijing: Zhongguo Fazhi Chubanshe, 1993).

12. *Haiyangfa Wenti Yanjiu* 海洋法问题研究 [A Study on Issues of the Law of the Sea] (Beijing: Beijing Daxue Chubanshe, 1996).

13. Legal nihilism asserts that international law is not really law because of the lack of an international legal system that features an enforcement mechanism for its rules, courts with universal and compulsory jurisdiction, and a rule of recognition, a criterion for determining which laws are in the system. The British legal philosopher H. L. A. Hart is well known in this regard.

Charter); and (3) the legal issues in the Kokario case,[14] through which he discussed the recognition and inheritance systems in international law.

Concerning the law of the sea, he published several articles to evaluate the United Nations Convention on the Law of the Sea (UNCLOS) and addressed international seabed issues. Based on his comprehensive analysis of UNCLOS, he presented the pros and cons for China to join the convention and urged China to join. After China ratified the convention in 1996, he advocated the drafting of the Law on the Exclusive Economic Zone and the Continental Shelf and the Law of Fisheries Protection and Management in order to protect China's marine rights.

Zhao proposed six principles in delimitation of the continental shelf in the East China Sea. He conducted extensive research on China's sovereignty in the South China Sea and used various sources and relevant international treaties, conventions, and practice to support his argument.

In his discussions on the revision of the UN Charter, Zhao examined the general attitudes and positions of different countries and the battles over the deliberation and revision of the charter. He predicted that revision of the charter would be inevitable in the future, but the work could be difficult. He addressed the membership of small countries to the United Nations and other issues within the organization. His opinions on the revision of the UN Charter and the reform of the United Nations Security Council are instrumental and valuable even today.

Bibliography of English Publications by Professor Zhao Lihai

Chao Li-hai. *The Common Heritage of Mankind: An Important Principle of Contemporary Law of the Sea*. Washington, DC: World Peace through Law Center, 1990.

Mensah, Thomas A., Rüdiger Wolfrum, Lihai Zhao, Gritakumar E. Chitty, and Vicente Marotta Rangel. *The M/V "Saiga" (N. 2) Case: Judgment (Saint Vincent and the Grenadines v. Guinea)*. Hamburg: International Tribunal for the Law of the Sea, 1999.

Rao, P. Chandrasekhara, L. Dolliver, M. Nelson, Hugo Caminos, Lihai Zhao, Gritakumar E. Chitty, and Vicente Marotta Rangel. *The "Camouco" Case: Judgment (Panama*

---

14. Republic of China v. U. Heikan (Case for Evaluation for Land and Building), case no. 1967(WA) 1025 (Kyoto Dist. Ct., 4th Civ. Dept. 16, 1977).

v. France): Application for Prompt Release—Affaire du "Camouco": Arrêt (Panama c. France): Demande de Prompte Mainlevée. Hamburg: International Tribunal for the Law of the Sea, 2000.

Rao, P. Chandrasekhara, Thomas A. Mensah, Rüdiger Wolfrum, Lihai Zhao, Ivan Shearer, Gritakumar E. Chitty, and Vicente Marotta Rangel. *Southern Bluefin Tuna Case: Order (New Zealand v. Japan; Australia v. Japan): Request for Provisional Measures—Affaires du Thon à Nageoire Bleue: Ordonnance (Nouvelle-Zélande c. Japon; Australie c. Japon): Demandes En Prescription De Mesures Conservatoires*. Hamburg: International Tribunal for the Law of the Sea, 1999.

Zhao Lihai. "The Main Legal Problems in the Bilateral Relations between China and the United States." *New York University Journal of International Law and Politics* 16, no. 3 (1984): 543–79.

———. *Papers and Materials on Chinese Views of International Law*. New York: n.p., 1983.

References

Bai Guimei 白桂梅. "Zhao Lihai Zhu *Guojifa Jiben Lilun*" 赵理海著《国际法基本理论》 [On Zhao Lihai's *The Fundamental Theories of International Law*]. *Zhongwai Faxue* 中外法学 2 (1991).

Qiao Shitong 乔仕彤. "Zhao Lihai" 赵理海 [Zhao Lihai]. In *Luojia Guojifa: Xueren Yu Xuewen* 珞珈国际法: 学人与学问 [Luojia International Law: Scholars and Their Scholarship], edited by He Qisheng 何其生, 322–42. Wuhan: Wuhan Daxue Chubanshe, 2011.

Yang Qinyun 杨钦云. "Zhao Lihai" 赵理海 [Zhao Lihai]. In *20 Shiji Zhongguo Zhiming Kexuejia Xueshu Chengjiu Gailan: Faxuejuan* 20 世纪中国知名科学家学术成就概览: 法学卷 [Introduction to the Achievements of the Famous Chinese Scientists in the Twentieth Century: Law Volumes], vol. 2, edited by Jiang Ping 江平 et al. 277–87. Beijing: Kexue Chubanshe, 2014.

12. Wang Mingyang (王名扬)

(1916–2008)

Administrative Law

Professor of law at the China University of Political Science and Law, Wang Mingyang was a prominent scholar of administrative law. His books *Administrative Law of Britain*,[1] *Administrative Law of France*,[2] and *Administrative Law of the United States*[3] are known as the "administrative law trilogy." They are regarded as a milestone in the study of administrative law in China. Because of these publications, a "Wang Mingyang Age" emerged in the study of administrative law in China.[4]

Educational Background

Wang was born in Hengyang (衡阳) County of Hunan Province. He entered Wuhan University and began to study law in 1937. With a thesis titled "Status of the People in an Enemy Country,"[5] he received his bachelor's

---

1. Wang Mingyang 王名扬, *Yingguo Xingzhengfa* 英国行政法 [Administrative Law of Britain] (Beijing: Zhongguo Zhengfa Daxue Chubanshe, 1987).

2. Wang Mingyang 王名扬, *Faguo Xingzhengfa* 法国行政法 [Administrative Law of France] (Beijing: Zhongguo Zhengfa Daxue Chubanshe, 1989).

3. Wang Mingyang 王名扬, *Meiguo Xingzhengfa* 美国行政法 [Administrative Law of the United States] (Beijing: Zhongguo Fazhi Chubanshe, 1995).

4. See "Wang Mingyang."

5. "Diguo Renmin De Diwei" 敌国人民的地位 [Status of the People in an Enemy Country].

degree in 1940. He then went to the National Central University in Chongqing and became a graduate student under Professor Zhang Hui-wen (张汇文), an authority of administrative law in China. Three years later, with a thesis titled "Study on the Neutrality of Office Clerks,"[6] he obtained a master's degree. In 1946, Wang passed the government's study abroad exam. He entered the school of law at the University of Paris in 1948. With a dissertation titled "Civil Liability of Civil Servants towards Individuals under Chinese Law,"[7] he earned a doctoral degree in 1953. For the following three years, he studied Russian and Japanese in France.

Career Highlights

Still living in France, Wang worked as the editor of an overseas Chinese newspaper[8] from 1956 to 1958. He returned to China in 1958 and was assigned a teaching position at the Beijing College of Political Science and Law (now the China University of Political Science and Law). However, for many years, he was not able to teach law because of the interruption of the Anti-Rightist Movement. In 1963, he went to teach French at the Beijing Foreign Trade College (now the University of International Business and Economics). During the Cultural Revolution, Wang was sent to work on a farm and dig ditches in Henan Province. When he was allowed to come back to his teaching position at the Beijing Foreign Trade College, it was 1976, and the Cultural Revolution had ended. In 1983, at the invitation of Professor Ying Songnian (应松年), who was building an administrative law program, Wang returned to the Beijing College of Political Science and Law. At the age of sixty-seven, he began to teach Chinese administrative law and foreign administrative law. Meanwhile, he was adviser to the Administrative Law Group of the China Law Society.

6. "Shiwuguan Zhongli Wenti De Yantao" 事务官中立问题的研讨 [Study on the Neutrality of Office Clerks].

7. Wang Ming Yang, "La Responsabilité civile des fonctionnaires envers les particuliers en droit chinois" (PhD diss., University of Paris, 1953).

8. The newspaper, titled *Qiaozhong* 侨众 [The Overseas Crowd], provided information on the development of the newly established communist China to Chinese people living in France.

Research Areas and Publications

Forced away from teaching law and legal research during the 1960s and 1970s, Wang put his language skills to use. He translated foreign publications, including Hans Kelsen's *The Communist Theory of Law*,[9] and compiled a French textbook.

An opportunity for Wang to present himself as an outstanding scholar came when he was asked to write the chapter on administrative action for China's first textbook of administrative law.[10] In the early 1980s, administrative law was an unfamiliar subject to most scholars in China. Administrative action was a new concept to the writers and chief editor of the textbook. Based on Wang's educational background, the textbook's chief editor invited him to write the chapter. He surpassed expectations and crafted one of the best chapters in the publication. His definition and classification of administrative action was so vital that it continues to be influential even today. It was said that his concept of administrative action has provided theoretical foundations for much administrative legislation, including Administrative Procedure, Administrative Review Law, Administrative Penalties Law, and so on.[11]

Wang became one of the most respected administrative law scholars when he was invited to teach graduate students in 1985. Facing a shortage of textbooks in the field, he set out to write five books on his own: *Administrative Law of Britain*, *Administrative Law of France*, *Administrative Law of the United States*, *Comparative Administrative Law*, and *Administrative Law of China*. The first three books were published in 1987, 1989, and 1995, respectively. By then, he was seventy-nine years old. With advanced age and poor health, he was not able to finish his fourth book, which was published incomplete in 2006.[12] He never started the fifth book.

9. *Gongchanzhuyi De Falü Lilun* 共产主义的法律理论 [The Communist Theory of Law] Hans Kelsen (1955), (Beijing: Zhongguo Fazhi Chubanshe, 1962).

10. Wang Mincan 王岷灿, ed., *Xingzhengfa Gaiyao* 行政法概要 [Introduction to Administrative Law] (Beijing: Falü Chubanshe, 1983), was the first authorized textbook published on the subject in mainland China after 1949.

11. See Gao Jiawei, "Wang Mingyang," 291.

12. Wang Mingyang 王名扬, *Bijiao Xingzhengfa* 比较行政法 [Comparative Administrative Law] (Beijing: Beijing Daxue Chubanshe, 2006).

Wang had many other publications, including fifteen articles, *A Concise Textbook of French, American, British, and Japanese Administrative Law* (1991),[13] and *Foreign Administrative Litigation System* (1991).[14] However, none of these works has had such a profound impact on administrative law studies in China as his administrative law trilogy of *Administrative Law of Britain*, *Administrative Law of France*, and *Administrative Law of the United States*. The most significant contribution of his publications was to introduce Chinese scholars to foreign administrative law concepts, systems, and scholarship. These include natural justice, administrative remedies, judicial review, due process of law, freedom of information, and other topics. According to Professor Zhu Suli (朱苏力) of Peking University, Wang's trilogy was one of the most cited works in legal textbooks in China from 1998 to 2002 (with *Administrative Law of the United States* as number one).[15] These three publications, plus the unfinished *Comparative Administrative Law*, have been recognized as a milestone and represented the arrival of a "Wang Mingyang Age" in China's administrative law study.[16]

To Wang, the most important thing in writing his administrative law trilogy was to use firsthand materials. From 1990 to 1992, he spent two years at Columbia University to do research for his book *Administrative Law of the United States*. According to Wang, to collect materials for this book, "I mainly relied on the library of Columbia University."[17] His overseas students provided some materials for the first two books in the trilogy. The long-lasting influence of the trilogy has been rooted in these features of his works: they fill theoretical gaps and answer the calls of legal development; they are conceptually accurate and systematic; and they are rich and original in material and simple and professional in language.

13. Wang Mingyang 王名扬, *Fa, Mei, Ying, Ri Xingzhengfa Jianming Jiaocheng* 法，美，英，日行政法简明教程 [A Concise Textbook of French, American, British, and Japanese Administrative Law] (Taiyuan: Shanxi Renmin Chubanshe, 1991).

14. Wang Mingyang 王名扬, *Waiguo Xingzheng Susong Zhidu* 外国行政诉讼制度 [Foreign Administrative Litigation System] (Beijing: Renmin Fayuan Chubanshe, 1991).

15. Zhu Suli 朱苏力, "Cong Faxue Zhuzuo Yinzheng Kan Zhongguo Faxue" 从法学著作引证看中国法学 [On Chinese Legal Studies from Citations of Legal Publications], *Zhongguo Faxue* 中国法学 2 (2003).

16. Chen Xiahong, "Shenju Loushi Mingyang Tianxia."

17. Chen Xiahong, "Shenju Loushi Mingyang Tianxia."

In 2016, a six-volume publication titled *A Complete Collection of Wang Mingyang's Works*[18] was published by Peking University Press. This set is a complete collection of all articles, dictionary entries, textbooks, translation works, and published books by Wang. His works have enlightened new generations of administrative law scholars and have had a significant influence on the development of administrative law in China.

References

Chen Xiahong 陈夏红. "Shenju Loushi Mingyang Tianxia—Wang Mingyang De Zhibi Rensheng" 身居陋室，名扬天下-王名扬的纸笔人生 [Wang Mingyang's Academic Life]. In Chen Xiahong 陈夏红, *Bainian Zhongguo Falüren Jianying* 百年中国法律人剪影 [Profiles of Chinese Jurists in a Hundred Years]. Beijing: Zhongguo Fazhi Chubanshe, 2006.

Gao Jiawei 高家伟. "Wang Mingyang" 王名扬 [Wang Mingyang]. In *20 Shiji Zhongguo Zhiming Kexuejia Xueshu Chengjiu Gailan: Faxuejuan* 20 世纪中国知名科学家学术成就概览: 法学卷 [Introduction to the Achievements of Famous Chinese Scientists in the Twentieth Century: Law Volumes], vol. 2, edited by Jiang Ping et al., 289–99. Beijing: Kexue Chubanshe, 2014.

Liu Dongliang 刘东亮, Si Posen 司坡森, and Wang Yan 王彦. "Wang Mingyang Xiansheng Faxue Sixiang Shuping" 王名扬先生法学思想述评 [A Discussion on Mr. Wang Mingyang's Legal Thought]. http://www.lawtime.cn/info/lunwen/xzqtxzflw /2007011960806.html (accessed Mar. 12, 2017).

"Wang Mingyang" 王名扬 [Wang Mingyang]. http://baike.baidu.com/item /%E7%8E%8B%E5%90%8D%E6%89%AC/6388608 (accessed Mar. 12, 2017).

Xiao Ping 萧评. "Zhongguo Xingzheng Faxue de 'Puluomixiusi'—Wang Mingyang Xiansheng Fangtan" 中国行政法学的"普罗米修斯"-王名扬先生访谈 [Prometheus of China's Administrative Law—an Interview with Wang Mingyang]. *Falü Pinglun* 法律评论 5 (2002).

Ying Songnian 应松年. "Xu" 序 [Preface]. In Wang Mingyang 王名扬, *Bijiao Xingzhengfa* 比较行政法 [Comparative Administrative Law]. Beijing: Beijing Daxue Chubanshe, 2006.

Ying Songnian 应松年 and Ma Huaide 马怀德, eds. *Dangdai Zhongguo Xingzhengfa De Yuanliu—Wang Mingyang Jiaoshou Jiushi Huadan Zhushou Wenji* 当代中国行政法的源流-王名扬教授九十华诞祝寿文集 [The Origins of Contemporary Chinese Administrative Law—Collective Articles to Celebrate Professor Wang Mingyang's Ninetieth Birthday]. Beijing: Zhongguo Fazhi Chubanshe, 2006.

18. Wang Mingyang 王名扬, *Wang Mingyang Quanji* 王名扬全集 [A Complete Collection of Wang Mingyang's Works] (Beijing: Beijing Daxue Chubanshe, 2016).

13. Chen Tiqiang (陈体强)

(1917–1983)

International Law

Professor at China Foreign Affairs University, Chen Tiqiang was one of the most important philosophers of international law in contemporary China. His book *The International Law of Recognition, with Special Reference to Practice in Great Britain and the United States*[1] (1951) earned him a reputation as a formidable scholar and intellect on the world stage.

Educational Background

Chen was born in Minhou (闽侯) County of Fujian Province. He graduated from the Department of Political Science at Tsinghua University in 1939. From 1945 to 1948, he studied international law at Oxford University and earned a doctoral degree under the supervision of Professor James Leslie Brierly. His doctoral dissertation was titled "Recognition in International Law: With Special Reference to Practice in Great Britain and the United States."[2] He returned to China in 1948.

1. Chen Ti-Chiang, *The International Law of Recognition, with Special Reference to Practice in Great Britain and the United States* (London: Stevens, 1951).
2. Chen Ti-Chiang, "Recognition in International Law: With Special Reference to Practice in Great Britain and the United States" (PhD diss., University of Oxford, Faculty of Law, 1949).

Career Highlights

Chen started his teaching career at Tsinghua University, where he taught in the Department of Political Science. After 1950, he became associate director of the Editorial Committee of the Association of China People's Foreign Affairs. He also worked at the Institute of International Relations and the Institute of International Law. In 1957, Chen was accused of being a Rightist for one of his newspaper articles. He was forced out of his academic position. In 1969, at the height of the Cultural Revolution, Chen was sent to the labor camp of the Ministry of Foreign Affairs in Hunan Province. Following his political rehabilitation, he became a researcher at the Institute of International Affairs. In 1981, he came to teach at China Foreign Affairs University and was an adjunct professor at Peking University. He was appointed consultant of the Ministry of Foreign Affairs and member of the Chinese People's Political Consultative Conference. He served as chief editor of the *Chinese Yearbook of International Law*. In 1981, Chen taught at Harvard University and the University of Geneva. He also taught at Dalhousie University and the University of London.

Research Areas and Publications

Despite his relatively short life span (he died at the age of sixty-six) and the interruption of China's political chaos in the 1950s and 1960s, Chen published sixty to seventy articles on international law in China. He also published articles and books in Canada, the United States, Belgium, and Great Britain.

The importance of his research starts with his dissertation at Oxford University. At the time, the value of his scholarship was challenged by Professor Hersch Lauterpacht's newly published book *Recognition in International Law*.[3] To prove the worth of his dissertation on the same

3. Hersch Lauterpacht, *Recognition in International Law* (Cambridge: Cambridge University Press, 1947).

topic, Chen made special efforts and used additional documents and cases in his dissertation. This work became a solid foundation for his best-known book: *The International Law of Recognition, with Special Reference to Practice in Great Britain and the United States* (1951).[4] The publication cited more than 450 cases and referenced an abundance of government records, international treaties, articles, and so on. It has been recognized as an authority on international law worldwide.

In this book, Chen presented different ideas from the traditional theories of the international law of recognition. He rejected the constitutive theory and partially disagreed with the declaratory theory. He believed that recognition was not simply a legal action or merely a political action. Recognition was a political action of the state with legal consequences. He disagreed with the constitutive theory and the declaratory theory. The former claims that as long as the people of a region possess the requirements of what constitutes a country, they certainly have the personality[5] under international law. According to declaratory theory, recognition can create the legal personality of a new country; that is, a new country can only acquire international personality through recognition by existing countries.

Before Chen went to Oxford, he published a book in 1943 titled *China's Administration of Foreign Affairs*.[6] Although the book was limited to the social conditions of the time, it provides rich materials for the study of history, foreign relations, and diplomacy of the Qing dynasty.

Between 1949 and 1956, and again between 1979 and 1983, Chen published many articles on the status of the People's Republic of China

---

4. See footnote 1.

5. Personality as a legal term refers to the legal qualifications of a legal person. That is, the capacities/conditions of having legal rights and duties within a certain legal system. Legal personality is a prerequisite to legal capacity. Legal persons are of two kinds: natural persons (i.e., people) and judicial persons (i.e., groups of people, such as corporations, which are treated by law as if they were persons). While people acquire legal personhood when they are born, judicial persons do so when they are incorporated in accordance with law. Personality as a concept in international law is principally employed to distinguish between those social entities relevant to the international legal system and those excluded from it.

6. *Zhongguo Waijiao Xingzheng* 中国外交行政 [China's Administration of Foreign Affairs] (Shanghai: Shangwu Yinshuguan, 1943).

in the United Nations, the sovereignty of Taiwan, border issues between China and India, world peace treaties, and so on. Many of these articles served to promote China's foreign policy and diplomacy. Before his death, Chen selected forty articles from his previously published works and assembled a volume titled *A Collection of Essays on International Law.*[7]

In 1982, Chen became one of the two inaugural chief editors of the prestigious journal *Chinese Yearbook of International Law.*[8] He had input in the composition of China's first textbook on international law. He wrote articles on recognition in international law and other related topics for the law volume of *The Encyclopedia of China.*[9] He also teamed up with Professor Wang Tieya to publish a Chinese translation of *Oppenheim's International Law* (1972).[10]

Bibliography of English Publications by Professor Chen Tiqiang

Chen Tiqiang. "Conclusions Confirmed by History—Some Legal Aspects Regarding Japan's Distortion of History in Textbooks." *Beijing Review* 25, no. 35 (1982): 26.
———. *The International Law of Recognition: with Special Reference to Practice in Great Britain and the United States.* Breinigsville, PA: Nabu Press, 2011.
———. *The International Law of Recognition, with Special Reference to Practice in Great Britain and the United States.* New York: Praeger, 1951.
Chen Tiqiang and Mark A. Cohen. "Some Legal Problems in Sino-U.S. Relations." *Columbia Journal of Transnational Law* 22 (1983): 41–60.
Chen Tiqiang and L. C. Green. *The International Law of Recognition, with Special Reference to Practice in Great Britain and the United States.* London: Stevens, 1951.

7. Guojifa Lunwenji 国际法论文集 [A Collection of Essays on International Law] (Beijing: Falü Chubanshe, 1985).
8. For information about this publication, see footnote 2 in chapter 3 on Li Haopei.
9. *Zhongguo Dabaike Quanshu* 中国大百科全书 [The Encyclopedia of China] (Beijing: Zhongguo Dabaike Quanshu Chubanshe, 1978–1993).
10. For information about this publication, see footnote 17 in chapter 9 on Wang Tieya.

References

"Chen Tiqiang" 陈体强 [Chen Tiqiang]. https://baike.baidu.com/item/%E9%99%88%E4%BD%93%E5%BC%BA (accessed Apr. 10, 2016).

"Chen Tiqiang" 陈体强 [Chen Tiqiang]. http://www.law.tsinghua.edu.cn/publish/law/6878/2011/20110317094533416842153/20110317094533416842153_.html (accessed Dec. 20, 2020).

Deng Zhenglai 邓正来. "Zheshi Wo Xiangqile Tamen: Wang Tieya, Li Haopei He Chen Tiqiang" 这时我想起了他们: 王铁崖, 李浩培和陈体强 [Now I Am Thinking about Them: Wang Tieya, Li Haopei, and Chen Tiqiang]. http://www.aisixiang.com/data/11292.html (accessed Apr. 10, 2016).

Liao Gailong 廖盖隆. *Makesi Zhuyi Baike Yaolan* 马克思主义百科要览 [An Encyclopedic Outline of Marxism]. Beijing: Renmin Ribao Chubanshe, 1993.

Tang Rongzhi 唐荣智, ed. *Shijie Faxue Mingren Cidian* 世界法学名人词典 [A Dictionary of World Jurists]. Shanghai: Lixin Kuaiji Chubanshe, 2002.

Wang Tieya 王铁崖. "Huainian Tiqiang Tongzhi" 怀念体强同志 [In Memory of Comrade Tiqiang]. In *Guojifa Lunwenji* 国际法论文集 [A Collection of Essays on International Law], edited by Chen Tiqiang 陈体强, Beijing: Falü Chubanshe, 1985.

Wang Yuming 王玉明, ed. *Zhongguo Faxuejia Cidian* 中国法学家词典 [A Dictionary of Chinese Jurists]. Beijing: Zhongguo Laodong Chubanshe, 1991.

Zhongguo Guojifa Niankan Bianji Weiyuanhui 《中国国际法年刊》编辑委员会 [The Editorial Committee of *Zhongguo Guojifa Niankan*]. "Chentong Daonian Chen Tiqiang Jiaoshou" 沉痛悼念陈体强教授 [A Profound Mourning for Professor Chen Tiqiang]. In *Zhongguo Guojifa Niankan* 中国国际法年刊 [Chinese Yearbook of International Law], edited by the Chinese Society of International Law, 424–26. Beijing: Zhongguo Duiwai Fanyi Chuban Gongsi, 1984.

14. Xie Huaishi (谢怀栻)

(1919–2003)

Civil Law

Professor of law at the Institute of Law, Chinese Academy of Social Sciences, Xie Huaishi was recognized as an "encyclopedia" in the field of civil law. Although trained domestically, he was fluent in English, German, Japanese, and Russian. As a prominent scholar in civil law, he is also known for his work in comparative law, intellectual property, and legal translation.

Educational Background

Xie was born in Zaoyang (枣阳) County of Hubei Province. He entered the Faculty of Mechanics of Tsinghua University in 1937. A year later, he changed his mind and switched to the Faculty of Law of the National Chengchi University[1] and graduated from there in 1942. He did an internship with a Chongqing Court in 1943 and then became a student in the judge training program of the National Chengchi University.

---

1. Zhongyang Zhengzhi Xuexiao Daxuebu 中央政治学校大学部 [National Chengchi University], a public university, was established in 1927 in Nanjing and reestablished in Taiwan in 1954. The school was established by the Chinese Nationalist Party to provide training for personnel in law, politics, management, and journalism.

From 1949 to 1951, he attended the Institute of New Legal Studies of China.[2]

Career Highlights

Xie worked briefly as a clerk in the Shanxi (陝西) government after he graduated from college in 1942. Following an internship, he became the youngest judge on the Civil Court of Chongqing Regional Court from 1943 to 1945. Post–World War II, the Nationalist government sent him to Taiwan to take over the court system from the Japanese. As a judge of the High Court, he worked in Taiwan in 1945 and 1946. A year later, he quit his position due to a disagreement with the government. He then took a job as a civil court judge on the Shanghai Regional Court between 1947 and 1949. During this time, he also taught civil law and civil procedure at the Faculty of Law of Tongji University. In 1949, Xie came to Beijing, first as a student and then as a teacher at the Institute of New Legal Studies of China. He taught philosophy at the Central Cadres School of Politics and Law[3] from 1952 to 1957. Due to his criticism of Communist Party leaders and promotion of professionalism in the legal system, he was classified as a Rightist and fired from his teaching position in 1958. He spent the next twenty years working on farms in Beijing and a labor camp in Xinjiang. In 1979, Xie's accusation was cleared, and he was allowed to return to Beijing. He began teaching at the Institute of Law, Chinese Academy of Social Sciences, in 1979 and retired in 1989. He continued research and writing after retirement and was honored as a "lifetime researcher/professor" by the Institute in 2002.

Xie was a senior arbitrator for the China International Economic and Trade Arbitration Commission. He was an adviser to the Drafting Committee of Trust Law. He contributed to legislation for the General Princi-

2. Zhongguo Xifaxue Yanjiuyuan 中国新法学研究院 [Institute of New Legal Studies of China]—the school was established by the Ministry of Justice to provide ideological training for academics.

3. See footnote 4 in chapter 7 on Gong Xiangrui.

ples of Civil Law, the Civil Procedure Law, the Copyright Law, the Securities Law, the Negotiable Instrument Law, and so on.[4]

Research Areas and Publications

An honest and truthful scholar, Xie's discussions on the rule of law and his criticisms of political chaos in the 1950s cost him more than twenty years of his academic life. However, some of his insights into the legal education and government policies, which can be found in *A Collection of the Fallacies of the Rightists in the Political and Legal Community* (1957),[5] are still inspiring today. Despite a long period (from 1958 to 1979) away from teaching and research, his solid academic background allowed him to immediately regain his status in the community upon returning to teaching. He became one of the most respected and authoritative scholars of civil law in China during the 1980s and 1990s. Many prominent civil law scholars today studied under him or received advice from him.

The renowned professor of civil law Jiang Ping (江平) called Xie "an encyclopedia of civil law."[6] Xie's most important publication is *An Introduction to Negotiable Instruments* (1990).[7] This book came out before the Law of Negotiable Instruments was promulgated and thus had a profound impact on the legislation. It earned him an award for outstanding research (1977–1991) by the Chinese Academy of Social Sciences and has become one of the most important works in the field. After the Law of Negotiable Instruments was promulgated in 1995, he wrote "On Our New Law of Negotiable Instruments,"[8] providing honest assessments of the

4. See Long Weiqiu, "Youfeng Zinan, Yibi Xinmiao," 172.

5. *Zhengfajie Youpai Fenzi Miulun Huiji* 政法界右派分子谬论汇集 [A Collection of the Fallacies of the Rightists in the Political and Legal Community] (Beijing: Falü Chubanshe, 1957).

6. See Jiang Ping, "Shensi Yu Huainian."

7. Xie Huaishi 谢怀栻, *Piaojufa Gailun* 票据法概论 [An Introduction to Negotiable Instruments] (Beijing: Falü Chubanshe, 1990).

8. "Ping Xinggongbu De Woguo Piaojufa" 评新公布的我国票据法 [On Our New Law of Negotiable Instruments], *Faxue Yanjiu* 法学研究 6 (1995).

law. This work became an excellent example of legislative review by an expert.

As a scholar of civil and commercial law, Xie was interested in the drafting of the civil code. Although he was not involved in the legislative work, his publications laid the groundwork for the creation of the civil code. These publications include "A Study of Civil Codes of the Countries of the Civil Law System" (1994),[9] "On China's Civil Code amid the Centennial of Germany's Civil Law" (2001),[10] "A Reflection on Japanese Civil Law" (2001),[11] "On the Interaction and Convergence of Civil Law Legislation across the Strait" (2002),[12] and so on.

A compilation titled *Selected Works on Legal Studies by Xie Huaishi* (2002)[13] contains Xie's most important essays. These writings addressed various topics in civil law, including the principles of civil law, the objective of civil law, and civil rights. Other topics he discussed include property rights, copyright law, contract law, Chinese corporate law, and the basic law of Hong Kong. He addressed the differences between civil law and economic law and pointed out that the mission of economic law was to enhance macroeconomic control, while the mission of civil law was to regulate microeconomic activities.

Xie emphasized the division between public law and private law and the independence of civil law. He promoted the "civil law spirit," which emphasized equality before the law, respecting and protecting private rights, and freedom of contract. The core of his legal thought was to protect citizens' rights. He believed that the person was the subject of

9. "Dalu Guojia Minfadian Yanjiu" 大陆国家民法典研究 [A Study of Civil Codes of the Countries of the Civil Law System], *Waiguofa Yiping* 外国法译评 3 and 4 (1994).

10. "Cong Deguo Minfa Baizhounian Shuodao Zhongguo Minfadian Wenti" 从德国民法百周年说到中国民法典问题 [On China's Civil Code amid the Centennial of German's Civil Law], *Zhongwai Faxue* 中外法学 1 (2001).

11. "Guanyu Riben Minfa De Sikao" 关于日本民法的思考 [A Reflection on Japanese Civil Law], *Huanqiu Falü Pinglun* 环球法律评论 3 (2001).

12. "Haixia Liangan Minshi Lifa De Hudong Yu Qutong" 海峡两岸民事立法的互动与趋同 [On the Interaction and Convergence of Civil Law Legislation across the Strait], in *Xie Huaishi Faxue Wenxuan* 谢怀栻法学文选 [Selected Works on Legal Studies by Xie Huaishi] (Beijing: Zhongguo Fazhi Chubanshe, 2002).

13. Xie Huaishi 谢怀栻, *Xie Huaishi Faxue Wenxuan* 谢怀栻法学文选 [Selected Works on Legal Studies by Xie Huaishi] (Beijing: Zhongguo Fazhi Chubanshe, 2002).

law. There was a part of personal life that was sacred and protected by law from government intrusion/intervention. Xie also emphasized the importance of equality and protection of personality. According to him, modern civil law was centered on the person and rights.[14]

Xie had in-depth knowledge of German law and published *The Civil Procedure Law of the Federal Republic of Germany*.[15] Through translations of the Soviet Civil Law, German Code of Civil Procedure, the General Part of the German Civil Code, the Revision of Hungary Civil Code, and the Features of Swiss Civil Code, among others, he introduced foreign laws to China and contributed to the study of comparative law.

Bibliography of English Publications by Professor Xie Huaishi

Henderson, Dan Fenno, Preston M. Torbert, and Xie Huaishi. *Contract in the Far East: China and Japan*. Tübingen: J. C. B. Mohr (Paul Siebeck); The Hague: Martinus Nijhoff, 1992.

Henderson, Dan Fenno, Preston M. Torbert, Xie Huaishi, and Arthur Taylor von Mehren. "Contracts in General." In *International Encyclopedia of Comparative Law*, edited by U. Drobnig, R. David, H. H. Egawa, R. Graveson, V. Knapp, A. T. Von Mehren, Y. Noda, S. Rozmaryn, V. M. Tschchikwadze, H. Valladão, H. Yntema, and K. Zweigert. Tübingen: J. C. B. Mohr, 1992.

Xie Huaishi. *Symposium on General Principles of Civil Law of the People's Republic of China in Comparative Perspective*, March 25–29, 1988, No. 7. Hong Kong: The Symposium, 1988.

14. Wang Liming 王利明, "Huainian Xie Lao—Xie Huaishi Xiansheng De Faxue Sixiang Jiqi Dui Woguo Minfa Shiye De Gongxian" 怀念谢老—谢怀栻先生的法学思想及其对我国民法事业的贡献 [In Memory of Master Xie: Mr. Xie Huaishi's Legal Thoughts and His Contributions to China's Civil Law Studies], in *Xie Huaishi Xiansheng Jinian Wenji* 谢怀栻先生纪念文集 [A Collection of Articles in Memory of Mr. Xie Huaishi], ed. Xie Ying 谢英 (Beijing: Zhongguo Fazhi Chubanshe, 2005).

15. *Deyizhi Lianbang Gongheguo Minshi Susongfa* 德意志联邦共和国民事诉讼法 [The Civil Procedure Law of the Federal Republic of Germany] (Beijing: Zhongguo Fazhi Chubanshe, 2001).

References

Chen Xiahong 陈夏红. "Xiangqile Xie Huaishi" 想起了谢怀栻 [Recalling Xie Huaishi]. In Chen Xiahong 陈夏红, *Bainian Zhongguo Falüren Jianying* 百年中国法律人剪影 [Profiles of Chinese Jurists in a Hundred Years]. Beijing: Zhongguo Fazhi Chubanshe, 2016.

Jiang Ping 江平. "Shensi Yu Huainian—Jinian Xie Huaishi Xiansheng" 深思与怀念–纪念谢怀栻先生 [Deep Thinking and Cherishing—in Memory of Mr. Xie Huaishi]. http://old.civillaw.com.cn/Article/default.asp?id=26107 (accessed May 2, 2017).

Xie Huaishi 谢怀栻. *Xie Huaishi Faxue Wenxuan* 谢怀栻法学文选 [Selected Works on Legal Studies by Xie Huaishi]. Beijing: Zhongguo Fazhi Chubanshe, 2002.

Xie Ying 谢英, ed. *Xie Huaishi Xiansheng Jinian Wenji* 谢怀栻先生纪念文集 [A Collection of Articles in Memory of Mr. Xie Huaishi]. Beijing: Zhongguo Fazhi Chubanshe, 2005.

15. Tong Rou (佟柔)

(1921–1990)

Civil Law

Professor of law at Renmin University, Tong Rou is regarded as a founding father of civil law in the People's Republic of China. He was one of the first civil law professors trained in Communist China. His consistent scholarship helped to shape the contemporary theory and practice of civil law in China.

Educational Background

Tong was born into a poor Manchurian family in Beizhen (北镇) County of Liaoning Province. Later, his family moved to Beijing and Baoding. In 1946, he entered the Law Department of Dongbei University in Shenyang. The university was moved to Beijing two years later. He was sent to Huabei University (which later became Renmin University) for graduate study in 1949. He graduated from the Night School of Renmin University in 1954.

Career Highlights

Tong worked briefly at Huabei University in 1949 and 1950. He was assigned to teach civil law and marriage law at Renmin University in 1950. At the same time, he studied at the night school of the university. In 1969,

Renmin University was closed. Along with the entire faculty and staff, Tong was sent to the labor camp in Jiangxi Province. He worked there until November 1972. Not long after he returned to Beijing, Tong and the Law Department of Renmin University were transferred to Peking University. He taught civil law and marriage law at the university until 1978, when the Law Department of Renmin University was reopened. He taught there until his death in 1990.

Tong was executive director of the China Law Society and director general of the Civil and Economic Law Research Group of the China Law Society. He was a member of the academic evaluation committee of Renmin University and the State Education Commission.

Research Areas and Publications

Tong was a student of both the traditional Chinese civil law in the pre-1949 era and the new Chinese civil law studies thereafter. His scholarship became the bridge between China's transforming social and economic conditions and the integrity of civil law studies in China. His most important scholarly contribution was his view on the objective of civil law. He promoted China's civil law theory of market economy.

Chinese civil law before 1949, for the most part, was an adaptation of the civil law system, especially from German and Japanese civil law. After the Communist Party seized political power, the civil law system of the Soviet Union became the mainstream of civil law studies in China. For a long time, the dominant concept in the field was to define civil law as a mechanism to deal with property relations within a certain scope and with personal nonproperty relations. This concept was established to work with China's planned economy. It became inadequate when China's economic reforms accelerated in the late 1970s. However, few scholars stood up to the challenge of this need for a change in doctrine because the ideology of the Communist Party had not changed. Scholars of a promarket economy faced the risk of being called "procapitalism." In his book, *Principles of Civil Law of the People's Republic of*

China,[1] Tong took the risk and pointed out that unlike what was described in Soviet-influenced textbooks, China's civil law was not meant to deal with abstract property relations. Instead, China's civil law regulated the commercial and economic relations of socialist society. This theory defined China's civil law system and structure within a market economy. It was a historical development in China's civil law studies. This theory provided a legislative foundation for the General Principles of Civil Law.[2]

Another important contribution of Tong's was to redefine the relationship between civil law and economic law. Under the influence of Soviet ideology, many scholars believed that civil law was an integral part of economic law. Tong suggested that civil law was an independent field of legal science, separate from economic law. He pointed out that economic law dealt with concrete economic matters through various legal mechanisms. Economic law did not have any defined objectives and methodologies and thus was not an independent field of legal study.

Tong believed that state ownership and distribution according to labor composed the basic system of socialism. He addressed the relationship between state ownership and the management rights of enterprises. He was not a supporter of privatization and shared ownership of state enterprises.

Tong participated in drafting the civil code and the General Principles of Civil Law. He also participated in drafting and discussions of the Economic Contract Law, the Marriage Law, the Inheritance Law, the Industrial Enterprise Law, the Bankruptcy Law, and the Copyright Law, among others. Although he did not publish as many works as some other prominent legal scholars, his work and theory were fundamental to the development of Chinese civil law.

1. *Zhonghua Renmin Gongheguo Minfa Yuanli* 中华人民共和国民法原理 [The Principles of Civil Law of the People's Republic of China] (Beijing: Zhongguo Renmin Daxue Chubanshe, 1981).

2. *Zhonghua Renmin Gongheguo Minfa Tongze* 中华人民共和国民法通则 [The General Principles of Civil Law] (promulgated by the National People's Congress, April 12, 1986, effective Jan. 1, 1987, expired Jan. 1 2021), http://www.npc.gov.cn/wxzl/wxzl/2000 -12/06/content_4470.htm (accessed Mar. 4, 2017).

Bibliography of English Publications by Professor Tong Rou

Tong Rou. "The General Principles of Civil Law of the PRC: Its Birth, Characteristics, and Role." *Law and Contemporary Problems* 52, no. 2 (1989): 151–75.

References

"Faxue Mingjia—Tong Rou" 法学名家–佟柔 [The Famous Jurist: Tong Rou]. http://eastlawlibrary.court.gov.cn/court-digital-library-search/page/judgeLawyer/jurist.html (accessed Dec. 21, 2020).

Sun Peicheng 孙沛成. *Bengkui Yu Chongjian: Tong Rou Minfa Sixiang De Xingcheng Ji Yanbian* 崩溃与重建: 佟柔民法思想的形成及演变 [Collapse and Rebuild: The Formation and Development of Tong Rou's Civil Law Theory]. Beijing: Zhongguo Renmin Daxue Chubanshe, 2010.

Tong Rou 佟柔. *Tong Rou Zhongguo Minfa Jianggao* 佟柔中国民法讲稿 [Professor Tong Rou's Lecture Notes on Chinese Civil Law]. Beijing: Beijing Daxue Chubanshe, 2008.

"Tong Rou Wenji" Bianji Weiyuanhui 《佟柔文集》编辑委员会. *Tong Rou Wenji–Jinian Tong Rou Jiaoshou Danchen 75 Zhounian* 佟柔文集–纪念佟柔教授诞辰 75 周年 [A Collection of Tong Rou's Works: A Commemoration of Professor Tong Rou's Seventy-Fifth Birthday]. Beijing: Zhongguo Zhengfa Daxue Chubanshe, 1996.

16. Zhang Guohua (张国华)

(1922–1995)

Historical Studies of Chinese Law

Professor of law at Peking University, Zhang Guohua was director of the Law Department. He was one of the founders of the study of Chinese legal history under the guidance of Marxism. He taught and wrote important works on Chinese politics and legal thought and served as cochair of the Committee on Legal Education Exchange with China (CLEEC).[1]

Educational Background

Zhang was born in Liling (醴陵) County of Hunan Province. In 1942, he entered the Department of Architecture of Zhongshan University. A year later, he transferred to the Department of Engineering at Hunan University. From 1944 to 1946, Zhang studied at the Department of Philosophy and the Department of Political Science of the National Southwest Associated University.[2] In 1947, he began studying in the Political Science Department of Peking University and graduated in 1949.

---

1. Funded by the Ford Foundation, the Committee on Legal Education Exchange with China (CLEEC) (1982–1995) provided support for approximately 219 Chinese legal scholars and students to study or conduct research at U.S. law schools and institutions. For more information regarding the CLEEC, see Stanley Lubman, "The Study of Chinese law in the United States: Reflections on the Past and Concerns about the Future," *Washington University Global Studies Law Review* 2, no. 1 (2003).

2. See footnote 2 in chapter 6 on Rui Mu.

Career Highlights

Zhang started his teaching career at Peking University right after his graduation. He worked as a teacher's assistant to Professor Qian Duansheng (钱端升), then director of the Law Department of Peking University. In 1952, the Law Department was merged with the Beijing College of Political Science and Law (now the China University of Political Science and Law). Zhang went to work for the college until 1954 when the Law Department at Peking University was reopened. Returning to Peking University, he remained on the staff until his retirement, except for during the Cultural Revolution, when he was sent back to his hometown and employed in physical labor. He came back to his teaching position in 1977 and was director of the Law Department from 1981 to 1986. He served as part-time director of the Law Department of Ningbo University from 1986 to 1990.

Zhang was a member of the Legal Review Group of the Academic Degrees Committee of the State Council and cochairman of the Committee on Legal Education Exchange with China. He served as director of the China Institute of Legal History and vice president of the China Law Society. He gave lectures on historical theories of Chinese law at Columbia Law School and Yale Law School and conducted academic exchanges in Canada, England, and the United States.

Research Areas and Publications

At Peking University, Zhang taught history of the Chinese Communist Party, history of the Soviet State, law and power, history of Chinese political thought, and history of Chinese legal thought. Because of the heavy load of his administrative duties, Zhang published fewer works than his peers, but the works he published are regarded as major contributions to scholarship. His research focused on the legal theories of Confucianism, legalism, Taoism, and Mohism.

Zhang was the chief editor of China's first textbook on the history of Chinese legal thought.[3] This book was considered the first in the field to be published in China since Professor Yang Honglie's book of the same title published in 1937. It is also the first book on Chinese legal thought based on the guidance of Marxist ideology. Different from Yang's book, which focused on the period from the Qin and Han dynasties[4] to the Opium Wars,[5] Zhang's book explored the legal history of the Spring and Autumn and Warring States periods,[6] as well as modern Chinese legal history.[7] Zhang believed that the focus of the study of Chinese legal thought should be social transition periods when various theoretical debates emerged. The Spring and Autumn and Warring States periods and the modern China period were major transformational periods in Chinese history. They naturally became the focus of his first book.

Between 1984 and 1987, Zhang, together with his colleague Professor Rao Xinxian (饶鑫贤), published a two-volume set titled *An Outline of the History of Chinese Legal Thought*.[8] The innovative structure and updated contents of this publication earned it a national excellent textbook award.

In 1991, Zhang published *A New Edition of the History of Chinese Legal Thought*.[9] This book features a new chapter structure. Instead of being arranged by individual philosophers, this book is organized by topics,

---

3. *Zhongguo Falü Sixiangshi* 中国法律思想史 [History of Chinese Legal Thought] (Beijing: Falü Chubanshe, 1982].

4. The Qin and Han dynasties began in 221 BCE, when China was first united by the Qin state. The head of the Qin state became China's first emperor.

5. The Opium Wars occurred between 1839 and 1842 and again between 1856 and 1860. They involved Anglo-Chinese disputes over British trade in China and China's sovereignty.

6. The Spring and Autumn and Warring States periods started in 771 BCE and ended in 221 BCE when the Qin state conquered the Han state and united China.

7. Modern Chinese legal history is commonly considered to cover the period from the mid-nineteenth century through 1949.

8. *Zhongguo Falü Sixiang Shigang* 中国法律思想史纲 [An Outline of the History of Chinese Legal Thought] (Lanzhou: Gansu Renmin Chubanshe, 1984–1987).

9. *Zhongguo Falü Sixiangshi Xinbian* 中国法律思想史新编 [A New Edition of the History of Chinese Legal Thought] (Beijing: Beijing Daxue Chubanshe, 1991).

issues, and theories. It is also a combination of discussions on both legal theories and legal systems, which appeared separately in publications at the time.

In 1994, Zhang teamed up with Professor Li Guangcan (李光灿) to initiate, organize, and coedit a four-volume set titled *A General History of Chinese Legal Thought*.[10] In crediting his colleague, who passed away before the set was published, Zhang expressed his regret for the limited time for research. He encouraged his students to explore unknown and difficult topics and issues in Chinese legal history.[11]

The late Qing dynasty and early republic of China scholar Yang Honglie (杨鸿烈)[12] pulled Chinese legal history apart from historical studies of Chinese thought. However, until the early 1980s, the study of Chinese legal thought was still part of general studies of legal history. When Zhang published his textbook *History of Chinese Legal Thought* (1982), he became one of the founders of historical studies of Chinese legal thought, which was separated from general studies of legal history. It is now an independent research discipline.

Zhang made breakthroughs and innovations on many theoretical issues. These include the period divisions of Chinese legal thought; the assessment of traditional Chinese legal culture; the formation of feudal orthodox legal thought; the features of feudal legal studies; the comparison of the legal philosophies of Confucianism, Legalism, Taoism, and Mohism; the role of the legal philosophies of pioneer thinkers during the Ming and Qing dynasties; and so on. He opposed the approach of total affirmation or total denial and advocated dialectic and historical views on traditional Chinese legal culture.

10. *Zhongguo Falü Sixiang Tongshi* 中国法律思想通史 [A General History of Chinese Legal Thought] (Taiyuan: Shanxi Renmin Chubanshe, 1994–2001).

11. Wu Shuchen, "Huainian Enshi Zhang Guohua Xiansheng."

12. Yang Honglie 杨鸿烈 (1903–1977), legal scholar, author of *Zhongguo Falü Fadashi* 中国法律发达史 [History of Chinese Legal Development] (1930), *Zhongguo Falü Zai Dongya Zhuguo Zhi Yingxiang* 中国法律在东亚诸国之影响 [The Influence of Chinese Law in East Asian Countries] (1934), and *Zhongguo Falü Sixiangshi* 中国法律思想史 [History of Chinese Legal Thought] (1937).

References

Bo Yong 薄勇 and Wang Yong 王永. "Zhang Guohua Xiansheng Xueshu Sixiang Ji 21 Shiji Zhongguo Faxue Zhanwang Yantaohui Zongshu" 张国华先生学术思想暨 21 世纪中国法学展望研讨会综述 [Summaries of the Conference on Mr. Zhang Guohua's Academic Thought and the Future of 21st Century Chinese Legal Studies]. http://db .cicjc.com.cn/sfwm/nrlb/96/node/22711 (accessed Mar. 26, 2017).

Li Guilian 李贵连, ed. *Chuantong Zhongguo Fali Tanyuan: Zhang Guohua Jiaoshou Bazhi Mingshou Jinianji* 传统中国法理探源: 张国华教授八秩冥寿纪念集 [On the Origins of Traditional Chinese Legal Theory: A Commemoration of Professor Zhang Guohua's Eightieth Birthday]. Beijing: Beijing Daxue Chubanshe, 2004.

Wu Shuchen 武树臣. "Huainian Enshi Zhang Guohua Xiansheng" 怀念恩师张国华先生 [In Memory of My Mentor, Mr. Zhang Guohua]. In *Falüshi Lunji Di Si Juan* 法律史论集第四卷 [Collected Essays on Legal History], vol. 4, edited by Han Yanlong 韩延龙. Beijing: Falü Chubanshe, 2002.

Yu Ronggen 余荣根. "Xunqiu 'Ziwo'—Zhongguo Falü Sixiang De Chuancheng Yu Quxiang" 寻求 "自我"–中国法律思想的传承与趋向 [On the Pursuit of Oneself—the Inheritance and Trend of Chinese Legal Thought]. *Xiandai Faxue* 现代法学 2 (2005): 166.

"Zhang Guohua" 张国华 [Zhang Guohua]. In *Yanyuan Shilin—Beijing Daxue Boshisheng Daoshi Jianjie* 燕园师林: 北京大学博士生导师简介 [Professors of Yanyuan Campus: Introduction to PhD Advisers of Peking University], edited by the Graduate School of Peking University, 58. Beijing: Beijing Daxue Chubanshe, 1991.

17. Shen Zongling (沈宗灵)

(1923–2012)

Jurisprudence and Comparative Law

Professor of law at Peking University, Shen Zongling was one of the founding scholars of contemporary Chinese jurisprudence. He was an expert in comparative law and Western legal philosophy. Known for his integrity, honesty, and diligence, Shen was one of the most respected legal scholars in China.

Educational Background

Shen was born in Hangzhou (杭州) and grew up in a merchant family in Shanghai. In 1942, he went to Guanghua (光华) University[1] and majored in political science. A year later, he transferred to Fudan University Department of Law and graduated with a bachelor of laws degree in 1946. The following year, he went to the United States and enrolled in the Department of Political Science at the University of Pennsylvania (UPenn). Having graduated from law school in China, he avoided the JD program at UPenn. However, he managed to take many law classes, including constitutional law, labor law, business law, international law, and international

---

1. Guanghua University was a private university in the foreign settlement in Shanghai. It was merged with East China Normal University in 1952.

organizations. He graduated with a master of liberal arts degree in 1948 and returned to China in the same year.

Career Highlights

Shen started his teaching career in the Department of Law of Fudan University in 1948. He taught introduction to law and comparative constitutional law. From 1951 to 1953, he was sent to study at and later taught at the China Institute of New Legal Studies.[2] Established by the Ministry of Justice to provide ideological training for academics, Soviet Russian scholars taught part of the curriculum of the institute. In 1954, the Department of Law at Peking University was reestablished, and Shen went to teach there. He was the head of the State and Theory of Law Division. After thirty-nine years at Peking University, he retired from teaching in 1993 and continued to advise doctoral students until 2000.

From 1958 to 1962, Shen was classified as a Rightist and was prohibited from teaching. During the Cultural Revolution, he was sent to the university's labor camp in Jiangxi Province and came back to Beijing in 1972. While the higher education system was still paralyzed, he teamed with other professors, including Rui Mu, Wang Tieya, and Gong Xiagnrui, to translate foreign works and documents. His career as a law professor and legal scholar eventually took off after the Cultural Revolution ended in the late 1970s. He became director of the Legal Theory Department and head of the Institute of Comparative Law and Sociology of Law at Peking University Law School. He was secretary general of the China Society of Legal Theory and of the China Society of Comparative Law under the China Law Society. He was the first chairperson of the Chinese Section of the International Association for the Philosophy of Law and Social Philosophy, among other academic positions.

2. See footnote 2 in chapter 14 on Xie Huaishi.

Research Areas and Publications

Shen's scholarship is best known in the areas of Chinese jurisprudence, Western legal philosophy, and comparative law. His research was based on empirical analysis, with an emphasis on the examination and comparison of different legal schools, systems, and theories. Believing in academic freedom, he refrained from attacking other ideas, theories, or opponents.

Chinese jurisprudence has been linked with the name of Shen Zongling since the 1980s. According to Professor Jiang Ping, Shen approached Chinese jurisprudence as if it were a subject of science rather than a political slogan. The study of Chinese jurisprudence often addresses issues intertwined with politics and therefore carries the risk of "political incorrectness." Shen took the risk and explored the subject as a reflection of the spirit of the time.[3] He was one of the early scholars who tried to separate Chinese jurisprudence from political science. From 1949 to the late 1970s, the Theory of State and Law, which was adopted from the Soviet Union, was the doctrine of Chinese jurisprudence. Law was defined as a tool of proletarian dictatorship. Law was regarded as a representation of the ruling class's ideology. In 1982, in the preface of *An Introduction to Legal Theory*,[4] Shen discussed the objectives and scope of legal studies and the status of jurisprudence in legal studies. These discussions were inspirations for the formation of an independent study of jurisprudence in China.

Shen redefined many concepts of law, including the nature, functions, structure, value, and application of law. He provided unique explanations of many important issues of Chinese jurisprudence. His three-level model of the nature of law[5] was revolutionary at the time.

3. Qiang Shigong, "Shen Zongling Xueshu Sixiang," 92.

4. Sun Guohua 孙国华, Shen Zongling 沈宗灵, and Wang Zilin 王子琳, eds., *Faxue Jichu Lilun* 法学基础理论 [An Introduction to Legal Theory] (Beijing: Falü Chubanshe, 1982).

5. In "Yanjiu Fade Gainian De Fangfalun Wenti" 研究法的概念的方法论问题 [Research Methodology for the Study of Legal Concept], *Faxue Yanjiu* 法学研究 4 (1986),

The most important work on jurisprudence by Shen is *Jurisprudence* (1994),[6] which is a primary textbook assigned by the Educational Commission. Combining current theoretical developments in the field, this landmark publication addresses the principles and concepts of law from new perspectives. It provides an improved framework for the study of jurisprudence and is still influential today.

Shen was also a pioneer in the study of Western legal philosophy. When criticisms and denials were the common attitudes toward Western scholarship in China's academic circles from the 1960s to the early 1980s, Shen took political risks to introduce Western legal philosophy. He published many articles on U.S. law, Roman law, schools of legal theories, and Western legal history. His article "Roscoe Pound's Sociological Studies of Law"[7] was published in the *Journal of Peking University* in 1964. Shen's publications explored a wide range of Western legal scholarship, from Roscoe Pound to R. A. Posner. His books *The American Political System* (1980)[8] and *On Modern Western Legal Philosophy* (1983)[9] are early works in the field. These two publications earned him acclaim and awards[10] and, along with his 1992 book, *Modern Western Jurisprudence*,[11] are his most important works and considered classics in the field.

Instead of simply examining the meanings of Western legal theory, Shen wanted to find their implications in China. He tried to uncover the scientific, neutral, and plural nature of legal studies by addressing legal reasoning, legal interpretation, case law systems, and other concepts.

Shen pointed out that the notion "law represents the ideology of the ruling class" was no longer applicable to China since the exploiting class had ceased to exist. He offered his insight on the concept of law with his three-level model of the nature of law.

6. *Falixue* 法理学 [Jurisprudence] (Beijing: Gaodeng Jiaoyu Chubanshe, 1994).

7. Wang Lin 王林 (Shen's pseudonym), "Pangde De Shehuixue Faxue" 庞德的社会学法学 [Roscoe Pound's Sociological Studies of Law], *Beijing Daxue Xuebao* 北京大学学报 3 (1964).

8. *Meiguo Zhengzhi Zhidu* 美国政治制度 [The American Political System] (Beijing: Shangwu Yinshuguan, 1980).

9. *Xiandai Xifang Falü Zhexue* 现代西方法律哲学 [On Modern Western Legal Philosophy] (Beijing: Falü Chubanshe, 1983).

10. "Shen Zongling."

11. *Xiandai Xifang Falixue* 现代西方法理学 [Modern Western Jurisprudence] (Beijing: Beijing Daxue Chubanshe, 1992).

Beginning in the 1980s, Shen was the most important cultivator in the field of contemporary Chinese comparative law. In his famous 1987 book, *An Overview of Comparative Law*,[12] Shen systematically addressed the following essential issues: the concepts of comparative law and comparative legal studies, the relationship between comparative legal studies and other fields of legal studies, legal systems, divisions of comparative legal studies, and micro and macro comparative legal studies. This publication earned him the prestigious Impact China Rule of Law Book Award.[13]

In the early 1990s, Shen began to discuss the concept of legal transplant.[14] In his famous article "On Legal Transplant and Comparative Law Studies,"[15] Shen addressed the Western concept of legal transplant and its implications for Chinese law. His *A Study of Comparative Law* (1998)[16] and *Comparative Constitutional Law: A Comparative Study on Constitutional Laws from Eight Countries* (2002)[17] are his most important works in the field. His analysis of China's adaptability of case law is also influential.

To facilitate the study and research of foreign law and comparative law, Shen made considerable efforts to translate important works of Western legal studies. *An Introduction to United States Law* by Peter Hay,[18]

12. *Bijiaofa Zonglun* 比较法总论 [An Overview of Comparative Law] (Beijing: Beijing Daxue Chubanshe, 1987).

13. For information regarding this book award, see footnote 11 in chapter 7 on Gong Xiangrui.

14. *Legal transplant*, also known as *legal diffusion*, is the term "used to refer to the method of adopting and enacting some laws of another country, by some other country on the same line of the provisions existing in the adoptive country. This borrowing of laws or enactment of new laws, on inspiration by some foreign examples is called legal transplant." See https://definitions.uslegal.com/l/legal-transplant/ (accessed Mar. 30, 2017).

15. "Lun Falü Yizhi Yu Bijiao Faxue" 论法律移植与比较法学 [On Legal Transplant and Comparative Law Studies], *Waiguofa Yiping* 外国法译评 1 (1995).

16. *Bijiaofa Yanjiu* 比较法研究 [A Study of Comparative Law] (Beijing: Beijing Daxue Chubanshe, 1998).

17. *Bijiao Xianfa: Dui Baguo Xianfa De Bijiao Yanjiu* 比较宪法: 对八国宪法的比较研究 [Comparative Constitutional Law: A Comparative Study on Constitutional Laws from Eight Countries] (Beijing: Beijing Daxue Chubanshe, 2002).

18. Peter Hay, *Meiguo Falü Gailun* 美国法律概论 [An Introduction to United States Law], trans. Shen Zongling (Beijing: Beijing Daxue Chubanshe, 1983).

The General Theory of Law and State by Hans Kelsen,[19] and *Social Control through Law* by Roscoe Pound[20] are his major translation works. His last translation, *Man and State* by Jacques Maritain,[21] was published just a year before his death in 2011.

As a productive scholar, Shen published more than 110 essays and articles. Many of these works are included in a two-volume publication titled *A Collection of Theses on Jurisprudence and Comparative Law.*[22]

Bibliography of English Publications by Professor Shen Zongling

Shen Zongling. "Comparative Law Studies in China." In *Law in East and West: On the Occasion of the 30th Anniversary of the Institute of Comparative Law, Waseda University,* edited by Institute of Comparative Law, Waseda University, 333–40. Tokyo: Waseda University Press, 1988.

——. "Judicial Precedents in China Today: A Comparative Study of Law." *Asia Pacific Law Review* 3, no. S1 (1994): 109–15.

——. "Legal Transplant and Comparative Law." In *L'avenir Du Droit Comparé: Un Défi Pour Les Juristes Du Nouveau Millénaire,* edited by X. Blanc-Jouvan, 117–21. Paris: Société de Législation Comparée, 2000.

——. "Legal Transplant and Comparative Law." *Revue Internationale De Droit Comparé: Revue Trimestrielle Publiée Avec Le Concours Du C.N.R.S. Et Sous Les Auspices Du Centre Français De Droit Comparé* 51, no. 4 (1999): 853–57.

——. "The Role of Lawyers in Social Change: China." *Case Western Reserve Journal of International Law* 25, no. 2 (1993).

19. Hans Kelsen, *Fa Yu Guojia De Yiban Lilun* 法与国家的一般理论 [The General Theory of Law and State], trans. Shen Zongling (Beijing: Zhongguo Dabaike Quanshu Chubanshe, 1996).

20. Roscoe Pound, *Tongguo Falü De Shehui Kongzhi* 通过法律的社会控制 [Social Control through Law], trans. Shen Zongling (Beijing: Shangwu Yinshuguan, 2009).

21. Jacques Maritain, *Ren Yu Guojia* 人与国家 [Man and State], trans. Shen Zongling (Beijing: Zhongguo Fazhi Chubanshe, 2011).

22. Shen Zongling, Luo Yuzhong, and Zhang Qi, *Falixue Yu Bijiao Faxue Lunji.*

References

Ji Weidong 李卫东. "Daonian Shen Zongling Jiaoshou" 悼念沈宗灵教授 [A Tribute to Professor Shen Zongling]. http://china.caixin.com/2012-02-28/100361299.html (accessed Feb. 28, 2016).

Shen Zongling 沈宗灵, Luo Yuzhong 罗玉中, and Zhang Qi 张骐, eds. *Falixue Yu Bijiao Faxue Lunji—Shen Zongling Xueshu Sixiang Ji Dangdai Zhongguo Falixue De Gaige Yu Fazhan* 法理学与比较法学论集－沈宗灵学术思想暨当代中国法理学的改革与发展 [A Collection of Essays on Jurisprudence and Comparative Law: Shen Zongling's Legal Thought and the Development and Reform of Contemporary Chinese Jurisprudence]. Beijing: Beijing Daxue Chubanshe; Guangzhou: Guangdong Gaodeng Jiaoyu Chubanshe, 1999.

"Shen Zongling" 沈宗灵 [Shen Zongling]. http://baike.baidu.com/view/1328997.htm (accessed Dec. 4, 2016).

Zhang Wei 张伟 and Zhang Xue 张雪. "Shen Zongling" 沈宗灵 [Shen Zongling]. In *Zhongguo Faxuejia Fangtanlu* 中国法学家访谈录 [Interviews with Chinese Jurists], edited by He Qinhua 何勤华. Beijing: Beijing Daxue Chubanshe, 2010.

Zheng Qiang 郑强 and Li Qingwei 李清伟. "Shen Zongling Xiansheng Fangtanlu" 沈宗灵先生访谈录 [An Interview with Mr. Shen Zongling]. *Zhongguo Faxue* 中国法学 6 (1998).

18. Xiao Weiyun (肖蔚云)

(1924–2005)

Constitutional Law

Professor of law at Peking University, Xiao Weiyun's scholarship focused on constitutional law and administrative law. He played an important role in the creation and development of constitutional law in the People's Republic of China. His work on the making of the Hong Kong Basic Law and the Macao Basic Law was also instrumental.

Educational Background

Xiao was born in Qiyang (祁阳) County of Hunan Province. In 1944, he was admitted to the National Southwest Associated University[1] but did not study there due to the Second Sino-Japanese War (1937–1945).[2] After the war, he entered the Law Department of Peking University and graduated in 1951. Three years later, he received an opportunity to study at the Faculty of Law of Leningrad State University in the Soviet Union. He received a graduate degree in law in 1959.

---

1. See footnote 2 in chapter 6 on Rui Mu.

2. Also known the War of Resistance against Japanese Aggression, the Second Sino-Japanese War (1937–1945) was a military conflict that mainly took place between the Republic of China and Japan. For more information, see *Encyclopedia Britannica Online*, s.v. "Second Sino-Japanese War," https://www.britannica.com/event/Second-Sino-Japanese-War (accessed Dec. 21, 2020).

Career Highlights

After graduating from Peking University, Xiao took a teaching position at his alma mater. He taught political science and later held political positions in the Department of Eastern Languages and in the university. In a universitywide departmental reorganization in 1954, then vice president of Peking University Jiang Longji (江隆基) recommended Xiao to study law in the Soviet Union. Upon his graduation, Xiao was put to work as associate director of the Law Department of Peking University. He taught at the university for nearly sixty years except for during the Cultural Revolution.

Xiao participated in the drafting of the current Constitution of the PRC[3] between 1980 and 1982. He played an important role in drafting the Basic Law of the Hong Kong Special Administrative Region[4] (the Hong Kong Basic Law, 1990) and the Basic Law of the Macau Special Administrative Region[5] (the Macau Basic Law, 1993). Starting in 1985, he spent the next fifteen years working in various committees concerning the drafting of the basic laws and the return of the two special administrative regions to Chinese sovereignty. In 2000, he was invited to establish the Law School at Macau University of Science and Technology and became its dean. He was honorary president of the Beijing Law Society and the China Constitutional Law Society.

3. See footnote 20 in chapter 1 on Zhang Youyu.

4. Zhonghua Renmin Gongheguo Xianggang Tebie Xingzhengqu Jibenfa 中华人民共和国香港特别行政区基本法 [The Basic Law of the Hong Kong Special Administrative Region of the People's Republic of China] (promulgated by the National People's Congress, Apr. 4, 1990, effective July 1, 1997). Please see http://www.gov.cn/test/2005-07/29/content_18298.htm (accessed Dec. 23, 2020).

5. Zhonghua Renmin Gongheguo Aomen Tebie Xingzhengqu Jibenfa 中华人民共和国澳门特别行政区基本法) [The Basic Law of the Macao Special Administrative Region of the People's Republic of China] (promulgated by the National People's Congress, Mar. 31, 1993, effective Dec. 20, 1999). Please see http://www.gov.cn/test/2005-07/29/content_18300.htm (accessed Dec. 23, 2020).

Research Areas and Publications

Xiao is one of the founding scholars of constitutional law study in China. He is also one of the founding scholars of the "one country, two systems" policy.[6] His scholarship is embedded in his legislative work on China's constitutional law and the two basic laws of Hong Kong and Macau. As a member of the Secretariat of the Constitution Revision Committee under the Third Session of the Fifth National People's Congress (NPC), Xiao was tasked to work on the general principles. He drafted article 3 and article 5 of the Constitution.[7] These articles set forth that the delegates of the National and Local People's Congresses should come from democratic elections. They are responsible to the people and subject to their supervision. No organization or individual is privileged to be above the Constitution or the law.[8] Some of his ideas that were incorporated

6. "One country, two systems" refers to the strategic direction that, as a nation, mainland China has a socialist system. Meanwhile, Hong Kong, Macau, and Taiwan remain capitalist societies. This policy design was initiated by China's leader Deng Xiaoping in the early 1980s.

7. See "Xiao Weiyun."

8. Article 3 states:

The state organs of the People's Republic of China apply the principle of democratic centralism. The National People's Congress and the local people's congresses at various levels are constituted through democratic elections. They are responsible to the people and subject to their supervision. All administrative, judicial and procuratorial organs of the state are created by the people's congresses to which they are responsible and by which they are supervised.

The division of functions and powers between the central and local state organs is guided by the principle of giving full scope to the initiative and enthusiasm of the local authorities under the unified leadership of the central authorities.

Article 5 says: "The state upholds the uniformity and dignity of the socialist legal system. No laws or administrative or local rules and regulations may contravene the Constitution. All state organs, the armed forces, all political parties and public organizations, and all enterprises and institutions must abide by the Constitution and the law. All acts in violation of the Constitution or the law must be investigated. No organization or individual is privileged to be beyond the Constitution or the law."

Please see http://en.pkulaw.cn/display.aspx?cgid=1457&lib=law (accessed Mar. 12, 2017).

in the 1982 Constitution are still valid today. During this period, Xiao published many articles. He coauthored China's first constitutional law textbook: *Introduction to Constitutional Law*.[9] His 1983 book, *On the New Development of the New Constitutional Law*,[10] and his 1986 book, *The Birth of Our Current Constitutional Law*,[11] have been important sources for the study of China's 1982 Constitution. His 2004 publication, *On Constitutional Law*,[12] is a collection of his essays on the revision and development of China's constitutional law.

Xiao led important discussions on constitutional law, which include the guiding theory of constitutional law; the awareness, authority, and safeguard of constitutional law; the assessment of China's constitutional law; the structure and development of the People's Congress; and the rule of law and democracy in constitutional law, as well as the application of constitutional law in judicial trials. His legislation work and scholarship have been recognized as a major contribution to the development of constitutional law study in China.

As a member of the Drafting Committee of the Hong Kong Basic Law, Xiao led the work of drafting chapter 4 ("The Political Structure"), appendix 1 ("Method for the Selection of the Chief Executive of the Hong Kong Special Administrative Region"), and appendix 2 ("Method for the Formation of the Legislative Council of the Hong Kong Special Administrative Region"). With his partner team leader, Cha Liangyong (查良镛, Louis Cha Leung-yung in English), they proposed a political system complying with the principles of judicial independence, mutual restrictions, and cooperation between administrative organs and legislative bodies, and under the leadership of the administration. The proposal was accepted and incorporated into the "one country, two systems" design of the Hong Kong Basic Law.

---

9. Xiao Weiyun 肖蔚云, Wei Dingren 魏定仁, and Baoyinhuriyakeqi 宝音胡日雅克琪, *Xianfaxue Gailun* 宪法学概论 [Introduction to Constitutional Law] (Beijing: Beijing Daxue Chubanshe, 1982).

10. *Lun Xinxianfa De Xinfazhan* 论新宪法的新发展 [On the New Development of the New Constitutional Law] (Taiyuan: Shanxi Renmin Chubanshe, 1983).

11. *Woguo Xianxing Xianfa De Dansheng* 我国现行宪法的诞生 [The Birth of Our Current Constitutional Law] (Beijing: Beijing Daxue Chubanshe, 1986).

12. Xiao Weiyun 肖蔚云, *Lun Xianfa* 论宪法 [On Constitutional Law] (Beijing: Beijing Daxue Chubanshe, 2004).

As a member of the Drafting Committee of the Macau Basic Law, Xiao once again led the work of drafting chapter 4 ("The Political Structure") and appendixes 1 and 2. To adapt to Macau's situation, the team came up with different specifications for the residency of administrative executives and the judicial system from the Hong Kong Basic Law. In 2002, he was honored by the chief executive of the Macau Special Administrative Region for his work on Macau-related legislation and teaching.[13]

Besides *On Constitutional Law* (2004), Xiao's publications *On Hong Kong Basic Law* (2003)[14] and *On Macau Basic Law* (2003)[15] constitute a complete landscape of his scholarship. His works are still influential in China today.

English Publications by Professor Xiao Weiyun

Hsiao Wei-yün. *Chinese Constitution Aiming at Protection of the Fundamental Rights of Citizens and Upholding World Peace.* Washington, DC: World Peace through Law Center, 1990.

Xiao Weiyun, Haocai Luo, and Xieying Wu. "How Marxism Views the Human Rights Question." In *The Chinese Human Rights Reader: Documents and Commentary, 1900–2000,* edited by Steven C. Angle and Marina Svensson, 281–88. Armonk, NY: M. E. Sharpe, 2001.

———. *One Country, Two Systems: An Account of the Drafting of the Hong Kong Basic Law.* Beijing: Peking University Press, 2001.

———. "Why the Court of Final Appeal Was Wrong: Comments of the Mainland Scholars on the Judgment of the Court of Final Appeal." In *Hong Kong's Constitutional Debate: Conflict Over Interpretation,* edited by Johannes M. M. Chan, H. L. Fu, and Yash Ghai, 53–59. Hong Kong: Hong Kong University Press, 2000.

13. See Jiang Chaoyang 蒋朝阳, Wang Yu 王禹, and Zhang Xiang 张翔, "Xiao Weiyun" 肖蔚云 [Xiao Weiyun], in *20 Shiji Zhongguo Zhiming Kexuejia Xueshu Chengjiu Gailan: Faxuejuan* 20 世纪中国知名科学家学术成就概览: 法学卷 [Introduction to the Achievements of Famous Chinese Scientists in the Twentieth Century: Law Volumes], vol. 2, edited by Jiang Ping et al. (Beijing: Kexue Chubanshe, 2014), 464–68.

14. *Lun Xianggang Jibenfa* 论香港基本法 [On the Hong Kong Basic Law] (Beijing: Beijing Daxue Chubanshe, 2003).

15. *Lun Aomen Jibenfa* 论澳门基本法 [On the Macau Basic Law] (Beijing: Beijing Daxue Chubanshe, 2003).

References

Beijing Daxue Xianfa Yu Xingzhengfa Yanjiu Zhongxin 北京大学宪法与行政法研究中心, ed. *Xianfa Yu Gang Ao Jibenfa Lilun Yu Shijian Yanjiu: Jinian Xiao Weiyun Jiaoshou Bashi Huadan Zhiqingji* 宪法与港澳基本法理论与实践研究: 纪念肖蔚云教授八十华诞志庆集 [A Study of the Theory and Practice of the Constitutional Law and the Hong Kong and Macau Basic Laws: Commemoration of Professor Xiao Weiyun's Eightieth Birthday]. Beijing: Beijing Daxue Chubanshe, 2004.

Wang Ying 王英. "Xiao Weiyun: Qinli Lishi De Zhuanzhe" 肖蔚云: 亲历历史的转折 [Xiao Weiyun: Experiencing the Historical Transition]. *Guoji Rencai Jiaoliu* 国际人才交流 10 (2000).

Xiao Weiyun 肖蔚云. "Xianggang Tebie Xingzhengqu Zhengzhi Tizhi Zhong De Jige Zhuyao Falü Wenti" 香港特别行政区政治体制中的几个主要法律问题 [A Few Major Issues Concerning the Political System of the Hong Kong Special Administrative Region]. *Zhongguo Faxue* 中国法学 4 (1990): 3–9.

———. "Xiao Weiyun Zizhuan: Laoji Dangde Jiaodao" 肖蔚云自传: 牢记党的教导 [The Autobiography of Xiao Weiyun: Firmly Keeping in Mind the Party's Guidance]. http://news.pku.edu.cn/xwzh/129-74376.htm (accessed Dec. 21, 2020).

"Xiao Weiyun" 肖蔚云 [Xiao Weiyun]. https://zh.wikipedia.org/wiki/%E8%82%96%E8%94%9A%E9%9B%B2 (accessed Mar. 19, 2016).

Yu Hao 于浩. "Xiao Weiyun: Zizi Tansuo Zhongguo Xianfaxue" 肖蔚云: 孜孜探索中国宪法学 [Xiao Weiyun: Diligently Explore Chinese Constitutional Law]. *Zhongguo Renda* 中国人大 21 (2011): 52–53.

Zhang Xiang 张翔. "Xiao Weiyun Jiaoshou Yu Zhongguo Xianfaxue" 肖蔚云教授与中国宪法学 [Professor Xiao Weiyun and the Study of Chinese Constitutional Law]. http://www.calaw.cn/article/default.asp?id=2712 (accessed Mar. 12, 2017).

19. Liang Xi (梁西)

(1924–2020)

International Organizations

Professor of law at Wuhan University, Liang Xi was known for his work in the law of international organizations. As a pioneer in the field, he published major works on the subject. Also, as one of the first part-time lawyers during the 1950s, Liang represented clients in many high-profile trials at the Beijing People's Courts and the Supreme People's Court.

Educational Background

Liang was born in Anhua (安化) County of Hunan Province. In 1946, he entered Wuhan University and studied international law under Professor Zhou Gengsheng (周鲠生), then president of the university, and Professor Han Depei (韩德培). Influenced by his professors, Liang decided to make international law his subject of lifetime study. After graduating from the Law Department in 1950, he spent some time studying the legal systems of the Soviet Union and Western countries at Renmin University.

Career Highlights

Liang taught at the Law Department of Peking University from 1953 to 1982. The courses he taught included the law of the Soviet Union, U.S. and European criminal law, international law, and the law of international

organizations. In the mid-1950s, he became a pioneer part-time lawyer in
Beijing. Serving as one of the defense lawyers, he played an important
role in the Supreme People's Court case involving an American pilot, Lt.
Lyle Cameron, who flew fighter bomber missions during the Korean War
and was shot down, captured, and held prisoner in China in 1952 until
his release in 1955. This case was influential in China-U.S. relations at the
time.

While teaching at Peking University, he was invited to prepare materials for China's participation in the third United Nations Convention
on the Law of the Sea. During the Cultural Revolution, Liang spent two
years in Peking University's labor camp in Jiangxi Province. Upon returning to the campus, he joined a faculty translation team that included
Wang Tieya, Shen Zongling, Rui Mu, and Zhao Lihai. They translated
and published many international documents and materials on international relations, which were referenced by the government in preparing
for the recognition of the People's Republic of China as the legal representative of China in the United Nations in 1971.

Invited by Professor Han Depei to teach at Wuhan University, Liang returned to his alma mater in 1983. He assisted Han in creating the
Wuhan University Institute of International Law and published his best-
selling books there. He was also a part-time arbitrator for the China Mar-
itime Arbitration Commission. Among other responsibilities, he was a
board member of the Chinese Society of International Law and legal adviser to the Chinese Ministry of Posts and Telecommunications.

Research Areas and Publications

Liang was the first person in China to create and teach a course on the
law of international organizations. His *Modern International Organizations* (1984)[1] was a foundational work for the study of the law of international organizations. He revised this book six times and changed the
title of its last edition to *Liang's Writings on the Law of International Organ-*

---

1. *Xiandai Guoji Zuzhi* 现代国际组织 [Modern International Organizations] (Wuhan: Wuhan Daxue Chubanshe, 1984).

izations (2011).[2] Filling a gap in legal studies in China, this book earned him a first prize from the State Education Commission in 1996. His *International Law*[3] has become one of the most circulated textbooks in the field. Liang's most important essays include "On the International Social Organization and Its Impact on International Law" (1997),[4] "The Call for the International Legal Order" (2002),[5] "The Crises of International Law" (2004),[6] and "A Restatement of the United Nations Security Council Reform" (2006).[7]

Liang's scholarship is best known in the following areas: fundamental theories of international law, principles of international organizations, the system of the United Nations, and the developmental trends of international law. His theories of international law emerged mainly in his essays published after the 1980s and in his book *International Law* (2000). According to Liu Min (柳敏), Liang's wife, his views of international law were based on a social foundation, including the following: (1) independently coexisting sovereign countries and international societies are the social foundations of the rise, existence, and development of international law; (2) the increase of international organizations elevates the status of international law; such organizations have become important actors in society and have major impacts on international relations; (3) among nations, there are differences and conflicts, as well as common interests that bind countries together in the international regime; international law is

2. *Guoji Zuzhifa* 国际组织法 [The Law of International Organizations] (Wuhan: Wuhan Daxue Chubanshe, 1993). The sixth edition of this book is titled *Liangzhu Guoji Zuzhifa* 梁著国际组织法 [Liang's Writings on the Law of International Organizations] (Wuhan: Wuhan Daxue Chubanshe, 2011).

3. *Guojifa* 国际法 [International Law] (Wuhan: Wuhan Daxue Chubanshe, 1993).

4. "Lun Guoji Shehui Zuzhihua Jiqi Dui Guojifa De Yingxiang" 论国际社会组织化及其对国际法的影响 [On the International Social Organization and Its Impact on International Law], *Faxue Pinglun* 法学评论 4 (1997): 1–7.

5. "Guoji Falü Zhixu De Huhuan—9/11 Shijianhou De Lixing Fansi" 国际法律秩序的呼唤—"9 11"事件后的理性反思 [The Call for the International Legal Order: A Rational Reflection on Post-9/11], *Faxue Pinglun* 法学评论 1 (2002): 3–11.

6. "Guojifa De Weiji" 国际法的危机 [The Crises of International Law], *Faxue Pinglun* 法学评论 1 (2004): 3–9.

7. "Anlihui Gaige Rechao Zaixi" 安理会改革热潮再析 [A Restatement of the United Nations Security Council Reform], *Wuda Guojifa Pinglun* 武大国际法评论 5 (2006): 1–7.

the mechanism to coordinate various national interests; (4) the changing needs of international society promote the evolution of international law; the establishment of an international legal order is beneficial for international peace and progress; (5) from time to time, international law has its limitations due to international politics, but, as a code of conduct, international law also provides relative restrictions for international political activities; (6) today, both international society and international law recognize and confirm the equality of the sovereignty of all nations, which is an important advancement compared to the nineteenth-century class of nations.[8]

Regarding theories of international law, Liang explored alternative origins of international law. Besides international customs and treaties, he believed that the scope of the origins of international law could also expand into the decisions of international judiciaries, important international and diplomatic documents, theories of well-known international jurists, and the resolutions of international government organizations. He discussed the relationship between international law and domestic law.

On principles of international organizations, Liang examined international organizations from an anthropological perspective and presented a theory of "balanced structure." At an advanced seminar, he discussed the legal status of international organizations and proposed a principle of "compromised functionality."[9] He analyzed the structure of international organizations and suggested various divisions of international organizations.

On the system of the United Nations, Liang elaborated on its Security Council's veto power defined in article 27 of the UN Charter.[10] Based on his theory of balanced structure, he pointed out that international society should pay close attention to the balance of interests between the state and the world, and among nations, as well as how to achieve a veto

8. See Liu Min 柳敏, "Liang Xi Xiansheng Jiqi Jiaoxue Shengya" 梁西先生及其教学生涯 [Mr. Liang Xi and His Teaching Career], in *Quanqiuhua Shidai De Guojifa—Jichu, Jiegou Yu Tiaozhan* 全球化时代的国际法—基础、结构与挑战 [International Law in Globalization: Foundations, Structures, and Challenges], ed. Zeng Lingliang 曾令良 and Yu Minyou 余敏友 (Wuhan: Wuhan Daxue Chubanshe, 2005), 463–80.

9. See Ma Ran, "Liang Xi."

10. See the Charter of the United Nations, https://legal.un.org/repertory/art27.shtml (accessed Oct. 15, 2020).

power wherein the advantages outweigh the disadvantages. He provided descriptions of what "collective security might look like in the future."[11]

Finally, on the developmental trends of international law, Liang addressed the nature and effect of international law. He predicted that the successful enforcement of dispute resolution mechanisms, such as the GATT/WTO, would change the nature of international law from a "soft law" to a "forceful law."[12]

References

Guojifa Yanjiusuo Bangongshi 国际法研究所办公室 [The Office of Wuhan University Institute of International Law]. "Duyou Luojia Guihuaxiang—Liang Xi Jiaoshou Fangtanlu" 独有珞珈桂花香—梁西教授访谈录 [The Scent of Luojia's Osmanthus Flowers Is the Best—Interview with Professor Liang Xi]. *Renmin Ribao* 人民日报, April 20, 2016.

"Ji Guoji Zuzhifa Zhuanjia Liang Xi Jiaoshou: Pushi De Rensheng Zuimeili" 记国际组织法专家梁西教授：朴实的人生最美丽 [On International Organization Law Expert Professor Liang Xi: Simple Life Is Most Beautiful]. http://edu.cnhubei.com/hbrb /hbrbsglk/hbrb05/201112/t1919282.shtml (accessed Dec. 22, 2020).

"Liang Xi" 梁西 [Liang Xi]. http://baike.baidu.com/view/660517.htm (accessed Mar. 13, 2016).

"Liang Xi: Zhongguo Guoji Zuzhifa De Kaituozhe (Fazhi Rensheng)" 梁西：中国国际组织法的开拓者 (法治人生) [Liang Xi: China's Pioneer of International Organization Law]. *China Daily*, April 20, 2016, C18.

Ma Ran 马冉. "Liang Xi" 梁西 [Liang Xi]. In *20 Shiji Zhongguo Zhiming Kexuejia Xueshu Chengjiu Gailan: Faxuejuan* 20 世纪中国知名科学家学术成就概览：法学卷 [Introduction to the Achievements of Famous Chinese Scientists in the Twentieth Century: Law Volumes], edited by Jiang Ping et al. 450–61. Beijing: Kexue Chubanshe, 2014.

Zhao Haiyan 赵海燕. "Liang Xi: Momo Gengyun, Manzai Ergui" 梁西：默默耕耘，满载而归 [Liang Xi: A Quiet Cultivator Returning from a Rewarding Journey]. http:// news.whu.edu.cn/info/1005/23991.htm (accessed June 5, 2017).

11. See his article, "Lun Xiandai Guojifa Zhongde Jiti Anquan Zhidu" 论现代国际法中的集体安全制度 [On the Collective Security System in Modern International Law], *Faxue Pinglun* 法学评论 3 (1988): 6–13.

12. See his article, "Lun Guoji Shehui Zuzhihua Jiqi Dui Guojifa De Yingxiang," in footnote 4.

20. Sun Guohua (孙国华)

(1925–2017)

Jurisprudence and Legal Philosophy

Professor of law at Renmin University, Sun Guohua was one of the founders of Marxist jurisprudence in China. He was an author and editor of one of China's earliest jurisprudence textbooks. His research focused on Marxist legal philosophy, socialist legal theory, legal sociology, comparative law, and legal theory of the Soviet Union.

Educational Background

Sun was born in Yanggao (阳高) County of Shanxi Province. In 1946, he entered Chaoyang University and began to study law. During his college years, he was arrested and put in jail for several months due to his involvement in student activities against the Nationalist government.[1] He was released in 1949. A year later, he became one of the first graduate students at the Faculty of Law of Renmin University. He studied under Professor He Sijing (何思敬) and a Soviet legal scholar and graduated in 1952.

---

1. The Nationalist government led by the Nationalist Party (known as the Kuomintang) and its leader Chiang Kai-shek worked and competed with the Communist Party, led by Mao Zedong, to reunify and modernize China and to oppose the Japanese invasion between 1937 and 1945.

Career Highlights

Before entering Renmin University, Sun worked briefly at the China University of Political Science and Law. He started his teaching career at Renmin University in 1952. During his long career at the university, he founded the Doctoral Program of Jurisprudence. He was a visiting professor at many law schools and was often invited to provide legal training to high-level government officials.

Among many academic positions, he was a member of the Academic Committee of the China Law Society, adviser of the China Jurisprudence Research Society, and member of the Expert Advisory Committee of the Supreme People's Procuratorate (SPP). In 2012, Sun was named National Outstanding Senior Jurist by the China Law Society.[2]

Research Areas and Publications

Sun was a productive scholar. He published over two hundred articles and more than fifty books. His first publication was "The Function of Our People's Democratic Legal System on the Socialist Construction" (1955).[3] He later turned this article into a book.[4] In these publications, he established one of his main research topics for the years to come: the necessity to create and improve a socialist legal system after the Communist Party rose to power. Based on the theories of Marxist and Mao Zedong thought, he discussed the effect of a people's democratic legal sys-

2. See "Woyuan Wuwei Jiaoshou Huo 'Quanguo Zishen Jiechu Faxuejia' Chenghao" 我院五位教授获 "全国资深杰出法学家" 称号 [Five Professors of Our Law School Received the Honor of "National Outstanding Senior Jurist"], http://www.law.ruc.edu.cn /article/?id=38326 (accessed May 5, 2020). For information about this award, see footnote 3 in chapter 25 on Wu Changzhen.

3. "Lun Woguo Renmin Minzhu Fazhi Zai Shehuizhuyi Jianshe Zhongde Zuoyong" 论我国人民民主法制在社会主义建设中的作用 [The Function of Our People's Democratic Legal System on Socialist Construction], *Zhengfa Yanjiu* 政法研究 1 (1955).

4. *Woguo Renmin Minzhu Fazhi Zai Shehuizhuyi Jianshe Zhongde Zuoyong* 我国人民民主法制在社会主义建设中的作用 [The Function of Our People's Democratic Legal System on Socialist Construction] (Wuhan: Hubei Renmin Chubanshe, 1955).

tem on the socialist construction and formed a theoretical foundation for his future research.

After a relatively silent period of academic life in the 1960s and 1970s, Sun published a series of articles in the late 1970s and early 1980s. His articles, including "The Necessity of Enhancing a Socialist Legal System" (1978),[5] "The Relationship between Party Policies and Law" (1978),[6] and "Law's Functions in the Modernization of a Socialist Construction" (1980),[7] called for the awareness of rule by law and denounced "legal nihilism."[8] He then took the lead and teamed up with colleagues, including Professor Shen Zongling, to publish a national unified textbook titled *The Fundamental Theories of Legal Studies*[9] in 1982. This pioneer law textbook not only broke the sales records for legal publications but also made a few theoretical breakthroughs. It recognized the historical value of law, or the legacy of law, and the social value of law. It provided new definitions and explanations of the concepts of law, the nature of socialist law, and the rule of law. The publication of this textbook was seen as a milestone in the study of Chinese legal theory. Built on the same topic, he later wrote or edited several books published in the 1980s and 1990s.[10] Three of them were award winners.

5. "Yidingyao Jiaqiang Shehuizhuyi Fazhi" 一定要加强社会主义法制 [The Necessity for Enhancing a Socialist Legal System], *Renmin Ribao* 人民日报, Nov. 24, 1978, 12.

6. "Dang De Zhengce Yu Falü De Guanxi" 党的政策与法律的关系 [The Relationship between Party Policies and Law], *Faxue Yanjiu* 法学研究 1 (1978).

7. "Fa Zai Shehuizhuyi Xiandaihua Jianshezhong De Zuoyong" 法在社会主义现代化建设中的作用 [Law's Functions in the Modernization of a Socialist Construction], *Faxue Yanjiu* 法学研究 1 (1980).

8. Legal nihilism is "a trend in sociopolitical thought that denies the social value of law and considers it to be the least perfect means of regulating social relations." See *The Great Soviet Encyclopedia*, 3rd ed. (1970–1979), s.v. "Legal Nihilism," https://encyclopedia2.thefreedictionary.com/Legal+Nihilism (accessed May 7, 2020).

9. Sun Guohua 孙国华, Shen Zongling 沈宗灵, and Wang Zilin 王子琳, eds., *Faxue Jichu Lilun* 法学基础理论 [The Fundamental Theories of Legal Studies] (Beijing: Falü Chubanshe, 1982).

10. *Faxue Jichu Lilun* 法学基础理论 [The Fundamental Theories of Legal Studies] (Tianjin: Tianjin Renmin Chubanshe, 1986, 1995); *Faxue Jichu Lilun* 法学基础理论 [The Fundamental Theories of Legal Studies] (Beijing: Zhongguo Renmin Daxue Chubanshe, 1987); *Falixue Jiaocheng* 法理学教程 [A Textbook of Jurisprudence] (Beijing: Zhongguo Renmin Daxue Chubanshe, 1994); *Falixue* 法理学 [Jurisprudence] (Beijing: Zhongguo Renmin Daxue Chubanshe, 1999). The last three titles received textbook awards.

Sun wrote extensively on various topics of Chinese jurisprudence and emerging issues in Chinese legal studies, including human rights. In his 1994 publication, *Human Rights: The Measure toward Freedom*, Sun explored the relationship between socialist countries and human rights, as well as the origin of human rights. He pointed out that human rights were issues involving the freedom of human beings.

Sun's teaching and research life yielded more than two hundred essays. The most important of these have been compiled and published in a volume titled *A Self-Selected Collection of Essays by Sun Guohua* (2007),[11] which has a newer edition published in 2015.[12] Because of his pioneer research role and long-lasting academic life, this book could serve as a testament to the development of Chinese jurisprudence. His latest publications include *A Study on Democracy and the Rule of Law with Chinese Characteristics* (2015),[13] *Equity and Justice: The Core Value of a Socialist Rule of Law* (2014),[14] *Marxist Legal Study and Social Harmony* (2014),[15] *Jurisprudence* (2015),[16] *Research on the Socialist Democracy and the Rule of Law with Chinese Characteristics* (2015),[17] and *The Truthfulness of Law* (2015).[18]

Sun took a theoretical approach to the study of Marxist jurisprudence. He believed that Marxist jurisprudence was not simply the per-

11. *Sun Guohua Zixuanji* 孙国华自选集 [A Self-Selected Collection of Essays by Sun Guohua] (Beijing: Zhongguo Renmin Daxue Chubanshe, 2007).

12. *Fa De Zhendi: Sun Guohua Zixuanji* 法的真谛: 孙国华自选集 [The Truthfulness of Law: A Self-Selected Collection of Essays by Sun Guohua] (Beijing: Zhongguo Renmin Daxue Chubanshe, 2015).

13. *Zhongguo Tese Shehui Zhuyi Minzhu Fazhi Yanjiu* 中国特色社会主义民主法治研究 [A Study on Democracy and the Rule of Law with Chinese Characteristics] (Beijing: Zhongguo Renmin Daxue Chubanshe, 2015).

14. *Gongping Zhengyi: Shehui Zhuyi Fazhi De Hexin Jiazhi* 公平正义: 社会主义法治的核心价值 [Equity and Justice: The Core Value of a Socialist Rule of Law] (Beijing: Zhongguo Renmin Daxue Chubanshe, 2014).

15. *Makesi Zhuyi Faxue Yu Shehui Hexie* 马克思主义法学与社会和谐 [Marxist Legal Study and Social Harmony] (Beijing: Falü Chubanshe, 2014).

16. *Falixue* 法理学 [Jurisprudence] (Beijing: Zhongguo Renmin Daxue Chubanshe, 2015).

17. *Zhongguo Tese Shehuizhuyi Minzhu Fazhi Yanjiu* 中国特色社会主义民主法治研究 [Research on the Socialist Democracy and the Rule of Law with Chinese Characteristics] (Beijing: Zhongguo Renmin Daxue Chubanshe, 2015).

18. *Fa De Zhendi.*

sonal thoughts and views on law of Karl Marx and Friedrich Engels. The two laid theoretical foundations for Marxist jurisprudence and provided worldviews and methodology for its study. During different historical periods, Marxists faced different challenges and tasks and had different needs in solving various problems. Therefore, he perceived Marxist jurisprudence as a fluid and constantly evolving science that responded to the varying needs of Marxists over time and to their changing focus on different jurisprudential issues.

According to Sun, Marxist jurisprudence could be divided into two parts: the legal view concerning revolution and the legal theory concerning socialist construction. The first part, created by Marx, Engels, Lenin, and Mao, was relatively mature. The second part, guided by Deng Xiaoping's ideas, had not been established yet.[19]

Sun believed that legal research should be separate from politics. He regarded legal studies as a social science and had always based his theoretical perspective on Marxist and socialist ideologies. Because of his persistent and independent approach to the study of Chinese jurisprudence, he was often labeled a Rightist before and during the Cultural Revolution and then a Leftist in the post-opening-up and economic-reform period in the academic circles of contemporary China.[20]

References

Sun Guohua 孙国华. *Fa De Zhendi: Sun Guohua Zixuanji* 法的真谛: 孙国华自选集 [The Truthfulness of Law: A Self-Selected Collection of Essays by Sun Guohua]. Beijing: Zhongguo Renmin Daxue Chubanshe, 2015.

19. Sun Guohua 孙国华, "Wo Dui Makesi Zhuyi Faxue De Yidian Renshi" 我对马克斯主义法学的一点认识 [My Understanding on Marxist Legal Studies], in *Makesi Zhuyi Faxue Yu Dangdai* 马克思主义法学与当代 [Marxist Legal Studies and Present], ed. Sun Guohua 孙国华 (Beijing: Zhongguo Jinrong Chubanshe, 2004).

20. Feng Yujun 冯玉军, "Fali Qingshen, Zhongsheng Qiusuo—Sun Guohua Jiaoshou Falixue Sixiang Shuyao" 法理情深，终生求索−孙国华教授法理学思想述要 [A Deep Feeling for Jurisprudence and a Lifetime of Exploring—Introduction to Professor Sun Guohua's Legal Thought], in *Makesi Zhuyi Faxue Yu Dangdai* 马克思主义法学与当代 [Marxist Legal Studies and Present], ed. Sun Guohua 孙国华 (Beijing: Zhongguo Jinrong Chubanshe, 2004).

————. *Fali Qiusuo* 法理求索 [Pursuing Jurisprudence]. Beijing: Zhongguo Jiancha Chubanshe, 2003.

————. *Sun Guohua Zixuanji* 孙国华自选集 [A Self-Selected Collection of Essays by Sun Guohua]. Beijing: Zhongguo Renmin Daxue Chubanshe, 2007.

————, ed. *Makesi Zhuyi Faxue Yu Dangdai* 马克思主义法学与当代 [Marxist Legal Studies and the Present]. Beijing: Zhongguo Jinrong Chubanshe, 2004.

"Sun Guohua" 孙国华 [Sun Guohua]. http://baike.baidu.com/subview/932468/15644623 .htm (accessed July 30, 2016).

21. Wang Shuwen (王叔文)

(1927–2006)

Constitutional Law

Professor of law at the Institute of Law of the Chinese Academy of Social Sciences (CASS), Wang Shuwen was a renowned constitutional law scholar. He was known for his Marxist and socialist view of constitutional law. A member of the Legal Committee of the Standing Committee of the National People's Congress (NPC), he was active in both academic and political arenas.

Educational Background

Wang was born in Qingshen (青神) County of Sichuan Province. He graduated from the Law Department of Sichuan University in 1950. After studying at the Law Faculty of Lomonosov Moscow State University (Moscow University), he graduated with a bachelor's degree in law in 1957. In 1988, he was awarded an honorary doctoral degree in law by Ritsumeikan University in Japan.

Career Highlights

Upon graduation from Sichuan University, Wang worked at the university for a while until he went to Moscow University. After returning from Moscow, he was assigned an academic position at the Institute of Law of

CASS. He worked there until his death in 2006. Wang's career as a constitutional law scholar and politician lasted for forty-nine years. He became one of the first PhD degree advisers of constitutional law studies in China in 1984. He worked as director of the Institute of Law of CASS from 1982 to 1988 and was a member of the Academic Degree Committee of CASS.

Outside CASS, Wang served as vice president of the China Law Society and president of the Chinese Association of Constitutional Law. He was a member of the Academic Degree Committee of the State Council. He was actively involved in legislation and was a people's representative and a member of the Legal Committee of the Seventh and Eighth National People's Congresses. He participated in the drafting of China's 1982 Constitution, the Basic Law of the Hong Kong Special Administrative Region (1990), and the Basic Law of the Macau Special Administrative Region (1993). He proposed the bill to create the Law on Legislation.[1]

Research Areas and Publications

Wang was a leading scholar of constitutional law in China. He published nearly two hundred articles and twenty-two books on the subject. His book *The Basics of Constitutional Law* (1962),[2] coauthored with Wang Min (王珉), was the first publication on constitutional theories written by a Chinese scholar. This book provided comprehensive and systematic explanations on the principles and viewpoints of Marxist constitutional law. It addressed the key issues and concepts of Chinese constitutional law and thus remains relevant even today.

1. Zhonghua Remin Gongheguo Lifafa 中华人民共和国立法法 [The Law on Legislation of the People's Republic of China] (promulgated by the National People's Congress, Mar. 15, 2000, effective July 1, 2000, amended Mar. 15, 2015).

2. Wang Min 王珉 and Wang Shuwen 王叔文, *Xianfa Jiben Zhishi Jianghua* 宪法基本知识讲话 [The Basics of Constitutional Law] (Beijing: Zhongguo Qingnian Chubanshe, 1962).

Wang's most influential publications include "On the Supreme Legal Authority of Constitutional Law" (1981),[3] *Introduction to the Basic Law of the Hong Kong Special Administrative Region* (1990),[4] and *Introduction to the Basic Law of the Macau Special Administrative Region* (1994).[5] Among them, "On the Supreme Legal Authority of Constitutional Law" earned him an award for excellent essay by the China Law Society. The other two books were based on his real-life law-drafting experience of the basic laws and thus have both theoretical and practical values. They have become important textbooks for the study of the Hong Kong Basic Law and the Macau Basic Law. An English translation of *Introduction to the Basic Law of the Hong Kong Special Administrative Region* was published in 2009.[6]

Wang pointed out that the key feature of the Hong Kong Basic Law was the tight integration of China's sovereignty and Hong Kong's high-level autonomy. Therefore, this was a national law enforcing the policy of "one country, two systems."[7] Many issues arose from this unprecedented law, including the relationship between the central government and the special administrative region; the status, interpretation, and revision of the basic law; and so on.

Wang's scholarship focuses on the principles, concepts, history, features, functionalities, revision, implementation, and supervision of constitutional law, as well as the people's congress system and citizens' rights and responsibilities. Some of his most important essays were selected and published in a book titled *Selected Works of Wang Shuwen* (2003).[8]

3. "Lun Xianfa De Zuigao Falü Xiaoli" 论宪法的最高法律效力 [On the Supreme Legal Authority of Constitutional Law], *Faxue Yanjiu* 法学研究 1 (1981): 1–9.

4. *Xianggang Tebie Xingzhengqu Jibenfa Daolun* 香港特别行政区基本法导论 [Introduction to the Basic Law of the Hong Kong Special Administrative Region] (Beijing: Zhongyang Dangxiao Chubanshe, 1990).

5. *Aomen Tebie Xingzhengqu Jibenfa Daolun* 澳门特别行政区基本法导论 [Introduction to the Basic Law of the Macau Special Administrative Region] (Beijing: Zhongguo Renmin Gongan Daxue Chubanshe, 1994).

6. Wang Shu-wen, *Introduction to the Basic*.

7. See footnote 6 in chapter 18 on Xiao Weiyun.

8. *Wang Shuwen Wenxuan* 王叔文文选 [Selected Works of Wang Shuwen] (Beijing: Falü Chubanshe, 2003).

His other notable publications include "The New Constitutional Law Is the General Charter for Ruling the Country and Stabilizing the State in the New Era" (1983),[9] *Research on the Hong Kong Civil Servant System* (1997),[10] *The Marxist Legal Theory with Chinese Characteristics* (1997),[11] and *Market Economy and the Development of Constitutional Politics* (2001).[12]

Wang addressed constitutional supervision extensively. He stressed the importance of surveillance in constitutional law enforcement, which had two components: constitutional supervision and constitutional interpretation. Calling for an independent entity to conduct constitutional supervision, he suggested that a special committee under the People's Congress named the Constitutional Committee was most suitable. However, an independent constitutional court was not viable in China's circumstances.

Wang believed that legal research and political science shared some common features. Like political science, Marxism was the ideology and principle of legal studies. In his scholarship, he integrated Mao Zedong's thought and Deng Xiaoping's ideas into the study of constitutional law. Based on socialist ideology, Wang addressed the democratic system known as people's congresses and citizens' rights. He presented three essences of Chinese citizens' rights: (1) they complied with socialist democratic principles; (2) they supported citizens' equality before the law; and (3) they were comprehensive and real. He emphasized that citizens' rights and responsibilities were inseparable.

---

9. "Xinxianfa Shi Xinshiqi Zhiguo Anbang De Zongzhangcheng" 新宪法是新时期治国安帮的总章程 [The New Constitutional Law Is the General Charter for Ruling the Country and Stabilizing the State in the New Era], *Hongqi* 红旗 1 (1983).

10. *Xianggang Gongwuyuan Zhidu Yanjiu* 香港公务员制度研究 [Research on the Hong Kong Civil Servant System] (Beijing: Zhongyang Dangxiao Chubanshe, 1997).

11. *You Zhongguo Tese De Makesi Zhuyi Faxue Lilun* 有中国特色的马克思主义法学理论 [The Marxist Legal Theory with Chinese Characteristics] (Beijing: Qunzhong Chubanshe, 1997).

12. *Shichang Jingji Yu Xianzheng Jianshe* 市场经济与宪政建设 [Market Economy and the Development of Constitutional Politics] (Beijing: Zhongguo Shehui Kexue Chubanshe, 2001).

Bibliography of English Publications by Professor Wang Shuwen

Wang Min and Wang Shuwen. *Lectures on Constitutions of Communist China and Other Socialist States.* Washington, DC: U.S. Joint Publications Research Service, 1963.

Wang Shu-wen. *The Basic Content and Characteristics of the Current Constitution of China.* Vienna: Gesellschaft zur Förderung freundschaftlicher und kultureller Beziehungen zur VR China, 1984.

———. *Development of Socialist Constitutions of China.* Washington, DC: World Peace through Law Center, 1990.

———. *Introduction to the Basic Law of the Hong Kong Special Administrative Region.* Beijing: Law Press, 2000.

———. *Introduction to the Basic Law of the Hong Kong Special Administrative Region.* Beijing: Law Press; Hong Kong: Joint Publishing, 2009.

References

Li Xiaojian 李小建. "Xianfaxue Shengengzhe Wang Shuwen" 宪法学深耕者王叔文 [Wang Shuwen: An Extensive Cultivator of Constitutional Law Study]. *People's Congress of China* 2 (2012): 53.

Wang Shuwen 王叔文. *Wang Shuwen Wenxuan* 王叔文文选 [Selected Works of Wang Shuwen]. Beijing: Falü Chubanshe, 2003.

"Wang Shuwen (Xiandai Xianfa Xuejia)" 王叔文（现代宪法学家）[Wang Shuwen (Contemporary Constitutional Law Scholar)]. http://baike.baidu.com/subview/102109 /8696669.htm (accessed May 22, 2015).

Zhongguo Xianfa Xuehui 中国宪法学会 [The Chinese Association of Constitutional Law]. *Dangdai Zhongguo Xianfa Xuejia* 当代中国宪法学家 [Contemporary Chinese Constitutional Scholars]. Beijing: Falü Chubanshe, 2015.

22. Gao Mingxuan (高铭暄)

(1928–)

Criminal Law

Professor of law at Renmin University, Gao Mingxuan is an explorer and cultivator of the new criminal law study in China. A 2015 Beccaria Award winner,[1] Gao was the first scholar in China to be appointed academic adviser for PhD students in criminal law. He cowrote several best-selling textbooks on criminal law and conducted in-depth research on the structure of criminal law, criminal legislation, criminal obligation, the death penalty, and other topics.

Educational Background

Gao was born in Yuhuan (玉环) County of Zhejiang Province. His father worked as a court clerk in Shanghai. During the Japanese occupation, his father quit his job and became a teacher at a normal college in Zhejiang. After World War II, his father worked as a judge in the local and high courts in Zhejiang.

Influenced by his father and having a desire to be close to home, Gao entered the Law Department at Zhejiang University in 1947. He took a criminal law class at Zhejiang University with then dean of the law school, Professor Li Haopei (李浩培), and became interested in the study of

---

1. See "Gao Mingxuan Maodie Zhinian."

criminal law. In 1949, the law school was closed, and Gao transferred to the Law Department of Peking University. There he studied under Professor Cai Shuheng (蔡枢衡). In 1951, Gao graduated from Peking University. He then moved on to Renmin University for graduate study in criminal law. At Renmin University, he received systematic training by Soviet scholars and graduated in 1953.

Career Highlights

Gao started teaching criminal law at Renmin University right after his graduation. In 1954, he was invited to participate in the drafting of the PRC's first Criminal Law. Along with teaching, he and his colleagues worked on drafting the Criminal Law for nine years. They produced thirty-three draft versions before they were ordered to stop working in the midst of the Cultural Revolution. In 1969, the Law Department of Renmin University was forced to close. Gao was sent to a factory and then a labor camp for two years. In 1971, he was granted permission to come back to Beijing but faced the reality of the law school's closure. Therefore, he was assigned to Beijing Medical College and worked there for seven years. He first worked in an administrative position and then as a researcher. During this period, he published a few articles in medical journals.

Upon the reestablishment of the Law Department of Renmin University in 1978, Gao returned to teaching. He also resumed his work in criminal law drafting and became the only legal scholar who worked on all thirty-eight drafts of the Criminal Law[2] before the law was promulgated. During the drafting process, he provided many opinions and suggestions and compiled various legislative materials, including documents from the Communist Party–occupied areas and the Nationalist government before 1949, as well as from the Soviet Union, Germany, France,

---

2. Zhonghua Renmin Gongheguo Xingfa 中华人民共和国刑法 [The Criminal Law of the People's Republic of China] (promulgated by the National People's Congress, July 6, 1979, effective Jan. 1, 1980, amended in 1997, 1998, 1999, 2001, 2002, 2005, 2006, 2009, 2011, 2015, 2017, and 2020).

and Eastern Europe. He participated in subsequent revisions of the law and the drafting of other criminal laws.

Gao was director of the Law Department at Renmin University between 1983 and 1986. He was appointed China's first academic adviser for PhD students in the field of criminal law. As an outstanding educator and scholar, he won several prestigious awards, including the People's Educator, presented by President Xi Jinping in 2019.[3] He was vice president of the China Law Society and a member of the Academic Degree Committee of the State Council. Now he is honorary director of the Criminal Law Institute of Beijing Normal University.

In 1988, at the suggestion of Gao, the State Council granted permission to the China Law Society to join the International Association of Penal Law (IAPL/AIDP). Gao became vice president of the IAPL between 1999 and 2009. He was also vice president of the China branch of the IAPL between 1988 and 2011.

Research Areas and Publications

Gao believes that criminal law scholars should think independently. There should be no taboos in science and research.[4] As early as the 1950s, he began researching criminal rehabilitation through labor in China. He was the first Chinese scholar to suggest that criminal liability should be part of criminal law study. According to Gao, criminal liability was the connector between crime and punishment.[5]

In his long career as a criminal law professor, Gao has addressed many important topics and issues in criminal law. He emphasizes the study of

---

3. See "Qingxi Xingfa De 'Renmin Jiaoyujia' Gao Mingxuan" 情系刑法的 "人民教育家" 高铭暄 [Gao Mingxuan, "People's Educator" Who Loves Criminal Law], http://www.xinhuanet.com/politics/2019-10/16/c_1125110766.htm (accessed Dec. 22, 2020).

4. See Gao Mingxuan 高铭暄, "Shinianlai De Xingfaxue Yanjiu" 十年来的刑法学研究 [Ten Year's Study of Criminal Law], *Falü Xuexi Yu Yanjiu* 法律学习与研究 3 (1989): 8.

5. See Gao Mingxuan 高铭暄, "Luelun Xingfaxue Yanjiu De Duixiang He Fangfa" 略论刑法学研究的对象和方法 [A Brief Discussion on the Object and Methodologies of Criminal Law Studies], *Zhongyang Zhengfa Guanli Ganbu Xueyuan Xuebao* 中央政法管理干部学院学报 1 (1992): 28.

criminal law theory. He was the earliest scholar to promote the separation among crime, criminal liability, and criminal punishment. In the 1990s, Gao recommended ten viewpoints of criminal law, which include economic, legal, democratic, nonpartisan, human rights, appropriate, moderate, efficient, open, and forward-thinking approaches to the study of criminal law.

In his 1982 book, *On Criminal Law*,[6] Gao proposed the principles of Chinese criminal law, which include the following: (1) there is no crime without the law defining it as so; (2) the punishment should be appropriate for the crime; (3) criminal liability is one's own responsibility; and (4) punishment should be combined with education. He also discussed other important topics, including the legal person as the subject of crime, criminal liability, the death penalty, and regional and international criminal law.

Gao has been a productive scholar. He has authored or coauthored more than one hundred books and more than three hundred articles. *A Collection of Selected Essays by Gao Mingxuan* (2007)[7] contains articles published throughout his career. *The Continuation of Criminal Law Studies* (2013)[8] features his essays published in recent years. After China's Criminal Law was promulgated in 1979, Gao promptly published his first book: *The Development and Creation of the Criminal Law of the People's Republic of China*.[9] As the first book on the subject in China, it explains the arduous legislative history of the Criminal Law and how various opinions and ideas emerged during the legislative process. It has become an important source of background material for the study of China's Criminal Law. To support subsequent revisions of the 1979 Criminal Law, Gao published over forty articles that expounded on individual crimes in ques-

6. Gao Mingxuan 高铭暄, ed., *Xingfaxue* 刑法学 [On Criminal Law] (Beijing: Falü Chubanshe, 1982).

7. *Gao Mingxuan Zixuanji* 高铭暄自选集 [A Collection of Selected Essays by Gao Mingxuan] (Beijing: Zhongguo Renmin Daxue Chubanshe, 2007).

8. *Xingfa Xuyan: Gao Mingxuan Xingfaxue Wenji* 刑法续言: 高铭暄刑法学文集 [The Continuation of Criminal Law Studies—a Collection of Gao Mingxuan's Essays on Criminal Law] (Beijing: Beijing Daxue Chubanshe, 2013).

9. *Zhonghua Remin Gongheguo Xingfa De Yunyu He Dansheng* 中华人民共和国刑法的孕育和诞生 [The Development and Creation of the Criminal Law of the People's Republic of China] (Beijing: Falü Chubanshe, 1981).

tion. Because of his recommendation, the crime of violating military duty by soldiers was incorporated in chapter 10 of the 1997 amendment. His effort to improve China's criminal law also extended to abolishment of the death penalty for some criminal charges and the standardization of criminal sentencing.

In 1986, Gao published his second book, *The General Principles of Criminal Law*.[10] He then worked with other colleagues and coauthored several important publications, including *Theories and Practice of China's New Criminal Law* (1988),[11] *A Concise History of the Criminal Law Study in the New China* (1993)[12] and *The Fundamentals of Criminal Law* (1993–1994).[13] For the latter, he was one of the authors and the chief editor. This three-volume work has been regarded as a high achievement in criminal law study and received three national book awards.[14]

In 2012, at the age of eighty-four, Gao published another important book titled *The Birth and Development of the Criminal Law of the People's Republic of China*.[15] This is a revision of and supplement to his 1981 publication that elaborates the development of every article of the Criminal Law. It provides detailed explanations of the legislative reasoning, debates, and background. It has become an important resource for understanding the Criminal Law and the study of legal history. Because of this book, Gao was awarded First Prize for Excellent Chinese Legal Books from the

10. *Xingfa Zongze Yaoyi* 刑法总则要义 [The General Principles of Criminal Law] (Tianjin: Tianjin Renmin Chubanshe, 1986).

11. *Xin Zhongguo Xingfa De Lilun Yu Shijian* 新中国刑法的理论与实践 [Theories and Practice of China's New Criminal Law] (Shijiazhuang: Hebei Renmin Chubanshe, 1988).

12. *Xin Zhongguo Xingfa Kexueshi* 新中国刑法科学史 [A Concise History of the Criminal Law Study in the New China] (Beijing: Zhongguo Renmin Gongan Daxue Chubanshe, 1993).

13. *Xingfaxue Yuanli* 刑法学原理 [The Fundamentals of Criminal Law] (Beijing: Zhongguo Renmin Daxue Chubanshe, 1993–1994).

14. See "Zhongguo Renmin Daxue Faxue Kaoyan Zhuanye Jieshao Zhi Xingfa Zhuanye" 中国人民大学法学考研专业介绍之刑法学专业 [An Introduction to the Criminal Law Major at Renmin University Law School], http://mt.sohu.com/learning /d20161229/122965528_498035.shtml (accessed Feb. 4, 2017).

15. *Zhonghua Renmin Gongheguo Xingfa De Yunyu Dansheng He Fazhan Wanshan* 中华人民共和国刑法的孕育诞生和发展完善 [The Birth and Development of the Criminal Law of the People's Republic of China] (Beijing: Beijing Daxue Chubanshe, 2012).

China Law Society in 2015.[16] At ninety years old, Gao published his book *Me and Criminal Law for Seventy Years* in 2018.[17]

Bibliography of English Publications by Professor Gao Mingxuan

Gao Mingxuan and Zhao Bingzhi. *The Evolution of Criminal Legislation of China.* Beijing: Law Press China, 2007.

———. *Overseas Experience of Death Penalty Reform: English-Chinese Bilingual Version.* Beijing: China Legal, 2011.

———. *Study on Application Standards of Death Penalty: English-Chinese Bilingual Version.* Beijing: China Legal, 2011.

References

"Gao Mingxuan" 高铭暄 [Gao Mingxuan]. http://baike.baidu.com/view/316153.htm (accessed Oct. 16, 2016).

"Gao Mingxuan Maodie Zhinian Ronghuo Guoji Shehui Fangwei Xuehui 'Qiesalei Beikaliya' Jiang" 高铭暄耄耋之年荣获国际社会防卫学会 "切萨雷•贝卡里亚" 奖 [Gao Mingxuan, the Beccaria Award Winner at His Old Age]. http://www.chinalaw.org.cn/portal/article/index/id/16086/cid/71.html (accessed Dec. 22, 2020).

Sun Daocui 孙道萃 and Zhao Bingzhi 赵秉志. *Gao Mingxuan Xingfa Sixiang Shuping* 高铭暄刑法思想述评 [A Review of Gao Mingxuan's Criminal Law Theories]. Beijing: Beijing Shifan Daxue Chubanshe, 2013.

Zhao Bingzhi 赵秉志, ed. *Dangdai Xingshi Faxue Xinsichao: Gao Mingxuan Jiaoshou, Wang Zuofu Jiaoshou Bashiwu Huadan Ji Lianmei Zhijiao Liushi Zhounian Gonghe Wenji* 当代刑事法学新思潮: 高铭暄教授, 王作富教授八十五华诞暨联袂执教六十周年恭贺文集 [The New Ideological Trend of Criminal Law Study: A Celebration Collection for Professor Gao Mingxuan's and Professor Wang Zuofu's Eighty-Fifth Birthdays and Sixty Years of Teaching]. Beijing: Beijing Daxue Chubanshe, 2013.

Zhao Bingzhi 赵秉志 and Wang Junping 王俊平. "Xinzhongguo Xingfaxue De Kaituozhe: Gao Mingxuan" 新中国刑法学的开拓者——高铭暄 [The Cultivator of Criminal

---

16. See Professor Gao's award acceptance speech, http://www.chinalaw.org.cn/portal/article/index/id/21971.html (accessed Dec. 22, 2020).

17. Gao Mingxuan, *Woyu Xingfu Qishinian* 我与刑法七十年 [Me and Criminal Law for Seventy Years], ed. Fu Yuejian 傅跃建 (Beijing: Beijing Daxue Chubanshe, 2018).

Law Studies in the New China—Gao Mingxuan]. *Zhongguo Shenpan* 中国审判 9 (2007).

Zhang Xue 张雪 and Zhang Wei 张伟. "Xinzhongguo Xingfa Mingke Tade Xinji: Fang Xingfa Faxuejia Gao Mingxuan" 新中国刑法铭刻他的心迹：访刑法法学家高铭暄 [His State of Mind Is in the New Criminal Law of China: Interview with the Criminal Law Scholar Gao Mingxuan]. *Jiancha Fengyun* 检察风云 13 (2009).

Ye Liangfang 叶良芳. "Gao Mingxuan Jiaoshou: Fayuan Gengyun Xiandanxin" 高铭暄 教授：法苑耕耘献丹心 [Professor Gao Mingxuan: Cultivating and Contributing to the Law Land]. *Zhongguo Dizhi Daxue Xuebao* 中国地质大学学报 4 (2004).

23. Guo Daohui (郭道晖)

(1928–)

Jurisprudence and Legal Philosophy

Adjunct professor of law at several universities, Guo Daohui is a self-made legal scholar who was trained to be an engineer. As an "independent thinker" and one of "the three deans of the rule of law,"[1] he is one of the most influential legal philosophers in China today.

Educational Background

Guo was born into a family of intellectuals in Changsha (长沙), Hunan Province. His father was a famous high school chemistry teacher, who believed that advanced technology and industry would save China from wars and foreign invasion. Influenced by his father, Guo entered China's best science and technology college, Tsinghua University, in 1947, and majored in electrical engineering. He graduated from Tsinghua in 1951.

---

1. To honor their tireless and exceptional advocacy and contributions to promote human rights, private property, and the rule of law in China, Guo Daohui, Jiang Ping, and Li Buyun are called "the three deans of the rule of law" by social media. See "'Fazhi Sanlao' Jiang Ping, Li Buyun, Guo Daohui Lunfazhi" "法治三老"江平李步云郭道晖论法治 [The Three Deans of the Rule of Law—Jiang Ping, Li Buyun, and Guo Daohui Discuss the Rule of Law], http://news.wenweipo.com/2014/12/03/IN1412030074.htm (accessed Dec. 3, 2016).

Career Highlights

While a student at Tsinghua University, Guo was an active member of the Communist Party and held different positions in the party. Upon graduation from college, he was assigned to teach philosophy as well as work as the propaganda director of the Communist Party at Tsinghua. He created the weekly university publication *Xin Qinghua*[2] in 1953 and was the first chief editor of the magazine. Due to his reserved attitude toward the Anti-Rightist Movement and his refusal to publish radical speeches in *Xin Qinghua*, he was classified as a Rightist in 1958. He was cleared of the accusation a year later but was hit hard once again during the Cultural Revolution. He was sent to a labor camp in Jiangxi Province in 1969 and returned to Tsinghua in 1971. After the Cultural Revolution, the nation's urgent demand for new legislation required a great deal of service by legal scholars and lawmakers. Peng Zhen (彭真), then president of the National People's Congress (NPC), invited Guo to work for the Legal Work Committee of the Standing Committee of the NPC. From 1979 to 1987, Guo participated in law-making processes and studied theories of democracy and the rule of law at the NPC. He then moved on to become director of the Research Department of the China Law Society (CLS). He retired in 1989 but later came back to CLS and worked as chief editor of *China Legal Science*,[3] the most prestigious law journal in China. Guo retired from this position in 1998. He is currently a member of the PhD Adviser Team of Administrative Law at Peking University, adjunct professor at Guangzhou University, and chief editor of *Yuelu Law Review*,[4] as well as holding other academic posts.

2. *Xin Qinghua* 新清华 [*New Tsinghua*] was created in 1953 and continues to this date.

3. *Zhongguo Faxue* 中国法学 [China Legal Science] (Beijing: Qunzhong Chubanshe, 1984–).

4. *Yuelu Faxue Pinglun* 岳麓法学评论 [Yuelu Law Review] (Changsha: Hunan Daxue Chubanshe, 2000–).

Research Areas and Publications

While he was teaching philosophy at Tsinghua University between 1953 and 1957, Guo read and studied classics of Marxism and philosophical works from ancient China, Greece, and Rome, as well as many illuminating publications of Western countries from the seventeenth and eighteenth centuries. This prepared him with a method of thinking and worldview for his future work in law and legal education. After the political ordeals between the 1950s and 1970s, his position at the Legal Work Committee of the NPC gave him the opportunity to learn law and legislation on the job. He delved into the theories and practice of democracy and rule of law and, at the same time, worked on law making. His job as chief editor of *China Legal Science* once again enhanced his knowledge and skills in law.

Guo authored or coauthored more than twenty books and more than two hundred articles. His research areas include legislation, jurisprudence, and constitutionalism. As a participant in the drafting of the Constitution Law (1982), Guo gained in-depth knowledge and understanding of the law-making process. His monograph *China's Legislative System* (1988)[5] provides a comprehensive introduction to the legislative system and its organization, procedures, principles, and methodology. He discussed the jurisdiction of legislative power and the unification of the legal system in particular.

On the topic of legislation, Guo has other publications, including "On the Remedies and Phenomenon of Legislative Disorder" (1990)[6] and *On the Essence of Jurisprudence* (2005),[7] which discusses the oversight of legislation, the objectives of legislation, legislative power, and the

5. *Zhongguo Lifa Zhidu* 中国立法制度 [China's Legislative System] (Beijing: Renmin Chubanshe, 1988).

6. "Lun Lifa Wuxu Xianxiang Jiqi Duice" 论立法无序现象及其对策 [On the Remedies and Phenomenon of Legislative Disorder], *Falü Xuexi Yu Yanjiu* 法律学习与研究 5 (1990).

7. *Falixue Jingyi* 法理学精义 [On the Essence of Jurisprudence] (Changsha: Hunan Renmin Chubanshe, 2005).

cost, effectiveness, and efficiency of legislation. He proposed the concept that the people's interests were the supreme law.

As for the study of jurisprudence, he wrote the article "On the Philosophical Analysis of the Essence of Law" (1985),[8] which addressed the issue of law's class nature. He believes that there is no simple answer to this question. From the perspective of wholeness, law possesses the feature of class. But some law, or some norms and specifications of a law, have no absolute class nature but rather a social nature. The essence of law has a diverse and layered nature.

His book *Democracy, Legal System, and the Awareness of Law* (1988)[9] elaborates the differences between rule by man and the rule of law and between the legal system and rule of law. To him, the key question is what kind of law (democratic law or autocratic law) is used to rule whom (officials/governments or ordinary citizens). In other words, are laws measures for restricting officials' and governments' power or citizens' rights? The distinction between rule by man and rule of law concerns whether personal interests are above the law or the law is above personal interests when the two come into conflict. His article "On Ruling Officials by Law" (1998)[10] suggests that the essence of rule by law is governing powers by law and managing officials by law. His trilogy, *The Epochal Spirit of Law*,[11] *The Epochal Calling for Law*,[12] and *The Epochal Challenge of Law*,[13] consists of highly regarded works of theoretical enlightenment for legal studies and the rule of law after China's economic reform. His book *On the Essence of Jurisprudence* (2005)[14] is a significant work that has

8. "Fa De Benzhi Wenti De Zhexue Sikao" 法的本质问题的哲学思考 [On the Philosophical Analysis of the Essence of Law], *Zhengzhi Yu Falü* 政治与法律 1 (1985): 19–21.

9. *Minzhu, Fazhi, Falü Yishi* 民主, 法制, 法律意识 [Democracy, Legal System, and the Awareness of Law] (Beijing: Renmin Chubanshe, 1988).

10. "Lun Yifa Zhiguan" 论依法治官 [On Ruling Officials by Law], *Zhongguo Faxue* 中国法学 7 (1998).

11. *Fa De Shidai Jingshen* 法的时代精神 [The Epochal Spirit of Law] (Changsha: Hunan Renmin Chubanshe, 1997).

12. *Fa De Shidai Huhuan* 法的时代呼唤 [The Epochal Calling for Law] (Beijing: Zhongguo Fazhi Chubanshe, 1998).

13. *Fa De Shidai Tiaozhan* 法的时代挑战 [The Epochal Challenge of Law] (Changsha: Hunan Renmin Chubanshe, 2003).

14. *Falixue Jingyi* 法理学精义 [On the Essence of Jurisprudence] (Changsha: Hunan Renmin Chubanshe, 2003).

helped move Chinese legal theory forward from class struggle to justice and freedom under law.[15] His 2009 publication, *Social Power and Civil Society,*[16] introduces the new concept of "social power" and addresses the relationship between power and rights, as well as social power and the state.

Finally, Guo has published many articles on constitutionalism. He has written extensive discussions on human rights and the relationship between the party's power and state power. He has pointed out that, as a leading party and the governing party, the Communist Party should receive oversight from the People's Congress. The power of the leading party is part of people's power.

At the time of this writing, he is ninety-two years old and still active in the academic world. Guo's latest publications include *Important Discussions on Human Rights* (2015),[17] *A Centennial Overview of the Rule of Law in China* (2015),[18] *Political Parties and Constitutionalism* (2016),[19] "The Mission of the Times of China's Legal Journals" (2017),[20] and *Building the Rule of Law in China* (2020).[21] According to Professor Li Buyun (李步云), there are three key features present in Guo's scholarship. First, humanity is seen throughout Guo's works. Guo regards the people's interests as the supreme law. Topics like democracy, equality, freedom, human rights, and the rule of law are his major concerns. In the introduction to *The Epochal Challenge of Law*, Guo says that his interests are to challenge the situations, systems, thinking, theories, and ideas associated with democracy, the rule of law, freedom, truth, and human rights.

---

15. See Yan Jiabin and Zhang Qian, "Guo Daohui," 325.

16. *Shehui Quanli Yu Gongmin Shehui* 社会权力与公民社会 [Social Power and Civil Society] (Nanjing: Yilin Chubanshe, 2009).

17. *Renquan Yaolun* 人权要论 [Important Discussions on Human Rights] (Beijing: Falü Chubanshe, 2015).

18. *Zhongguo Fazhi Bainian Jingwei* 中国法治百年经纬 [A Centennial Overview of the Rule of Law in China] (Beijing: Zhongguo Minzhu Fazhi Chubanshe, 2015).

19. Guo Daohui 郭道晖 and Li Yongyan 李永艳, *Zhengdang Yu Xianzhi* 政党与宪制 [Political Parties and Constitutionalism] (Beijing: Falü Chubanshe, 2016).

20. "Zhongguo Faxue Qikan De Shidai Shiming" 中国法学期刊的时代使命 [The Mission of the Times of China's Legal Journals], *Zhongguo Falü Pinglun* 中国法律评论 2 (2017): 1.

21. *Fazhi Zhongguo Zhi Jiangou* 法制中國之建構 [Building the Rule of Law in China] (Hong Kong: City University of Hong Kong Press, 2020).

Second, Guo's scholarship has always reflected the spirit of the times. He is a promoter of ideological reform and social change. Third, his views often come from his observations and analyses of social life and legal practice rather than from books and doctrines. He tries to solve real problems rather than just engage in an argument.[22]

Bibliography of English Publications by Professor Guo Daohui

Guo Daohui. "Comments on Strategy of Legislative Amendments and Changes." *Rechtstheorie* 22 (1991): 461–69.
———. "The Presumption of Rights." *Social Sciences in China* 14, no. 3 (1993): 43.

References

Guo Daohui 郭道晖. *Fa De Shidai Tiaozhan* 法的时代挑战 [The Epochal Challenge of Law]. Changsha: Hunan Renmin Chubanshe, 2003.
"Guo Daohui" 郭道晖 [Guo Daohui]. http://baike.sogou.com/v7174182.htm (accessed Sept. 18, 2016).
Hunan Daxue Faxueyuan 湖南大学法学院, ed. *Shidai De Liangzhi—Guo Daohui Jiao-shou Faxue Sixiang Yantaohui Wenji* 时代的良知–郭道晖教授法学思想研讨会文集 [The Conscience of Times—a Collection of Essays on Professor Guo Daohui's Legal Scholarship]. Beijing: Falü Chubanshe, 2008.
Kong Zhiqiang 孔志强. "Guo Daohui" 郭道晖 [Guo Daohui]. In *20 Shiji Zhongguo Zhiming Kexuejia Xueshu Chengjiu Gailan: Faxuejuan* 20 世纪中国知名科学家学术成就概览: 法学卷 [Introduction to the Achievements of Famous Chinese Scientists in the Twentieth Century: Law Volumes], vol. 3, edited by Jiang Ping et al., 148–59. Beijing: Kexue Chubanshe, 2014.
"Xingzheng Xueren Guo Daohui" 行政学人郭道晖 [A Scholar of Administration Studies: Guo Daohui]. *Xingzheng Luntan* 行政论坛 6 (2011).
Yan Jiabin 严佳斌 and Zhang Qian 张倩. "Guo Daohui" 郭道晖 [Guo Daohui]. In *Zhongguo Faxuejia Fangtanlu* 中国法学家访谈录 [Interviews with Chinese Jurists], edited by He Qinhua 何勤华, 325–30. Beijing: Beijing Daxue Chubanshe, 2013.

22. See the preface to Guo Daohui, *Fa De Shidai Tiaozhan*.

24. Xu Chongde (许崇德)

(1929–2014)

Constitutional Law

Professor of law at Renmin University, Xu Chongde was a constitutional law scholar, as well as a poet. He became the first full professor of constitutional law in the People's Republic of China. His involvement in the creation and revision of China's Constitution and other related laws earned him the reputation of "a witness of fifty years of development of constitutionalism in China."[1]

Educational Background

Xu was born in the Qingpu (青浦) District of Shanghai. In 1947, he entered the Law Department of Fudan University, where his favorite class was constitutional law, taught by Professor Zhang Zhirang (张志让), a graduate of Columbia University. After graduating from college in 1951, he attended graduate school and studied constitutional law under Soviet legal scholars at Renmin University. He graduated in 1953.

---

1. See Yu Wei 余玮, "Jianzheng Zhongguo Xianfa De Fazhan Jincheng" 见证中国宪法的发展进程 [Witnessing the Development of China's Constitution], http://dangshi.people.com.cn/n/2014/1127/c85037-26106265-2html (accessed July 8, 2021).

Career Highlights

Xu began teaching at Renmin University right after his graduation. This job lasted more than a half century, except for the time between 1971 and 1978, when he worked at Beijing Normal College (now Beijing Normal University). During the Cultural Revolution and other political movements, he was sent to work on farms and in a factory intermittently between 1958 and 1977. He resumed his teaching position at Renmin University in 1978. He then went on to establish and run the doctoral program in constitutional law and administrative law.

Xu witnessed the legislative process of China's first Constitution (1954).[2] He was tasked to collect and prepare documents and materials for the Constitutional Law Drafting Committee. In 1979, he participated in the drafting and revision of the Organic Law of the Local People's Congresses and Local People's Governments,[3] and the Election Law.[4] As a member of the Secretariat of the Constitution Revision Committee, he participated in the drafting of China's current Constitution (1982). He was also involved in the revision of the first four amendments of the Constitution.[5] In 1985 and 1988, the Standing Committee of the National

2. Zhonghua Renmin Gongheguo Xianfa 中华人民共和国宪法 [Constitution of the People's Republic of China] (promulgated by the National People's Congress, Sept. 20, 1954). Please see http://www.npc.gov.cn/wxzl/wxzl/2000-12/26/content_4264.htm (accessed Mar. 19, 2017).

3. Zhonghua Renmin Gongheguo Difang Geji Renmin Daibiao Dahui He Difang Geji Renmin Zhengfu Zuzhifa 中华人民共和国地方各级人民代表大会和地方各级人民政府组织法 [The Organic Law of the Local People's Congresses and Local People's Governments] (promulgated by the National People's Congress, July 1, 1979, revised in 1982, 1986, 1995, 2004, and 2015). Please see http://www.gov.cn/xinwen/2015-08/30/content_2922114.htm (accessed Dec. 23, 2020).

4. Zhonghua Renmin Gongheguo Quanguo Renmin Daibiao Dahui He Difang Geji Renmin Daibiao Dahui Xuanjufa 中华人民共和国全国人民代表大会和地方各级人民代表大会选举法 [The Election Law of the National People's Congress and the Local People's Congresses] (promulgated by the National People's Congress, July 1, 1979, revised in 1982, 1986, 1995, 2004, 2010, 2015, and 2020). Please see http://www.moj.gov.cn/Department/content/2020-11/19/592_3260622.html (accessed Dec. 23, 2020).

5. The Constitution was promulgated in 1982 and revised in 1988, 1993, 1999, 2004, and 2018.

People's Congress (NPC) assigned Xu to the drafting committees of the Basic Law of the Hong Kong Special Administrative Region and the Basic Law of the Macao Special Administrative Region.[6] He was the founder of the China Institute of Constitutional Law and a member of the Academic Committee of the China Law Society. Among many leadership roles, he was president of the Second Branch School of Renmin University, dean of the School of Humanities and Law of Beijing United University, and member of the Advisory Committee of the Supreme People's Procuratorate. He was invited to teach or speak about Chinese constitutional law, the legal system, and the Hong Kong and Macau Basic Laws at many universities in China and in the United States, South Korea, and Japan.

Research Areas and Publications

During his lifetime, Xu published more than 320 articles and 85 books, both authored and coauthored. He also published 4 books of poetry.[7] Most of his legal publications are included in his 12-volume work titled *A Complete Collection of Xu Chongde's Works* (2009).[8] His first solo authored book was *The Head of the State* (1982).[9] In addition, he authored or coauthored several important textbooks.

As mentioned earlier, Xu was involved in the legislation process of China's first Constitution (1954). Working with Hu Sheng (胡绳) and Zhang Youyu (张友渔), he also participated in the drafting of the current

6. For information about the two basic laws, see footnotes 4 and 5 in chapter 18 on Xiao Weiyun.

7. *Xu Chongde Shicao* 许崇德诗草 [Poetry of Xu Chongde] (Jinan: Shandong Wenyi Chubanshe, 1993); *Xiangcao Shici* 香草詩詞 [The Poetry of Vanilla] (Xianggang: "Xiangcao Shici" Bianjibu, 1997); and *Xueer Yonghuai: Xu Chongde Shiciji* 学而咏怀：许崇德诗词集 [A Collection of Xue Chongde's Poems] (China: n.p., 2000). Some of his poems and literary essays are also included in his twelve-volume collection of works; see the note below.

8. Xu Chongde 许崇德, *Xu Chongde Quanji* 许崇德全集 [A Complete Collection of Xu Chongde's Works], 12 vols. (Beijing: Zhongguo Minzhu Fazhi Chubanshe, 2009).

9. *Guojia Yuanshou* 国家元首 [The Head of the State] (Beijing: Renmin Chubanshe, 1982).

Constitution (1982). For this job, he collected rare historical materials regarding China's Constitutions promulgated in 1975 and 1978. He recalled his past legislation experience in the book *The Constitutional Law History of the People's Republic of China* (2003).[10] With much historical material, this book provides a comprehensive introduction to the development of China's constitutional law after 1949. Xu discussed the details of the constitutional revisions and presented the opinions, arguments, and debates of politicians, scholars, and citizens during the law-making processes. This book was received very well and earned him two social science awards.[11]

Xu held distinguished points of view on constitutional law. Among them, he suggested that the key for the rule of law was rule by constitutional law. Constitutional law was the foundation of the establishment of a socialist country with the rule of law. One of the important functions of constitutional law was to define political power. The nature of constitutional law was reflected in the relationship among various political powers. He opposed China's adoption of the concept of separation of powers and insisted that China should uphold the people's congress system, which was superior in his opinion. He pointed out that the equality of citizens before the law meant equal application of law rather than equal rights of legislation. Because of the class nature of law, it was impossible for the people and their enemies to enjoy equal rights of legislation. Trained by Soviet legal scholars, Xu's scholarship was influenced by Marxist ideology. He stressed that many new concepts borrowed from Western legal scholarship were difficult to understand and not suitable for Chinese society. Chinese scholars should study China's situation and examine Chinese characteristics.[12]

10. *Zhonghua Renmin Gongheguo Xianfashi* 中华人民共和国宪法史 [The Constitutional Law History of the People's Republic of China] (Fuzhou: Fujian Renmin Chubanshe, 2003).

11. In 2004, *The Constitutional History of the People's Republic of China* was granted an Outstanding Research Award in Philosophy and Social Science in Beijing. In 2007, this book was given the Grand Prize of the Fifth Wu Yuzhang (吴玉章) Humanities and Social Science Award. Please see http://news.sina.com.cn/c/2007-10-31/210514205996.shtml (accessed Dec. 23, 2020).

12. See Li Airan and Fang Yu, "Xu Chongde," 124.

As a constitutional law scholar, Xu addressed many important issues, including the essence, effect, and implementation of constitutional law, the people's democratic dictatorship, and the people's congress system. He gave emphasis to the clarity, accuracy, and concreteness of the clauses in constitutional legislation. In his article "On the Clarity of the Constitution's Clauses,"[13] Xu pointed out that the wording or language in the constitution's clauses should consist of precise legal terms rather than political or literary phrases; citizens' rights and responsibilities should be affirmed clearly rather than with advisory or persuasive expressions; and whenever the term "according to law" was used, there must be an actual law to follow.

As a member of the drafting committees of the Hong Kong Basic Law and the Macau Basic Law, Xu proposed a comprehensive understanding of "one country, two systems"[14] for the two special administrative regions and regarded "one country" as a prerequisite. He believed that "Hong Kong's rule by Hong Kong people" must be based on rule by people who are loyal to the People's Republic of China.[15] Therefore, in his view, an election based on universal suffrage would not guarantee such a result. He further elaborated on "one country, two systems" when he discussed the Anti-Secession Law[16] in 2005. He said that this law was related to "one country, two systems." Based on the Constitutional Law, this law was a domestic law, not international law. For the recognition of the international community, the name of this law should be Anti-Secession Law, not Anti-Separation Law, because its mission was to restrain Taiwan's independence.[17]

13. "Lun Xianfa Guifan De Mingxianxing" 论宪法规范的明显性 [On the Clarity of the Constitution's Clauses], *Shehui Kexue Bao* 社会科学报 6 (1979).

14. For information about "one country, two systems," see footnote 6 in chapter 18 on Xiao Weiyun.

15. See his article, "Deng Xiaopin Lilun Yongfang Guangmang" 邓小平理论永放光芒 [Deng Xiaoping's Theory Shines Forever], *Renmin Ribao* 人民日报, March 1, 2004, http://www.lnsgdb.com.cn/Lnsgdb/publish/html/30/content/2004/1344577686901 .html (accessed July 8, 2021).

16. Fanfenlie Guojiafa 反分裂国家法 [Anti-Secession Law] (promulgated by the National People's Congress, Mar. 14, 2005, effective Mar. 14, 2005). Please see http://www .npc.gov.cn/wxzl/gongbao/2005-05/08/content_5341734.htm (accessed June 26, 2020).

17. See his article, "'Fan Fenlie Guojiafa'" De Lifa Yiju He Xingzhi Tanxi" 《反分裂国家法》的立法依据和性质探析 [An Analysis of the Legislative Basis and Nature of "Anti-Secession Law"], *Zhongzhou Xuekan* 中州学刊 3 (2005): 94–96.

Bibliography of English Publications by Professor Xu Chongde

Xu Chongde and Niu Wenzhan. *Constitutional Law in China*. Alphen aan den Rijn, Netherlands: Wolters Kluwer, 2019.

Xu Chongde and Pi Chunxie. "Questions and Answers on the Election System (Selections)." *Chinese Law and Government* 15 no. 3–4 (1982): 134–62.

References

Han Dayuan 韩大元, Hu Jinguang 胡锦光, and Niu Wenzhan 牛文展. "Xu Chongde" 许崇德 [Xu Chongde]. In *20 Shiji Zhongguo Zhiming Kexuejia Xueshu Chengjiu Gailan: Faxuejuan* 20 世纪中国知名科学家学术成就概览：法学卷 [Introduction to the Achievements of Famous Chinese Scientists in the Twentieth Century: Law Volumes], vol. 3, edited by Jiang Ping et al., 179–194. Beijing: Kexue Chubanshe, 2014.

Li Airan 李爱然 and Fang Yu 方宇. "Xu Chongde" 许崇德 [Xu Chongde]. In *Zhongguo Faxuejia Fangtanlu* 中国法学家访谈录 [Interviews with Chinese Jurists], edited by He Qinhua 何勤华. Beijing: Beijing Daxue Chubanshe, 2010.

Xu Chongde 许崇德. "Wo Yu Xinzhongguo Xianfaxue" 我与新中国宪法学 [Me and Constitutional Law Study of the New China]. In *Xianzheng Yu Xingzheng Fazhi Tansuo* 宪政与行政法治探索 [An Exploration of Constitutionalism and Administrative Rule of Law], edited by Zhongguo Renmin Daxue Xianzheng Yu Xingzheng Fazhi Yanjiu Zhongxin 中国人民大学宪政与行政法治研究中心 [The Constitutional Law and Administrative Law Research Center of Renmin University]. Beijing: Zhongguo Renmin Daxue Chubanshe, 2004.

———. *Xu Chongde Quanji* 许崇德全集 [Complete Works of Xu Chongde]. Beijing: Zhongguo Minzhu Fazhi Chubanshe, 2009.

———. *Xueer Yanxian* 学而言宪 [Learning and Discussions on Constitutional Law]. Beijing: Falü Chubanshe, 2000.

———. *Zhonghua Renmin Gongheguo Xianfashi* 中华人民共和国宪法史 [The Constitutional Law History of the People's Republic of China]. Fuzhou: Fujian Renmin Chubanshe, 2003.

"Xu Chongde" 许崇德 [Xu Chongde]. http://www.calaw.cn/teacher/StarDetail.asp?pkno=12 (accessed Mar. 19, 2017).

25. Wu Changzhen (巫昌祯)

(1929–2020)

Marriage Law, Women's Rights, and Civil Law

Professor of law at the China University of Political Science and Law, Wu Changzhen was an expert in marriage law, women's rights, family relations, and civil law. She was the youngest member of the drafting team of the civil code during the 1950s and participated in the revision of the Marriage Law in 1978 and 2001. She was the only female scholar out of 156 jurists featured in the three-volume set *Introduction to the Achievements of Famous Chinese Scientists in the Twentieth Century*.[1]

Educational Background

Wu was born in Jurong (句容) City of Jiangsu Province. In 1948, she entered Chaoyang (朝阳) University in Beijing. The university became the China University of Political Science and Law in 1949 and then was incorporated into Renmin University in 1950. She studied the law of the Soviet Union, Eastern European law, and Chinese law. She graduated from the Law Department of Renmin University in 1954 as part of its first graduating class.

1. See footnote 3 in the introduction. There are a total of 156 jurists featured in the three-volume set, which includes jurists born between 1840 and 1951.

Career Highlights

Wu was assigned to teach at the China University of Political Science and Law after college. At first, she taught civil law of the Soviet Union. From 1955 to 1957, led by Beijing mayor Peng Zhen (彭真), along with such prominent scholars as Rui Mu (芮沐) and Tong Rou (佟柔), Wu participated in drafting the civil code. Fresh out of college, she was the youngest member of the drafting team. The team produced four draft versions of the code before it was dismissed in 1957.[2] A year later, Wu's department of civil law was shut down. She was assigned to teach Mao's works and ancient literature. Then the Cultural Revolution took place in 1966, and all classes were canceled. She worked as an accountant at a campus factory and then was sent to a labor camp in Anhui Province while retaining her position as an accountant. She left that job after coming back to Beijing. In 1978, Wu returned to teaching when the China University of Political Science and Law was reestablished. She retired from formal teaching in 2003 but continued to advise graduate students, attend academic conferences, and participate in public interest work.

Wu was active in both academic circles and the practice of law. She founded an all-women's public-interest law firm named Beijing No. 8 Law Firm in the 1980s. The firm serves female clients and protects women's rights. She also led a number of field research projects regarding marriage and family-related legislation. This experience allowed her to address real-life problems via a practical approach in research and legislation.

Wu participated in the legislative drafting of many laws, including the civil code, the Marriage Law, the Population and Family Planning Law, the Law of the Protection of Women's Rights and Interests, the Juveniles Protection Law, and the Anti-Domestic Violence Law. She was

---

2. Between 1955 and 2018, there were several attempts to produce a comprehensive civil code, but none came to fruition. As a result, China took an approach of producing individual branch laws and part of the civil code first, then the complete code. In 1986, China issued the General Principles of the Civil Law (invalid now), and in 2017, the General Provisions of the Civil Law was promulgated. Other laws, including the Marriage Law and the Contract Law, were promulgated over the years. Finally, the civil code was enacted on May 28, 2020, which replaced the individual branch laws.

the honorary president of the Marriage Law Association of the China Law Society. She was a member of the National Committee of the Seventh, Eighth, and Ninth Chinese People's Political Consultative Conferences. Wu was an adviser to the Chinese Women's Research Society and was named the National Outstanding Senior Jurist by the China Law Society[3] in 2012. As an exceptional educator, she received a number of awards in Beijing and nationwide.

Research Areas and Publications

One of Wu's most notable contributions is her work on Marriage Law legislation. She was called "a witness of the development of China's Marriage Law."[4] Her legislative ideas were incorporated in both the 1980 Marriage Law and its 2001 amendment. Before participating in the drafting of the 1980 Marriage Law, she did extensive field research and studied foreign laws. While discussing the draft, she proposed a new minimum marriage age of twenty-two for men and twenty for women. This marriage age proposal was believed to be applicable for China's population control and growth and compatible with other marriage legislation in the world. She also recommended that one of the conditions for divorce should be the breakdown of affection/relationship between husband and wife, which was a major departure from the then-mainstream reasoning for divorce. Both of her recommendations were incorporated in the 1980 Marriage Law. During the 2001 revision of the Marriage Law, Wu was labeled a "conservative" and "going backward"[5] because she

---

3. At the recommendation of the national and local Chinese Law Societies, major Chinese law schools, and the Law Institute of the Chinese Academy of Social Sciences, twenty-five senior professors, including Wu Changzhen, were selected and named National Outstanding Senior Jurists for their significant contributions to the study of Chinese law, the rule of law, and legal education. Many scholars featured in this book also received this honor. For the list of the twenty-five selected professors, see http://energylaw.chinalaw.org.cn/portal/article/index/id/158.html (accessed July 9. 2021).

4. See Wang Xiaochen 王晓晨, "Wu Changzhen: Xin Zhongguo Hunyinfa De Fazhan De Jianzhengzhe."

5. Wang Xiaochen 王晓晨, "Wu Changzhen: Fan Jiabao Lifa Ershinian."

proposed clauses that required husband and wife to be truthful and respectful to each other and that demanded the cheating/wrongdoing party to bear financial responsibilities in divorce. However, facing the emerging social problem of bigamy associated with rapid economic development in the late 1990s, the 2001 amendment of the Marriage Law incorporated her ideas in articles 4 and 46.[6]

Building on her field survey and public-interest work, Wu became a pioneer and strong advocate against domestic violence. Because of her persuasiveness and insistence, a clause on the prohibition of domestic violence was written into article 3 of the Marriage Law. In 2008, at the suggestion of Wu, the Applied Law Institute of the Supreme People's Court called for the establishment of a ruling system for personal protection.[7] In 2015, China's first Anti-Domestic Violence Law[8] was passed, and Wu was named the 2015 Rule of Law Figure by China Central Television.[9]

From marriage to domestic violence to family property, Wu's scholarship is reflected both in her legislation work and her academic works. Her major publications include *A Textbook of Marriage Law* (1986),[10] "Forty Years of China's Marriage Law Study" (1989),[11] "On Further Implementation of the Law of Protection of Women's Rights and Interests"

6. See Wang Xiaochen, "Wu Changzhen: Xin Zhongguo." China's first Marriage Law was promulgated in 1950. The second Marriage Law was enacted in 1980 and amended in 2001. It became obsolete in 2020 due to the enactment of the civil code.

7. Wang Xiaochen, "Wu Changzhen."

8. Zhonghua Renmin Gongheguo Fan Jiating Baolifa 中华人民共和国反家庭暴力法 [Anti-Domestic Violence Law of the People's Republic of China] (promulgated by the Standing Committee of the National People's Congress Dec. 27, 2015, effective Mar. 1, 2016), http://www.gov.cn/zhengce/2015-12/28/content_5029898.htm (accessed Dec. 24, 2020).

9. See Wang Xiaochen, "Wu Changzhen: Fan Jiabao." Ten people were named the 2015 Rule of Law Figure by a China Central TV program sponsored by the Ministry of Justice, the Supreme People's Court, and other organizations. For more information, see http://news.cntv.cn/special/ndfzrw2015/index.shtml (accessed Dec. 24, 2020).

10. *Hunyinfa Jiangyi* 婚姻法讲义 [A Textbook of Marriage Law] (Beijing: Zhongguo Zhengfa Daxue Chubanshe, 1986).

11. "Zhongguo Hunyin Jiating Faxue Sishinian" 中国婚姻家庭法学四十年 [Forty Years of China's Marriage Law Study] *Zhengfa Luntan* 政法论坛 4 and 5 (1989).

(1993),[12] *The Marriage Law and Me* (2001),[13] *China's Marriage Law* (2001),[14] "The Civil Law Codification and the Improvement of the Divorce System" (2003),[15] *A Survey on the Implementation of the Marriage Law* (2004),[16] "A Few Ideas to Improve the Marriage Law" (2006),[17] "A Review of China's Marriage Law over Sixty Years" (2011),[18] and *Marriage Law and Inheritance Law* (2011).[19] She was known for her insightful discussions on kinship, domestic relations, the family system, and family property. She provided concrete solutions for the establishment of the parental system, the improvement of the custody system, and the adoption and fostering of children.

Bibliography of English Publications by Professor Wu Changzhen

Wu Ch'ang-chen. *China's Family in Developmeat* [sic]. Washington, DC: World Peace through Law Center, 1990.

———. "A Review of China's Marriage Law over Sixty Years." *China Law* 6 (2011).

12. "Jinyibu Guanche Funü Quanyi Baozhangfa" 进一步贯彻妇女权益保障法 [On Further Implementation of the Law of Protection of Women's Rights and Interests], *Zhongguo Fa*xue 中国法学 4 (1993).

13. *Wo Yu Hunyinfa* 我与婚姻法 [Marriage Law and Me] (Beijing: Falü Chubanshe, 2001).

14. *Zhongguo Hunyinfa* 中国婚姻法 [China's Marriage Law] (Beijing: Zhongguo Zhengfa Daxue Chubanshe, 2001).

15. "Minfa Fadianhua Yu Lihun Zhidu De Wanshan" 民法法典化与离婚制度的完善 [The Civil Law Codification and the Improvement of the Divorce System], *Shandong Daxue Falü Pinglun* 山东大学法律评论 (2003): 14–20.

16. *Hunyinfa Zhixing Zhuangkuang Diaocha* 婚姻法执行状况调查 [A Survey on the Implementation of the Marriage Law] (Beijing: Zhongyang Wenxian Chubanshe, 2004).

17. "Jinyibu Wanshan Hunyinfa De Jidian Sikao" 进一步完善婚姻法的几点思考 [A Few Ideas to Improve the Marriage Law], *Jinling Falü Pinglun* 金陵法律评论 1 (2006).

18. "Jiedu Zhongguo Hunyinfa Liushinian" 解读中国婚姻法六十年 [A Review of China's Marriage Law over Sixty Years] (published in both Chinese and English), *Zhongguo Falü* 中国法律 6 (2011).

19. *Hunyin Yu Jicheng Faxue* 婚姻与继承法学 [Marriage Law and Inheritance Law] (Beijing: Zhongguo Zhengfa Daxue Chubanshe, 2011).

References

Jiang Wenxing 蒋文星 and Liao Canqiang 廖灿强. "Wu Changzhen" 巫昌祯 [Wu Chang-zhen]. In *Zhongguo Faxuejia Fangtanlu* 中国法学家访谈录 [Interviews with Chinese Jurists], vol. 2, edited by He Qinhua 何勤华, 269–78. Beijing: Beijing Daxue Chu-banshe, 2010.

Li Li 李丽. "Hunyin De Zhendi Shi Xingfu—Fang Hunyinfa Dajia Wu Changzhen Ji-aoshou" 婚姻的真谛是幸福–访婚姻法大家巫昌祯教授 [The Essence of Marriage Is Happiness: An Interview with Marriage Law Master, Professor Wu Changzhen]. *21 Shiji* 21 世纪 6 (2013): 37–39.

Li Meng 李蒙. "Wu Changzhen Sumiao" 巫昌祯素描 [A Sketch of Wu Changzhen]. *Zhengfu Fazhi* 政府法制 6 (2009): 36–37.

Wang Xiaochen 王晓晨. "Wu Changzhen: Fan Jiabao Lifa Ershinian" 巫昌祯: 反家暴立法二十年 [Wu Changzhen: Twenty Years of Anti-Domestic Violence Legislation]. *Fangyuan* 方圆 1 (2016): 50–53.

———. "Wu Changzhen: Xin Zhongguo Hunyinfa De Fazhan De Jianzhengzhe" 巫昌祯: 新中国婚姻法的见证者 [Wu Changzhen: A Witness of the Development of the Marriage Law in the New China]. *Fazhi Yu Shehui* 法治与社会 4 (2016): 73–75.

Wu Changzhen 巫昌祯. *Wo Yu Hunyinfa* 我与婚姻法 [Marriage Law and Me]. Beijing: Falü Chubanshe, 2001.

"Wu Changzhen" 巫昌祯 [Wu Changzhen]. http://baike.baidu.com/item /%E5%B7%AB%E6%98%8C%E7%A5%AF (accessed May 4, 2017).

Yi Mingwu 冀明武. "Wu Changzhen" 巫昌祯 [Wu Changzhen]. In *20 Shiji Zhongguo Zhiming Kexuejia Xueshu Chengjiu Gailan: Faxuejuan* 20 世纪中国知名科学家学术成就概览: 法学卷 [Introduction to the Achievements of the Famous Chinese Scientists in the Twenty Century: Law Volumes], vol. 3, edited by Jiang Ping et al. (Beijing: Kexue Chubanshe, 2014).

26. Chen Guangzhong (陈光中)

(1930–)

Criminal Procedure

Professor of law at the China University of Political Science and Law, Chen Guangzhong is regarded as a pioneer and founder of the study of criminal procedure law in China. He was also president of the university and vice president of the China Law Society. He is an award-winning author of several publications on criminal procedure law and criminal evidence law.

Educational Background

Chen was born in Yongjia (永嘉) County of Zhejiang Province. In 1948, he entered the Law Department of the Central University (now Nanjing University). He later transferred to Zhongshan University in Guangzhou. In 1950, he transferred to the Law Department of Peking University and graduated in 1952.

Career Highlights

Upon graduation, Chen was assigned to teach in the Law Department at Peking University. Two months later, the Law Department was closed and merged with the Beijing College of Political Science and Law (now the China University of Political Science and Law). He went to teach at this newly established law school. A year later, he was asked to teach criminal procedure law, which started his long career in criminal procedure law research.

In 1955, Chen was assigned to assist a criminal procedure law expert from the Soviet Union. He soon caught the attention of his colleagues by his publications. In 1955 and 1956, he published two articles in the prestigious national publication *Political and Legal Research*.[1] He also participated in the composition of Communist China's first criminal procedure law textbook. Besides teaching and research, he practiced law as a freelance lawyer.

Due to his criticism of official policies during the Anti-Rightist Movement in 1957, Chen was ordered to leave the politically sensitive post of teaching criminal procedure law. Instead, he was forced to teach Chinese history and legal history. He was later sent to a labor camp in Anhui Province. During the Cultural Revolution, he followed his wife to Guangxi University and taught modern Chinese history. In 1978, he came back to Beijing and worked at the People's Education Press. In 1982, he obtained a position at the Law Institution of the Chinese Academy of Social Science. He later returned to his teaching position at the China University of Political Science and Law in 1983. He was China's first professor to be appointed academic adviser for PhD students in the field of criminal procedure law. He became president of the university in 1992 and returned to full-time teaching in 1994. The next year he created the Criminal Law Research Center at the university. He was granted tenure (lifetime professor) in 2001.

Chen has also held various academic posts outside the university. He is the associate director of the Research Committee and the honorary president of the Criminal Procedure Law Association of the China Law

1. Chen Guangzhong 陈光中, "Sulian De Bianhu Zhidu" 苏联的辩护制度 [The Defense System of the Soviet Union], *Zhengfa Yanjiu* 政法研究 [Political and Legal Research] 2 (1955); Chen Guangzhong 陈光中 and Shi Weichao 时伟超, "Guanyu Xingshi Susongzhong Zhengju Fenlei Yu Jianjie Zhengju De Jige Wenti" 关于刑事诉讼中证据分类与间接证据的几个问题 [A Few Issues Concerning the Classification of Evidence and Indirect Evidence in Criminal Litigation] *Zhengfa Yanjiu* 政法研究 [Political and Legal Research] 2 (1956).

Society. He was a member of the Science Committee of the Educational Commission, an adviser to the Supreme People's Court, and an appraiser of the Academic Committee of the State Council. He was named one of the National Outstanding Senior Jurists[2] by the China Law Society in 2012.

Research Areas and Publications

Chen is a chief editor, author, or coauthor of over fifty books. He has also published more than two hundred articles. Many of his articles have been published overseas. His scholarship focuses on such issues as the protection of human rights in criminal litigation, judicial justice and trial procedure reform, and criminal evidence, as well as the dynamic balance between substance and procedure, prosecution and defense, and criminal punishment and human rights protection. As early as the 1950s, he published articles proposing a presumption of innocence in criminal procedure.

Chen's *The Ancient Judicial System of China* (1984)[3] and *A Comparative Study of Foreign Criminal Procedures* (1988)[4] are the first such books published in mainland China. He was an early explorer of the United Nations criminal justice standards and published *The United Nations Criminal Justice Standards and China's Criminal Justice System*[5] in 1998, the first such book published in China. This book provided a reference for China's ratification of the International Covenant on Civil and

2. See footnote 2 in chapter 20 on Sun Guohua.

3. *Zhongguo Gudai Sifa Zhidu* 中国古代司法制度 [The Ancient Judicial System of China] (Beijing: Qunzhong Chubanshe, 1984).

4. *Waiguo Xingshi Susong Chengxu Bijiao Yanjiu* 外国刑事诉讼程序比较研究 [A Comparative Study of Foreign Criminal Procedures] (Beijing: Falü Chubanshe, 1988).

5. Chen Guangzhong 陈光中 et al., *Lianheguo Xingshi Sifa Zhunze Yu Zhongguo Xingshi Fazhi* 联合国刑事司法准则与中国刑事法制 [The United Nations Criminal Justice Standards and China's Criminal Justice System] (Beijing: Falü Chubanshe, 1998).

Political Rights (ICCPR), which China signed two months after the book was published.[6]

Chen has participated in legislative discussions and consultations on many laws, including the Constitutional Law (1982), the Lawyer's Law (1996), and the State Compensation Law (1994). Perhaps his most influential work on legislation was his involvement in the revisions of the Criminal Procedure Law in 1996 and 2012. In 1993, on behalf of the Legal Work Committee of the People's Congress, he led the Revision Research Group of the Criminal Procedure Law.[7] The group created a Criminal Procedure Law Revision Proposal and published a book on this topic in 1995. The proposal suggested a combination of criminal punishment and protection of human rights, a shift from the law's previous focus on fighting crimes. It is said that 65 percent of the proposal was adopted in the 1996 amendment.[8] The book, *A Discussion and a Proposed Draft of the Criminal Procedure Law of the People's Republic of China*,[9] received two social science awards, from the Beijing government and also the Ministry of Education.[10] In 2003, to help with the new revision of the Crimi-

6. See Bian Jianlin 卞建林, "Chen Guangzhong: Xinzhongguo Xingshi Susong Faxue Taidou" 陈光中：新中国刑事诉讼法学泰斗 [Chen Guangzhong—a Leading Scholar of Criminal Procedure Law of the New China], in *Hexie Shehui Goujian Yu Susong Faxue Fanrong: Chen Guangzhong Jiaoshou Bashi Huadan Qinghe Wenji* 和谐社会构建与诉讼法学繁荣：陈光中教授八十华诞庆贺文集 [The Construction of a Harmonious Society and the Flourishing of Procedure Law: Collected Essays to Celebrate Professor Chen Guangzhong's Eightieth Birthday], edited by Chen Guangzhong Jiaoshou Baoshi Huadan Qinghe Huodong Choubeizu 陈光中教授八十华诞庆贺活动筹备组. (Beijing: Zhongguo Zhengfa Daxue Chubanshe, 2010).

7. *Zhonghua Renmin Gongheguo Xingshi Susongfa* 中华人民共和国刑事诉讼法 [The Criminal Procedure Law of the People's Republic of China] (promulgated by National People's Congress July 1, 1979, effective Jan. 1, 1980, amended in 1996, 2012, and 2018).

8. See Chen Guangzhong 陈光中, "Zixu" 自序 [Author's Prelude], in *Chen Guangzhong Faxue Wenji* 陈光中法学文集 [A Collection of Chen Guangzhong's Legal Essays] (Beijing: Zhongguo Fazhi Chubanshe, 2000), 7.

9. Chen Guangzhong 陈光中 et al., *Zhonghua Renmin Gongheguo Xingshi Susongfa Xiugai Jianyigao Yu Lunzheng* 中华人民共和国刑事诉讼法修改建议稿与论证 [A Discussion and a Proposed Draft of the Criminal Procedure Law of the People's Republic of China] (Beijing: Zhongguo Fangzheng Chubanshe, 1995).

10. The book was awarded First Prize for Humanities and Social Sciences Research by the Ministry of Education. Please see https://www.gmw.cn/01gmrb/1999-07/02/GB /18105%5EGM8-0210.HTM (accessed Dec. 24, 2020).

nal Procedure Law, Chen once again assembled a group of scholars and experts in the field. They published *A Discussion and an Expert's Draft for the Re-Amendment of the Criminal Procedure Law of the People's Republic of China and Its Annotations*[11] in 2006. This Chinese and English bilingual publication became influential in the fields of legislation, judiciary, and academia. It was a reference for the 2012 revision of the Criminal Procedure Law. His *A Study of the Fundamental Theories of China's Judicial System*[12] was awarded the grand prize for the Beijing Excellent Research Award in the Field of Philosophy and Social Science.[13]

Among his research topics, Chen provided insights into the theories of criminal procedure, the implications of ancient judicial systems, criminal evidence, comparative criminal procedure law, and the improvement of China's criminal procedure law. In terms of the theories of criminal procedure, he has had in-depth discussions on the value, objectives, structures, and efficiency of criminal litigation, as well as the independence of the judiciary. As for the improvement of China's criminal procedure law, he proposed the enhancement of defendants' human rights, increase of victims' rights, perfection of criminal investigation methods, reinforcement of death penalty review, an upgrade of juvenile criminal procedures, and reform of the education through labor system.

Chen published China's first book on comparative criminal procedure law[14] in 1988. He is the chief editor of *The Twenty-First Century New Development of Foreign Criminal Procedure Legislation*,[15] which provides

11. Chen Guangzhong 陈光中 et al., *Zhonghua Renmin Gongheguo Xingshi*.

12. Chen Guangzhong et al., *Zhongguo Sifa Zhidu De Jichu Lilun Wenti Yanjiu* 中国司法制度的基础理论问题研究 [A Study of the Fundamental Theories of China's Judicial System] (Beijing: Jingji Kexue Chubanshe, 2010).

13. Beijingshi Zhexue Shehui Kexue Youxiu Chengguojiang 北京市哲学社会科学优秀成果奖 (Beijing Excellent Research Award in the Field of Philosophy and Social Science) has been given by the Beijing government and the Communist Party of Beijing Committee to outstanding research projects biannually since 1987.

14. *Waiguo Xingshi Susong Chengxu Bijiao Yanjiu* 外国刑事诉讼程序比较研究 [A Comparative Study of Foreign Criminal Procedure Law] (Beijing: Falü Chubanshe, 1988).

15. Chen Guangzhong, ed., *21shiji Yuwai Xingshi Susong Lifa Zuixin Fazhan* 21 世纪域外刑事诉讼立法最新发展 [The Twenty-First Century New Development of Foreign Criminal Procedure Legislation] (Beijing: Zhongguo Zhengfa Daxue Chubanshe, 2004).

a good introduction to new developments in criminal procedure law in major countries and relevant international treaties by the United Nations. Since the 1990s, Chen has led an effort to introduce translated works on criminal procedure and evidence law from France, Germany, Italy, the United States, England, Russia, Japan, Canada, and South Korea.

Bibliography of English Publications by Professor Chen Guangzhong

Albrecht, Hans-Jörg, and Chen Guangzhong. *Coercive Measures in a Socio-Legal Comparison of the People's Republic of China and Germany.* Freiburg, Germany: Iuscrim, 2004.
————. *Non-Prosecution Policies: A Sino-German Comparison.* Freiburg, Germany: Iuscrim, 2002.
Chen Guangzhong. *Chen Guangzhong: Selected Works on Law.* Beijing: Zhongguo Zhengfa Daxue Chubanshe, 2010.

References

Chen Guangzhong 陈光中. *Chen Guangzhong Faxue Wenji* 陈光中法学文集 [A Collection of Legal Essays by Chen Guangzhong]. Beijing: Zhongguo Fazhi Chubanshe, 2000.
————. *Zhonghua Renmin Gongheguo Xingshi Susongfa Zaixiugai Zhuanjia Jianyigao Yu Lunzheng* 中华人民共和国刑事诉讼法再修改专家建议稿与论证 [A Discussion and an Expert's Draft for the Re-Amendment of the Criminal Procedure Law of the People's Republic of China]. Beijing: Zhongguo Fazhi Chubanshe, 2006.
"Chen Guangzhong" 陈光中 [Chen Guangzhong]. http://baike.baidu.com/item /%E9%99%88%E5%85%89%E4%B8%AD/81125 (accessed Sept. 18, 2016).
Chen Xiahong 陈夏红. "Wei Faxue Chengqi Yipian Tiankong—Ji Jiang Ping, Chen Guangzhong, Zhang Jinfan Xiansheng" 为法学撑起一片天空—记江平, 陈光中, 张晋藩先生 [To Support Legal Studies—on Mr. Jiang Ping, Chen Guangzhong, and Zhang Jinfan]. *Guangming Ribao* 光明日报, Nov. 4, 2002.
Editorial Team. *Hexie Shehui Goujian Yu Susong Faxue Fanrong: Chen Guangzhong Jiaoshou Bashi Huadan Qinghe Wenji* 和谐社会构建与诉讼法学繁荣：陈光中教授八十华诞庆贺文集 [The Construction of a Harmonious Society and the Flourishing of Procedure Law: Collected Essays to Celebrate Professor Chen Guangzhong's Eightieth Birthday]. Beijing: Zhongguo Zhengfa Daxue Chubanshe, 2010.
Fan Chongyi 樊崇义. *Susong Faxue Xintan—Chen Guangzhong Jiaoshou Qishi Huadan Zhuhe Wenji* 诉讼法学新探–陈光中教授七十华诞祝贺文集 [New Studies on the Proce-

dure Law—Collected Essays to Celebrate Professor Chen Guangzhong's Seventieth Birthday]. Beijing: Zhongguo Fazhi Chubanshe, 2000.

Li Legang 李乐刚. "Chen Guangzhong Xueshu Chengjiu Jianjie" 陈光中学术成就简介 [An Introduction to Chen Guangzhong's Academic Achievement]. *Jianghan Luntan* 江汉论坛 8 (2006): 144.

Xiong Qiuhong 熊秋红. "Chen Guangzhong Xiansheng Fangtanlu" 陈光中先生访谈录 [An Interview with Mr. Chen Guangzhong]. *Huanqiu Falü Pinglun* 环球法律评论 4 (2001): 441–44.

Zhang Xue 张雪 and Zhang Wei 张伟. "Chen Guangzhong" 陈光中 [Chen Guangzhong]. In *Zhongguo Faxuejia Fangtanlu* 中国法学家访谈录 [Interviews with Chinese Jurists], edited by He Qinhua 何勤华, 242–48. Beijing: Beijing Daxue Chubanshe, 2010.

27. Jiang Ping (江平)

(1930–)

Civil Law and Commercial Law

Professor of law at the China University of Political Science and Law, Jiang Ping is a world-renowned jurist. He is regarded as a "soul figure," or "conscience,"[1] of contemporary Chinese law. As a legal scholar, an educator, and a social activist, he is passionate about private rights, democracy, and the rule of law, which have made him an exceptional advocate for the development of China's civil and commercial law. His favorite saying is "Only bow to truth."[2] Today, as one of "the three deans of the rule of law"[3] in China, Jiang continues to play an important role in China's academic, political, and social scene.

Educational Background

Jiang was born in Dalian (大连) City of Liaoning Province. In 1948, he entered the Journalism Department of Yenching University in Beijing. A year later, he dropped out of college and went to work for the newly formed

1. Jiang is called the soul and/or conscience of Chinese law or Chinese civil law or the rule of law in China in many articles. For example, in "Lingren Zunjing De Jiang Ping Xiansheng 令人崇敬的江平先生 [The Respectable Mr. Jiang Ping], the author, Xie Zhihao (谢志浩) called Jiang Ping the "Linghun" 灵魂(soul) and "Liangxin" 良心(conscience) of China's civil law, http://m.aisixiang.com/data/37156.html (accessed July 9, 2021).

2. See "A Self Statement" in *Jiang Ping Wenji* 江平文集 [A Collection of Jiang Ping's Articles] (Beijing: Zhongguo Fazhi Chubanshe, 2000).

3. See footnote 1 in chapter 23 on Guo Daohui.

Beijing Communist government. In 1951, he was selected by the government to study in the Soviet Union. Originally, he was enrolled in Kazan (Volga Region) Federal University but transferred to Moscow State University two years later. He graduated from the Law Faculty of Moscow State University in 1956.

Career Highlights

Upon returning from the Soviet Union, Jiang went to teach at the Beijing College of Political Science and Law. He began teaching civil law and worked with Soviet legal experts. A year later, the Anti-Rightist Movement was launched. His recommendations to improve the Communist Party being viewed as criticism of the party, he was labeled a Rightist and was sent to a labor camp in the countryside. During this time, he lost a leg in a work accident. In 1960, he was allowed to come back to the Beijing College of Political Science and Law but was assigned to teach Russian. In 1972, the college was closed. Jiang first went to Anhui Province for odd jobs and later found a job as an English teacher in a middle school in Yanqing District of Beijing. He was eventually assigned to teach political science at the middle school.

In 1978, the disbanded Beijing College of Political Science and Law was reestablished, and Jiang's teaching position was resumed. He taught classes in Roman law and introductions to civil and commercial law in Western countries. He quickly became one of the most popular professors at the college[4] and, in 1983, became vice president of the college. The following year, the college was upgraded to become the China University of Political Science and Law. Jiang was appointed as president of the university in 1988. A year later, due to his support for the student movement in 1989, which led to the Tiananmen Square Massacre,[5] he was forced to resign from the position.

4. See "Jiang Ping: Minshang Faxue Mingjia" 江平：民商法学名家 [Jiang Ping: Famous Scholars of Civil and Commercial Law], http://www.qlfy.com/sxf/Article/fxmj /200604/62.html (accessed Dec. 14, 2018).

5. Known as the June Fourth Incident or Tiananmen Square Protests, these were student-led demonstrations in Beijing's Tiananmen Square in 1989. For more informa-

As an educator and activist of law, Jiang held many important positions. He was vice president of the China Law Society, vice president of the China Economic Law Association, and vice president of the Beijing Bar Association. He was a representative of the Seventh National People's Congress (NPC), a member of the Standing Committee, and vice chairman of the Legal Committee of the NPC. He participated in the drafting of many laws, including the General Principles of Civil Law (1986), the Administrative Law (1988), the Contract Law (1999), the Trust Law (2001), and the Property Law (2007), among others. He has been a special adviser to the Supreme People's Court and is an arbitrator of the International Arbitration Commission and associate director of the Beijing Arbitration Commission. He has been invited to teach and give talks at leading universities around the world and received honorary doctoral degrees in Belgium and Italy.

In 2000, Jiang used his savings to establish the first scholarship for legal studies in China. The Jiang Ping Civil and Commercial Law Scholarship was the first public-interest fund created by an individual in the field at the time.

Research Areas and Publications

Because of his political ordeals from 1957 to 1977, Jiang's research life only took off after he returned to teaching at the Beijing College of Political Science and Law. His publications mainly appeared after the 1980s. As an inspiring speaker and forward thinker, Jiang primarily discussed his theories and ideas in speeches rather than through writing. In an interview with the journalist Han Yong, Jiang said, "Compared to essay writing, I prefer to express myself on the podium."[6] However, he has published several books and many articles in recent years. His major books

tion, see https://www.history.com/this-day-in-history/tiananmen-square-massacre-takes
-place (accessed Dec. 24, 2020).

6. Han Yong 韩永. "Faxue Dajia Jiang Ping Rensheng Xiezhao: Fazhi Shi Weiyi Xinyang" 法学大家江平人生写照: 法治是唯一信仰 [The Rule of Law Is the Only Belief: A Reflection on Jiang Ping's Life], *Zhengfu Fazhi* 政府法制 35 (2009): 23.

include *An Introduction to Western Civil and Commercial Law* (1984),[7] *A Collection of Jiang Ping's Articles* (2000),[8] *A Selection of Jiang Ping's Speeches* (2003),[9] *Fundamentals of Roman Law* (2004),[10] *To Shout Is My Duty* (2007),[11] *A Call for Private Rights: A Self-Selection by Jiang Ping* (2008),[12] *Ups and Downs and Withered: A Self-Reflection* (2010),[13] *The Rule of Law Must Succeed* (2016),[14] *Essentials of Civil and Commercial Law* (2019),[15] and *The Related Development of China's Market Economy and Civil Code* (2020).[16]

    Jiang's scholarship focuses on private law, property, the rule of law, the relationships between the individual and the state, the relationships between enterprises and the state, and economic, political, and legal reforms. He was one of the early scholars to recognize the importance of the rule of law in a civilized society. As a civil law expert, he took political risks by introducing the study of Roman law and Western civil and commercial law in China. In 1981, he and his colleagues wrote a Roman law textbook. In 1984, he published his first book, *An Introduction to Western Civil and Commercial Law.*[17] In these books, he pointed out that the rule of law was a system that allowed space for the existence of civil law

---

7. *Xifang Guojia Minshangfa Gaiyao* 西方国家民商法概要 [An Introduction to Western Civil and Commercial Law] (Shijiazhuang Shi: Falü Chubanshe, 1984).

8. *Jiang Ping Wenji* 江平文集 [A Collection of Jiang Ping's Articles] (Beijing: Zhongguo Fazhi Chubanshe, 2000).

9. *Jiang Ping Jiangyan Wenxuan* 江平讲演文选 [A Selection of Jiang Ping's Speeches] (Beijing: Zhongguo Fazhi Chubanshe, 2003).

10. *Luomafa Jichu* 罗马法基础 [Fundamentals of Roman Law] (Beijing: Zhongguo Zhengfa Daxue Chubanshe, 2004).

11. *Wo Suonengzhuo De Shi Nahan* 我所能做的是呐喊 [To Shout Is My Duty] (Beijing: Falü Chubanshe, 2007).

12. *Siquan De Nahan: Jiang Ping Zixuanji* 私权的呐喊: 江平自选集 [A Call for Private Rights—a Self-Selection by Jiang Ping] (Beijing: Shoudu Shifan Daxue Chubanshe, 2008).

13. Jiang Ping, *Chenfu Yu Kurong.*

14. Jiang Ping, *Fazhi Bisheng.*

15. *Minshangfa Lunyao* 民商法论要 [Essentials of Civil and Commercial Law] (Beijing: Zhongguo Fazhi Chubanshe, 2019).

16. *Zhongguo Shichang Jingji Fazhan Yu Minfadian* 中國市場經濟發展與民法典 [The Related Development of China's Market Economy and Civil Code] (Hong Kong: Xianggang Chengshi Daxue Chubanshe, 2020).

17. *Xifang Guojia Minshangfa Gaiyao* 西方国家民商法概要 [An Introduction to Western Civil and Commercial Law] (Shijiazhuang Shi: Falü Chubanshe, 1984).

and individuality within the state. Personal dignity and self-governance
were the center of a civilized society. China's planned economy and political state were barriers to civil law. The key to individuality was to cor-
rectly deal with the property relations between the state and state-owned
enterprises. These ideas have helped the development of the concept of
enterprise right in self-governance and the creation of a relevant article
in the General Principles of Civil Law (1986).[18]

In the late 1980s, Jiang made another effort to promote economic and
legal reforms. He saw private companies and ownership by legal persons
as two mechanisms to curb the unfair relationship between state ownership and enterprise governance. He took the lead in addressing these issues in the legislative discussions regarding the Corporation Law. After
the Corporation Law was promulgated in 1993, he immediately recommended next steps for economic reform, which included separating the
shareholder personality and the corporation personality. In the first chapter of *On the Legal Person System*,[19] he pointed out that one of the characteristics of the legal person was independent personality. He believed
that in market and social life, individuals could use the legal person to
release themselves from state power. With in-depth discussions on the
legal person and personality, legal person and organization, legal person
and property, legal person and capability, legal person and intent, and
legal person and obligation, this book has become an important classic
for the study of the legal person.

Jiang is a leading expert on the Property Law and the Civil Law Code
drafting groups. Since 1997, he has published many articles and given
many speeches on issues related to these two laws. To him, the starting
point of the Civil Law Code is human rights. He pointed out that the
future of China's rule of law was the awakening of rights, the improvement of the judicial supervision system, and the progress of democratic
politics. He disapproved the absolute acceptance of the German Civil

18. See article 82 of the General Principles of Civil Law. It says that enterprises have
the right to manage their properties granted by the state. Zhonghua Renmin Gongheguo Minfa Tongze 中华人民共和国民法通则 [The General Principles of Civil Law]
(promulgated by the National People's Congress, Apr. 12, 1986, effective Jan. 1, 1987).

19. Jing Ping 江平 and Zhao Xudong 赵旭东, eds., *Faren Zhidu Lun* 法人制度论 [On
the Legal Person System] (Beijing: Zhongguo Zhengfa Daxue Chubanshe, 1994).

Code as a legislative model for China and suggested that separate laws would work if the creation of a unified code of civil law was not feasible in the current circumstance. Since the 1990s, Jiang has had renewed interests in Anglo-American law. He is open to the idea of learning from case law experience in the legislation and practice of law.

Jiang has also done important work in the field of comparative law. He engaged in the international exchange of civil law studies. He promoted the translation of prominent legal works by Western scholars and has led the publication of *The Series of Foreign Laws*[20] and *The Series of American Law*.[21] His frequent visits to foreign countries have introduced Chinese law to the world. He is regarded as a driver in the renaissance of China's legal studies and has helped to clarify many traditional ideas of law in today's context.

Jiang has also discussed widely issues of legal education and the practice of law. His addresses, speeches, and essays on these topics have had a lasting impact on students, scholars, and legal professionals in China. As Professor He Weifang (贺卫方) of Peking University put it: Jiang "is one of the most influential teachers. He is the law teacher of our nation."[22]

Bibliography of English Publications by Professor Jiang Ping

Jiang Ping. "Chinese Legal Reform: Achievements, Problems and Prospects." *Journal of Chinese Law* 9, no. 1 (1995): 67–75.

———. "Drafting the Uniform Contract Law in China." *Columbia Journal of Asian Law* 10, no. 1 (1996): 245–58.

———. *Introduction to Chinese Law: Een Voordrachtenreeks Door Prof. Jiang Ping, Gent, 3–27 November 1986.* Gent, Belgium: Rijksuniversiteit-Gent, Facuteit von de Rechtsgeleerheid, 1986.

20. Waiguo Falü Wenku 外国法律文库 [The Series of Foreign Laws] (Beijing: Zhongguo Dabaike Quanshu Chubanshe, 1993–).

21. Meiguo Falü Wenku 美国法律文库 [The Series of American Law] (Beijing: Zhongguo Zhengfa Daxue Chubanshe, 1997–).

22. He Weifang 贺卫方, "Jiang Laoshi De Jingshen" 江老师的精神 [The Spirit of Professor Jiang], in Jiang Ping, *Fazhi Bisheng*, 1–3.

References

Jiang Ping 江平. *Chenfu Yu Kurong: Bashi Zishu* 沉浮与枯荣: 八十自述 [Ups and Downs and Withered: A Self-Reflection]. Beijing: Falü Chubanshe, 2010.

———. *Fazhi Bisheng* 法治必胜 [The Rule of Law Must Succeed]. Beijing: Falü Chubanshe, 2016.

Jiang Ping 江平 and Zhao Xudong 赵旭东, eds. *Minshangfa Zonglun* 民商法综论 [A General Discussion on Civil and Commercial Law]. Beijing: Zhongguo Fazhi Chubanshe, 2000.

"Jing Ping" 江平 [Jing Ping]. https://baike.baidu.com/item/%E6%B1%9F%E5%B9%B3 /17297 (accessed Dec. 24, 2020).

Liu Bijun 刘璧君 and Yu Yongfan 余甬帆. "Jiang Ping" 江平 [Jiang Ping]. In *Zhongguo Faxuejia Fangtanlu* 中国法学家访谈录 [Interviews with Chinese Jurists], edited by He Qinhua 何勤华, 105–15. Beijing: Beijing Daxue Chubanshe, 2013.

Liu Renwen 刘仁文. "Jiang Ping Xiansheng Fangtanlu" 江平先生访谈录 [An Interview with Mr. Jiang Ping]. *Huanqiu Falü Pinglun* 环球法律评论 3 (2002).

Sun Guodong 孙国栋, ed. *Yongyuan De Xiaozhang: Jiang Ping Jiaoshou Bashi Huadan Qinghe Wenji* 永远的校长: 江平教授八十华诞庆贺文集 [The Forever University President: A Celebration Collection of Professor Jiang Ping's Eightieth Birthday]. Beijing: Zhongguo Fazhi Chubanshe, 2010.

Wen Yuzhong 文喻中. "Jiang Ping He Zhongguo Dangdai Faxue De Xingqi" 江平和中国 当代法学的兴起 [Jiang Ping and the Rise of Contemporary Chinese Legal Studies]. *Zhongguo Lüshi* 中国律师 4 (2011).

28. Zhang Jinfan (张晋藩)

(1930–)

Historical Studies of Chinese Law

Professor of law at the China University of Political Science and Law, Zhang Jinfan is one of the pioneers and leading scholars in the study of traditional Chinese law after 1949. He has lectured at Harvard, Yale, Duke, and Columbia Universities in the United States and many other international academic institutions. A prominent legal scholar and educator, Zhang is also a poet.

Educational Background

Zhang was born in Shenyang (沈阳) Municipality of Liaoning Province. In 1947, he was admitted into the English program in the Literature Department of Northeast Zhongzheng University in Shenyang. Because of the Chinese Civil War between the Communist Party and the Chinese Nationalist Party,[1] his college education was intermittent, and he moved among three area colleges. In 1949, he transferred to the Beijing College of Political Science and Law. A year later, his college was merged with Renmin University. He became a student at Renmin University and was chosen to be a graduate student of legal history. He graduated from the Law Department in 1952.

---

1. See footnote 11 in the introduction.

Career Highlights

Zhang was assigned to teach the history of the state and law at Renmin University right after his graduation. Except for 1972 to 1977, when he worked at the Institute of Qing Dynasty History of Beijing Normal University, Zhang taught at Renmin University until 1982. In 1983, he was invited to teach at the China University of Political Science and Law, and he spent the rest of his teaching career there. In 1985, he founded the Institute of Chinese Legal History (now the Academy of Legal History). He was dean of the graduate school and vice president of the university between 1983 and 1994. He served as a member of the Academic Evaluation Group of the State Council between 1985 and 1991. He was named discipline leader of legal history by the Academic Degree Committee of the State Council in 1988.

Research Areas and Publications

Zhang's research interests stretch from Chinese legal history and specialized topics within Chinese law to the chronological history of law, the comparative study of legal history, and legal culture. His most important essays have been published in three collections titled: *A Book of Dribbling* (1990),[2] *A Book of Pursuing* (1995),[3] and *A Book of Incompletion* (2000).[4] *A Book of Dribbling* features his essays published between 1949 and 1989. These essays explored important and fundamental issues of legal history.

2. *Juandi Ji* 涓滴集 [A Book of Dribbling] (Beijing: Zhongguo Guoji Guangbo Chubanshe, 1990).

3. *Qiusuo Ji: Zhang Jinfan Jiaoshou Yu Zhongguo Fazhi Shixue Sishinian* 求索集: 张晋藩教授与中国法制史学四十年 [A Book of Pursuing—Professor Zhang Jinfan and the Forty Years of China's Historical Studies of Law] (Nanjing: Nanjing Daxue Chubanshe, 1995).

4. *Weiyi Ji: Zhang Jinfa Jiaoshou Jiaoyan Wushi Zhounian Jinian* 未已集: 张晋藩教授教研五十周年纪念 [Weiyi Ji: A Book of Incompletion—a Commemoration of Professor Zhang Jinfan's Fifty Years of Teaching and Research] (Nanjing: Nanjing Daxue Chubanshe, 2000).

As early as 1957, Zhang wrote "Views on the Class Nature and Heritage Nature of Law."[5] In this article, he challenged the then popular idea of abolishing old Chinese law. He pointed out that the class nature of law did not work against the heritage nature of law. The key issue was how to scientifically understand the concept of the inheritance of law and how to adopt the positive aspects of old laws when creating new laws. On the eve of the Anti-Rightist Movement, Zhang's article demonstrated his courage and independent thinking. This collection also represented his ideas on the establishment of China's new legal views and research methodologies of legal studies. He addressed the objectives, goals, and methods of historical studies of law. He indicated that past studies of Chinese legal history merely focused on the history of criminal law, which was narrow-minded. He believed that historical studies of Chinese law needed to examine various subjects of laws (including economic, civil, procedural, administrative, and prison legislation) and in various levels.[6]

In the other two collections, *A Book of Pursuing* and *A Book of Incompletion*, Zhang presented his essays published between 1990 and 2000. During this period, Zhang published several articles on the legal history of the Qing dynasty. He is one of the early scholars who did in-depth research in this area. He later published a few books on this topic, including *The Legal History of the Qing Dynasty* (1994),[7] *On Civil Law of the Qing Dynasty* (1998),[8] and *System, Justice, and Reform: Special Topics on the Legal History of the Qing Dynasty* (2015).[9] Some of his works in this area have become classics in the field.

5. "Guanyu Fade Jiejixing He Jichengxing De Yijian" 关于法的阶级性和继承性的意见 [Views on the Class Nature and Heritage Nature of Law], *Zhengfa Yanjiu* 政法研究 2 (1957).

6. "Tantan Faxue Yanjiuzhong De Jige Wenti" 谈谈法学研究中的几个问题 [Discussions on a Few Issues in the Study of Law], in Zhang Jinfan, *Juandi Ji*.

7. *Qingchao Fazhishi* 清朝法制史 [The Legal History of the Qing Dynasty] (Beijing: Falü Chubanshe, 1994).

8. *Qingdai Minfa Zonglun* 清代民法综论 [On Civil Law of the Qing Dynasty] (Beijing: Zhongguo Zhengfa Daxue Chubanshe, 1998).

9. *Zhidu, Sifa, Yu Biange: Qingdai Falüshi Zhuanlun* 制度，司法，与变革：清代法律史专论 [System, Justice, and Reform: Special Topics on the Legal History of the Qing Dynasty] (Beijing: Falü Chubanshe, 2015).

In recent years, Zhang also published a few collections of his new articles. These include *Selected Essays of Zhang Jinfan* (2007),[10] *A Self-Selected Collection of Zhang Jinfan* (2015),[11] and *A Life with Legal History* (2015).[12] He continued to be very productive after 2015. He published *The Rule of Law and the Reflection of Legal History* (2015),[13] *The Great Chinese Legal Civilization* (2015),[14] *My Own Academic Account* (2015),[15] *History of Chinese Constitutional Law* (2016),[16] *Teachers Talk about Teachers— Zhang Jinfan Volume* (2016),[17] and other works. While dealing with health issues in 2016, Zhang teamed up with his wife, Lin Zhong, a retired professor from China University of Political Science and Law, to publish a book entitled *Discussions on Chinese Legal History*.[18] He dictated the contents while his wife wrote the manuscript. This book highlighted the features of the traditional Chinese legal system, the experiences and practice of ancient state governance, and the positive elements of Chinese legal culture.

Zhang has written several award-winning publications, including *The Ancient Legal System of China* (1992),[19] *China's Legal Heritage and Its Mod-*

10. *Zhang Jinfa Wenxuan* 张晋藩文选 [Selected Essays of Zhang Jinfan] (Beijing: Zhonghua Shuju, 2007).

11. *Xuesi Xinlu: Zhang Jinfan Zixuanji* 学思欣录: 张晋藩自选集 [A Self-Selected Collection of Zhang Jinfan] (Beijing: Shoudu Shifan Daxue Chubanshe, 2015).

12. *Fashi Rensheng* 法史人生 [A Life with Legal History] (Beijing: Falü Chubanshe, 2015).

13. *Yifa Zhiguo Yu Fashi Jingjian* 依法治国与法史镜鉴 [The Rule of Law and the Reflection of Legal History] (Beijing: Zhongguo Fazhi Chubanshe, 2015).

14. Zhang Jinfan 张晋藩 and Chen Yu 陈煜, *Huihuang De Zhonghua Fazhi Wenming* 辉煌的中华法制文明 [The Great Chinese Legal Civilization] (Nanjing: Jiangsu Renmin Chubanshe, 2015).

15. *Dankai Fengqi Buweixian, Wode Xueshu Zishu* 但开风气不为先, 我的学术自述 [My Own Academic Account] (Beijing: Zhongguo Minzhu Fazhi Chubanshe, 2015).

16. *Zhongguo Xianfashi* 中国宪法史 [History of Chinese Constitutional Law], rev. ed. (Beijing: Zhongguo Fazhi Chubanshe, 2016).

17. *Shidao Shuoshi: Zhang Jinfan Juan* 师道说师: 张晋藩卷 [Teachers Talk about Teachers—Zhang Jinfan Volume] (Beijing: Dongfang Chubanshe, 2016).

18. Zhang Jinfan 张晋藩 and Lin Zhong 林中, *Fashi Gouchen Huazhiku* 法史钩沉话智库 [Discussions on Chinese Legal History] (Beijing: Zhongguo Fazhi Chubanshe, 2016).

19. *Zhongguo Gudai Falü Zhidu* 中国古代法律制度 [The Ancient Legal System of China] (Beijing: Zhongguo Guangbo Dianshi Chubanshe, 1992).

ern Transformation (1997),[20] and *The Evolution of China's Legal Civilization* (1999).[21] He has published more than two hundred articles. Some of his works have been translated into English, Japanese, and Korean.

Perhaps his most significant scholarly contribution is his leadership and hard work on the ten-volume publication of *The General History of the Chinese Legal System* (1999).[22] As the project initiator and chief editor, Zhang led a group of seventy scholars and spent nineteen years completing the publication. This set concludes fifty years of research on the study of Chinese legal history. Each volume systematically used a variety of historical materials, such as archaeological relics, surveys of social habits, historical archives, private notes, official documents, statutes, doctrines, court judgments, and so on. The publication has been recognized as a monumental development in China's historical studies of law and received China's highest publication award—the China National Book Award.[23]

In 2013, Zhang began working on another important publication. Once again, he led a group of scholars to write a ten-volume legal history of China's ethnic minorities. This set was published in May 2017. It is called *An Overview of the Legal History of China's Minority Peoples*.[24] His latest publications include *History of Ancient Chinese Judicial Civilization* (2019),[25] *Outline of Chinese Legal Culture* (2019),[26] *History of Chinese Legal Supervision* (2019),[27] and *The Tradition and Modern Transformation of*

---

20. *Zhongguo Falü De Chuantong Yu Jindai Zhuanxing* 中国法律的传统与近代转型 [China's Legal Heritage and Its Modern Transformation] (Beijing: Falü Chubanshe, 1997).

21. *Zhonghua Fazhi Wenming De Yanjin* 中华法制文明的演进 [The Evolution of China's Legal Civilization] (Beijing: Zhongguo Zhengfa Daxue Chubanshe, 1999).

22. *Zhongguo Fazhi Tongshi* 中国法制通史 [The General History of the Chinese Legal System] (Beijing: Falü Chubanshe, 1999).

23. The China National Book Award, approved by the State Council and established in 1992, rewards the best publications in China every other year.

24. *Zhongguo Shaoshu Minzu Fashi Tonglan* 中国少数民族法史通览 [An Overview of the Legal History of China's Minority Peoples] (Xi'an: Shanxi Renmin Chubanshe, 2017).

25. *Zhongguo Gudai Sifa Wenmingshi* 中国古代司法文明史 [History of Ancient Chinese Judicial Civilization] (Beijing: Renmin Chubanshe, 2019).

26. *Zhonghua Fawenhua Yaolue* 中华法文化要略 [Outline of Chinese Legal Culture] (Beijing: Falü Chubanshe, 2019).

27. *Zhongguo Jiancha Fazhishi* 中国监察法制史 [History of Chinese Legal Supervision] (Beijing: Shangwu Yinshuguan, 2019).

Chinese Law (2019).[28] In 2020, he published two books in English: *The History of Chinese Legal Civilization: Ancient China—from about 21st Century B.C. to 1840 A.D.* and *The History of Chinese Legal Civilization: Modern and Contemporary China (from 1840–).*[29]

Zhang has also written more than two hundred poems. Some of these were published in 2005 and 2015.[30] In the collections of his poems, he expressed praise of nature and nostalgia for miracles to appreciate the harmony between man and nature and cultivate the feeling of self-satisfaction.

Bibliography of English Publications by Professor Zhang Jinfan

Zhang Jinfan. "Ancient China's Legal Tradition and Legal Thought." *Social Sciences in China* 34 (2013) 134–51.

———. *The History of Chinese Legal Civilization: Ancient China—from about 21st Century B.C. to 1840 A.D.* Singapore: Springer, 2020.

———. *The History of Chinese Legal Civilization: Modern and Contemporary China (from 1840–).* Singapore: Springer, 2020.

———. *The Tradition and Modern Transition of Chinese Law.* Berlin: Springer, 2014.

References

Chen Xiahong 陈夏红. "Shuzhong Suiyue Bixia Wenzhang—Ji Zhang Jinfan Jiaoshou De Xueshu Zhilu" 书中岁月笔下文章—记张晋藩教授的学术之路 [Years of Books and Writing—on the Research Path of Professor Zhang Jinfan]. *Renmin Ribao* 人民日报, Aug. 19, 2002, C6.

28. *Zhongguo Falü De Chuantong Yu Jindai Zhuanxing* 中国法律的传统与近代转型 [The Tradition and Modern Transformation of Chinese Law] (Beijing: Faü Chubanshe, 2019).

29. Zhang Jinfan, *History of Chinese Legal Civilization: Ancient China.*

30. *Siyouji Zhang Jinfan Shixuan* 思悠集 张晋藩诗选 [A Collection of Leisure Thoughts: A Collection of Zhang Jinfan's Poems] (Beijing: Zhongguo Zhengfa Daxue Chubanshe, 2005); *Siyouji Zengbuben* 思悠集 增补本 [A Collection of Leisure Thoughts, Supplement] (Beijing: Zhongguo Minzhu Fazhi Chubanshe, 2015).

———. "Wei Faxue Chengqi Yipian Tiankong—Ji Jiang Ping, Chen Guangzhong, Zhang Jinfan Xiansheng" 为法学撑起一片天空—记江平, 陈光中, 张晋藩先生 [To Support Legal Studies—on Jiang Ping, Chen Guangzhong, and Zhang Jinfan]. *Guangming Ribao* 光明日报, Nov. 4, 2002, C2.

Fan Zhongxin 范忠信. "Ping Zhang Jinfan Xiansheng Zhubian 'Zhongguo Fazhi Tong-shi'" 评张晋藩先生主编 《中国法制通史》 [Comments on *The General History of Chinese Legal System* Edited by Mr. Zhang Jinfan]. *Xiandai Faxue* 现代法学 2 (2002).

Gu Yuan 顾元. "Falü Shixue De Kaituo, Fazhan Yu Zhonghua Faxi De Fuxing: Zhang Jinfan Xiansheng Fangtanlu" 法律史学的开拓, 发展与中华法系的复兴: 张晋藩先生访谈录 [The Reclaiming and Development of Legal History and the Revival of the Chinese Legal System—an Interview with Mr. Zhang Jinfan]. *Shixue Yuekan* 史学月刊 9 (2006).

Li Airan 李爱然 and Fang Yu 方宇. "Zhang Jinfan" 张晋藩 [Zhang Jinfan]. In *Zhongguo Faxuejia Fangtanlu* 中国法学家访谈录 [Interviews with Chinese Jurists], edited by He Qinhua 何勤华. Beijing: Beijing Daxue Chubanshe, 2010.

Zhang Jinfan 张晋藩. *Fashi Rensheng* 法史人生 [My Life with Legal History]. Beijing: Falü Chubanshe, 2015.

———. *Weiyi Ji: Zhang Jinfan Jiaoshou Jiaoyan Wushi Zhounian Jinian* 未已集: 张晋藩教授教研五十周年纪念 [A Book of Incompletion: A Commemoration of Professor Zhang Jinfan's Fifty Years of Teaching and Research]. Nanjing: Nanjing Daxue Chubanshe, 2000.

"Zhang Jinfan" 张晋藩 [Zhang Jinfan]. http://baike.baidu.com/view/76455.htm#4 (accessed Oct. 10, 2016).

Zhu Yong 朱勇, ed. *Sixue Ji: Zhang Jinfan Xiansheng Zhijiao Liushi Zhounian Ji Bashi Huadan Jinian Wenji* 思学集: 张晋藩先生执教六十周年暨八十华诞纪年文集 [Sixue Ji: A Collection of Commemorating Articles for Mr. Zhang Jinfan's Sixty Years of Teaching and Eightieth Birthday]. Beijing: Zhongguo Zhengfa Daxue Chubanshe, 2010.

———. "Cong 'Juandi Ji' Dao 'Qinglan Ji'—Zhang Jinfan Xiansheng De Zhixue Jingli 从《涓滴集》到《青蓝集》—张晋藩先生的治学经历 [From *Juandi Ji* to *Qinglan Ji*—Mr. Zhang Jinfan's Academic Experience]. In *Dushu Duren* 读书读人 [Book Reading and People Reading], edited by Zhu Yong 朱勇. Beijing: Falü Chubanshe, 2007.

29. Wang Jiafu (王家福)

(1931–2019)

Civil Law

Professor of law at the Chinese Academy of Social Sciences (CASS), Wang Jiafu is regarded as "a trailblazer of Chinese legal studies."[1] A leader for many national research projects concerning economic reform since the 1990s, Wang was an influential scholar in legislation and the practice of civil and commercial law. He was a strong believer in the rule of law and promoted legal reform and human rights in his publications.

Educational Background

Wang was born in Nanchong (南充) County of Sichuan Province. He entered the Law Department of Peking University in 1950. In 1951 and 1952, he participated in the land reform in Jiangxi Province with fellow professors and students. By the time he came back to Peking University, the Law Department was closed and merged with the Beijing College of Political Science and Law (now the China University of Political Science and Law). He became a student of the college and graduated in 1953. The

---

1. Professor Wang Liming 王利明 called Wang Jiafu a "Kaituozhe" 开拓者 (trailblazer) and "Lingluren" 领路人 (leader) of civil law. See "Yongyuan Huainian Jingai De Wang Jiafu Jiaoshou" 永远怀念敬爱的王家福教授 [I Will Always Miss the Beloved Professor Wang Jiafu], https://www.civillaw.com.cn/gg/t/?id=36083 (accessed July 10, 2021).

next year, he was recommended to take the exam to study in Russia and passed it. He then spent a year learning Russian at the Beijing Russian School. In 1955, he was sent to study at the Faculty of Law of the Leningrad State University and received an associate doctoral degree in 1959.

Career Highlights

Wang started his research and teaching career at the Law Institute of CASS in 1959. During the Cultural Revolution, he was sent to a labor camp in Henan Province. Afterwards, he became director of the Civil Law and Economic Law Division of the Law Institute of CASS. From 1988 to 1994, he was director of the Law Institute of CASS. In 1990, he was the secretary general of the Civil Law and Economic Law Division of the China Law Society. Among many political and academic posts, he was a member of the Law Committee of the Standing Committee of the Eighth National People's Congress (NPC), a member of the Standing Committee of the Ninth NPC, a member of the Academic Degree Committee of the State Council, associate director of the China International Economic and Trade Arbitration Commission (CIETAC), director of the Human Rights Research Institute of the Chinese Academy of Social Sciences, legal adviser of the China Labor Union, and adjunct professor at Peking University, the China University of Political Science and Law, and Suzhou University.

Besides teaching and research, Wang also participated in the drafting of many important laws, including the General Principles of Civil Law, the Patent Law, the Copyright Law, and the Technology Contract Law.

Research Area and Publications

Wang's research interests extended from civil law to jurisprudence and human rights. He was one of the early scholars to explore the rule of law. As early as 1979, just three years after the end of the Cultural Revolution, Wang proposed the concept of rule of law in the Chinese Communist Party's Document No. 64,[2] which he codrafted with Professor Liu Hainian (刘海年) and Professor Li Buyun (李步云). In 1981, he published "Socialist Law Is an Inviolable Force"[3] with Professor Wang Baoshu (王保树). In 1996, he was invited to provide a training class on the theory and practice of the rule of law to members of the Politburo of the Communist Party. He told the party leaders that rule *of* law was better than the rule *by* law or the legal system. The former was a principle under which all persons, institutions, and entities are accountable to laws. The latter was a regime that used laws as an instrument to govern the country. A year later, being invited to draft the Work Report of the Party's Fifteenth Congress, Wang altered the wording of "constructing a socialist country with the legal system." He changed the phrase from the "legal system" to the "rule of law." According to Professor Jiang Ping (江平): "Turning the 'legal system' into the 'rule of law,' although only a difference in words, is a great advancement in the concept of legal studies. It changed the previous concept of only attaching importance to legal systems and legal norms, and instead attaching importance to the spirit of law."[4]

Wang wrote in-depth discussions on civil law and economic law, public law and private law, and the property rights of state-owned enterprises. He was one of the founders of civil law studies in contemporary China. To rebuild the legal system destroyed by the political movements between 1957 and 1976, Wang published many articles to promote the legislation of civil law. His notable articles include "What Kind of Civil

2. "Guanyu Jianjue Baozheng Xingfa, Xingshi Susongfa Qieshi Shishi De Zhishi" 关于坚决保证刑法、刑事诉讼法切实实施的指示 [The Guidance on the Guaranty of Practical Implementation of Criminal Law and Criminal Procedure Law], Zhongfa [1979] 64 Hao 中发 [1979] 64 号 [Zhongfa 1979 no. 64], in Zhonggong Zhongyao Lishi Wenxian Ziliao Huibian 中共重要历史文献汇编 [A Compilation of Important Historical Documents of the Communist Party of China], vol. 27, edited by Zhongwen Chubanwu Fuwu Zhongxin 中文出版物服务中心. (Los Angeles: Zhongwen Chubanwu Fuwu Zhongxin, 2005).

3. Wang Jiafu 王家福 and Wang Baoshu 王保树, "Shehuizhuyi Falü Shi Buke Qinfan De Liliang" 社会主义法律是不可侵犯的力量 [Socialist Law Is an Inviolable Force], *Xuexi Yu Yanjiu* 6 (1981).

4. See Pan Qi, "Minfa 'Qizhi' Wang Jiafu," 8.

Law We Ought to Make" (1980),[5] "A Few Opinions regarding the Civil Law Draft" (2003),[6] and "The 21st Century and the Development of China's Civil Law" (2003).[7] He defined principles of civil law legislation as the following: (1) civil law was public law dealing with economic relationships between public and public, public and private, and private and private equal entities; (2) both civil law and individual economic laws were needed; (3) based on China's reality, foreign expertise, including from both socialist and capitalist countries, could be useful; and (4) instead of political slogans, civil law must be concrete, clear, and precise to solve real-world problems. These ideas have been influential in the process of China's civil law legislation. According to Sun Xianzhong (孙宪忠) at the Chinese Academy of Social Sciences, Wang's theory of civil law dealing with the legal relationship between equal entities was widely accepted and incorporated in the General Principles of Civil Law.[8]

Wang saw economic law differently in the early years of his scholarship. Like Professor Tong Rou (佟柔), he originally believed that economic law was not an independent discipline of legal studies but a subfield of civil law.[9] He later changed his mind and recognized the independent status of economic law studies. He also published many works on the subject, such as "On Enhancing the Construction of a Socialist Economic Legal System" (1983),[10] *Introduction to Chinese Economic Law* (1987),[11] and *Economic Law* (1988).[12]

5. "Women Yinggai Zhiding Shenmoyang De Minfa" 我们应该制定什么样的民法 [What Kind of Civil Law We Ought to Make], *Faxue Yanjiu* 法学研究 1 (1980).

6. "Dui Minfa Caoan De Jidian Yijian" 对民法草案的几点意见 [A Few Opinions regarding the Civil Law Draft], *Falü Fuwu Shibao* 法律服务时报, Jan. 17, 2003.

7. "21 Shiji Yu Zhongguo Minfa De Fazhan" 21 世纪与中国民法的发展 [The 21st Century and the Development of China's Civil Law], *Faxuejia* 法学家 4 (2003).

8. See Pan Qi, "Minfa 'Qizhi' Wang Jiafu."

9. See He Jiaxin, "Wang Jiafu," 331.

10. "Lun Jiaqiang Shehuizhuyi Jinji Fazhi Jianshe" 论加强社会主义经济法治建设 [On Enhancing the Construction of a Socialist Economic Legal System], *Faxue Yanjiu* 法学研究 1 (1983).

11. *Zhongguo Jingjifa Xulun* 中国经济法绪论 [Introduction to Chinese Economic Law] (Beijing: Falü Chubanshe, 1987).

12. *Jingjifa* 经济法 [Economic Law] (Beijing: Zhongguo Jingji Chubanshe, 1988).

Wang's other major publications include *The Legal Issues in Economic Construction* (1982),[13] "General Principles of Civil Law with Chinese Characteristics" (1986),[14] *Contract Law* (1986),[15] *The Patent Law of China* (1987),[16] *China's Civil Law: Creditors' Rights* (1991),[17] *The Theory and Practice of Land Law* (1991),[18] *A Study of the Legal System of the Socialist Market Economy* (1992),[19] "WTO and the Construction of the Legal System of China's Socialist Market" (2001),[20] and so on. His most important articles have been assembled in a publication titled *Selected Works of Wang Jiafu in His Sixty Years of Legal Research and Teaching* (2010).[21]

In 2009, Wang was named one of the 10 "CCTV Annual Rule of Law Figures."[22] At the award ceremony, Professor Liang Huixing (梁慧星) of CASS summarized Wang's academic contributions. He said that

13. *Jingji Jianshezhong De Falü Wenti* 经济建设中的法律问题 [The Legal Issues in Economic Construction] (Beijing: Zhongguo Shehui Kexue Chubanshe, 1982).

14. "Yibu Juyou Zhongguo Tese De Minfa Tongze" 一部具有中国特色的民法通则 [General Principles of Civil Law with Chinese Characteristics], *Faxue Yanjiu* 法学研究 3 (1986).

15. *Hetongfa* 合同法 [Contract Law] (Beijing: Zhongguo Shehui Kexue Chubanshe, 1986).

16. *Zhongguo Zhuanlifa* 中国专利法 [The Patent Law of China] (Beijing: Qunzhong Chubanshe, 1987).

17. *Zhongguo Minfaxue: Minfa Zhaiquan* 中国民法学：民法债权 [China's Civil Law: Creditors' Rights] (Beijing: Zhongguo Shehui Kexue Chubanshe, 1991).

18. *Tudifa De Lilun Yu Shijian* 土地法的理论与实践 [The Theory and Practice of Land Law] (Beijing: Renmin Ribao Chubanshe, 1991).

19. *Shehuizhuyi Shangpin Jingji Falü Zhidu Yanjiu* 社会主义商品经济法律制度研究 [A Study on the Legal System of the Socialist Market Economy] (Beijing: Jingji Kexue Chubanshe, 1992).

20. "WTO Yu Zhongguo Shehuizhuyi Shichang Falü Zhidu Jianshe Wenti" WTO 与中国社会主义市场法律制度建设问题 [WTO and the Construction of the Legal System of China's Socialist Market], *Zhongguo Faxue* 中国法学 4 (2001).

21. Wang Jiafu, *Wang Jiafu Faxue Yanjiu*.

22. The CCTV Annual Rule of Law Figures is a China Central TV program, started fourteen years ago; see: https://baike.baidu.com/item/CCTV%E5%B9%B4%E5%BA%A6%E6%B3%95%E6%B2%BB%E4%BA%BA%E7%89%A9 (accessed July 10, 2021). The program features ten individuals and organizations that made significant contributions to the advancement of the rule of law in China. Wang Jiafu was named one of the CCTV Annual Rule of Law Figures in 2009; see http://www.fxcxw.org.cn/dyna/content.php?id=5432 (accessed July 10, 2021).

Wang had done two significant things in fifty years: (1) proposed the basic structure of the legal system of a socialist market economy and (2) proposed the rule of law as a basic model of governance for the country.[23]

Bibliography of English Publications by Professor Wang Jiafu

Wang Chia-fu. *Compensatory Transfer of the Right to Use Land.* Washington, DC: World Peace through Law Center, 1990.

References

He Jiaxin 何佳馨."Wang Jiafu" 王家福 [Wang Jiafu]. In *20 Shiji Zhongguo Zhiming Kexuejia Xueshu Chengjiu Gailan: Faxuejuan* 20 世纪中国知名科学家学术成就概览: 法学卷 [Introduction to the Achievements of Famous Chinese Scientists in the Twentieth Century: Law Volumes], vol. 3, edited by Jiang Ping, et al., 327–36. Beijing: Kexue Chubanshe, 2014.

Jiang Xihui 蒋熙辉. "Wang Jiafu Xuebu Weiyuan Fangtanlu" 王家福学部委员访谈录 [An Interview with a Member of the Academic Committee—Wang Jiafu]. In *Xuewen Youdao* 学问有道 [A Road to Knowledge]. Beijing: Fangzhi Chubanshe, 2007.

Pan Qi 潘琦. "Minfa 'Qizhi' Wang Jiafu" 民法 "旗帜" 王家福 [Civil Law's Banner Wang Jiafu]. *Fazhi Zhoumo* 法治周末, Apr. 18, 2013, 8.

Sun Xianzhong 孙宪忠, ed. *Wang Jiafu Faxue Yanjiu Yu Faxue Jiaoyu Liushi Zhounian Ji Bashi Shoudan Qinghe Wenji* 王家福法学研究与法学教育六十周年暨八十寿诞庆贺文集 [A Collection of Celebratory Essays of Sixty Years of Legal Research and Teaching and the Eightieth Birthday of Wang Jiafu]. Beijing: Falü Chubanshe, 2010.

Wang Jiafu 王家福. *Wang Jiafu Faxue Yanjiu Yu Faxue Jiaoyu Liushinian Wenxuanji* 王家福法学研究与法学教育六十年文选集 [Selected Works of Wang Jiafu in His Sixty Years of Legal Research and Teaching]. Beijing: Falü Chubanshe, 2010.

"Wang Jiafu" 王家福 [Wang Jiafu]. http://baike.baidu.com/subview/449810/18124641.htm (accessed May 28, 2016).

23. See Pan Qi, "Minfa 'Qizhi' Wang Jiafu."

30. Li Buyun (李步云)

(1933–)

Jurisprudence, Human Rights, and the Rule of Law

Professor of law at the Chinese Academy of Social Sciences, Li Buyun was one of the first scholars to systematically promote the rule of law in China. He is regarded as one of the "three deans of the rule of law" in China, along with Professor Jiang Ping and Professor Guo Daohui.[1] He is also a pioneer of the study of human rights law in China.

Educational Background

Li was born in Loudi (娄底) Municipality of Hunan Province. In 1949, he joined the People's Liberation Army and studied in the army school. From 1950 to 1952, he fought in the Korean War and lost his left hand. A disabled veteran, Li passed the entrance exam and was admitted to the Law Department of Peking University in 1957. He earned his undergraduate degree in 1962 and then became a graduate student of Zhang Youyu (张友渔). He earned his graduate degree in 1965 from Peking University.

---

1. See footnote 1 in chapter 23 on Guo Daohui.

Career Highlights

After his injury in the Korean War in 1952, Li retired from the Army in 1955 and went to work for the Jiangsu provincial government until he enrolled at Peking University. Upon graduation, he worked at Peking University for a year (1965–1966) and then moved on to the Institute of Law of CASS. He retired from CASS in 2001.

Li participated in the discussions and drafting of the 1982 Constitution. He was chief editor of *Faxue Yanjiu*.[2] Since his retirement, he has been very active in the academic world. He started human rights research centers at Hunan University, Guangzhou University, and Dongnan University. He is an adjunct professor at several universities and was a visiting scholar at New York University. He has visited England, Italy, Norway, Holland, Australia, and Japan for research and academic work.

In 2002, Li teamed up with Liu Hongru (刘鸿儒), former president of the Securities Regulatory Commission. Li founded the Shanghai Institute of Finance and Law (SIFL Institute), a nonprofit think tank. The organization created the Li Buyun Legal Study Award in 2013, which names and presents annual awards to one Chinese and one foreign individual or entity for their outstanding research on Chinese law and great achievements in legal education. The selection committee for the Li Buyun Legal Study Award is composed of prominent legal scholars, including Professor Zhang Wenxian (张文显) of Jilin University, Professor Han Dayuan (韩大元) of Renmin University, and so on. Past honorees include such distinguished scholars as Guo Daohui, Randle R. Edwards of Columbia Law School, Albert Hung-yee Chen of the University of Hong Kong, and William P. Alford of Harvard Law School. The Li Buyun Legal Study Award has become increasingly influential in China.

---

2. *Faxue Yanjiu* 法学研究 [Chinese Journal of Law], sponsored by the Law Institute of the Chinese Academy of Social Sciences (Beijing: Zhongguo Shehui Kexue Chubanshe, 1979–).

Research Areas and Publications

Li is a productive scholar and has published more than thirty books and three hundred articles. Some of his publications are available in English or Japanese.

Colleagues of Li have commented admiringly on his academic work and publications. Professor Zhang Wenxian called him "a pioneer of ideological emancipation, a master of theoretical innovation." Professor Yu Ronggen (俞荣根) of Southwest University of Political Science and Law put it this way: "To a scholar, it is not difficult to write a good article. It is difficult to always write good articles, never write a bureaucratic article, nor a superficial article. Mr. Li Buyun is a thinker who wrote better and better articles and wrote more and more thoughtful articles, therefore he has evolved from a scholar to a master thinker."[3] Li once said he would use the following words to describe his research principles: realistic, innovative, precise, and tolerant.[4]

During the academic renaissance period after the Cultural Revolution, China faced the urgent task of reconstructing its legal system. In 1979, Li and his colleagues published an article titled "On the Need for a Socialist Rule of Law"[5] in the *Guanming Daily*. This was the first time that the concept of the rule of law was addressed and promoted as a tool of governance in China. Back then, the legal system was the dominant idea, which emphasized rule by law, legislation, legalization of governance, and the implementation and enforcement of law. The rule of law, in contrast, pursued citizens' rights and equality before the law and asserted that no individual nor organization was above the law. This was a more comprehensive approach than the legal system doctrine and thus immediately inspired discussions among many people. Since then, Li has refined his views on the rule of law and

3. See Li Buyun, *Maixiang Fazhi Xinshidai*, 399–400.

4. Li Buyun, 399–400

5. Li Buyun 李步云, Wang Dexiang 王德祥, and Chen Chunlong 陈春龙, "Yao Shixing Shehuizhuyi Fazhi" 要实行社会主义法治 [On the Need for a Socialist Rule of Law], *Guangming Ribao* 光明日报 Dec. 2, 1979.

proposed ten measurements of it for China.[6] In 2008, he published his treatise *On the Rule of Law*.[7]

In 1978, his *People's Daily* article "On the Commitment to All Citizens' Equality before Law"[8] was regarded as a breakthrough against an ideological taboo. His 1979 article "On the Legal Status of China's Criminals"[9] called for the protection of human rights for the first time in China. Both articles had significant influence on the development of China's human rights theories. This was the beginning of Li's obsession with the study of human rights in China. He has published many articles and a book in 2010 on this topic.[10]

Besides the topics of rule of law and human rights, Li has led visionary discussions on law and jurisprudence, constitutional law, and legislation. His major publications include *An Introduction to the New Constitutional Law* (1984),[11] *Legal System, Democracy, and Freedom* (1986),[12] *A Comparative Study of Constitutional Law* (1998),[13] *Toward the Rule of Law* (1998),[14] *A General Discussion on the Socialist Rule of Law with Chinese Characteristics* (1999),[15] *On Jurisprudence* (2000),[16]

6. See "Fazhi Zhongguo De Shitiao Biaozhun" 法治中国的十条标准 [Ten Measurements of the Rule of Law for China], http://www.humanrights.cn/html/llyj/1/5/2016/0801/20669.html (accessed Dec. 2, 2016).

7. *Lun Fazhi* 论法治 [On the Rule of Law] (Beijing: Shehui Kexue Wenxian Chubanshe, 2008).

8. "Jianchi Gongmin Zai Falüshang Yilü Pingdeng" 坚持公民在法律上一律平等 [On the Commitment to All Citizens' Equality before Law], *Renmin Ribao* 人民日报, Dec. 6, 1978.

9. "Lun Woguo Zuifan De Falü Diwei" 论我国罪犯的法律地位 [On the Legal Status of China's Criminals], *Renmin Ribao* 人民日报, Dec. 27, 1979.

10. *Lun Renquan* 论人权 [On Human Rights] (Beijing: Sheke Wenxian Chubanshe, 2010).

11. *Xinxianfa Jianlun* 新宪法简论 [An Introduction to the New Constitutional Law] (Beijing: Falü chubanshe, 1984).

12. *Fazhi Minzhu Ziyou* 法制, 民主, 自由 [Legal System, Democracy, and Freedom] (Chengdu: Sichuan Renmin Chubanshe, 1986).

13. *Xianfa Bijiao Yanjiu* 宪法比较研究 [A Comparative Study of Constitutional Law] (Beijing: Falü Chubanshe, 1998).

14. *Zouxiang Fazhi* 走向法治 [Toward the Rule of Law] (Changsha: Hunan Renmin Chubanshe, 1998).

15. *Zhongguo Tese Shehuizhuyi Fazhi Tonglun* 中国特色社会主义法治通论 [A General Discussion on the Socialist Rule of Law with Chinese Characteristics] (Beijing: Sheke Wenxian Chubanshe, 1999).

16. *Falixue* 法理学 [On Jurisprudence] (Beijing: Jingji Kexue Chubanshe, 2000).

Constitutionalism and China (published in English, 2006),[17] *On Constitutional Law* (2013),[18] *On Jurisprudence* (2013),[19] *On Rule by the Constitution* (2013),[20] *The Road to Rule of Law in China* (2020),[21] and so on. A well-respected scholar, Li is known for his liberal voice on politically sensitive issues. "I admire his courage and honesty," said Professor Jiang Ping.[22]

Bibliography of English Publications by Professor Li Buyun

Li Buyun. "Constitutionalism and China." In *Democracy and the Rule of Law in China*, edited by Yu Keping, 197–229. Leiden, Netherlands: Brill, 2010.

———. *Constitutionalism and China*. Beijing: Law Press, 2006.

———. *Constitutionalism and China*. New York: Bridge, 2010.

———. "The Development of Jurisprudence in the New Era." *Social Science in China* 21, no. 2 (2000): 99–105.

———. "Explanations on the Proposed Law on Lawmaking of the People's Republic of China." In *Law-Making in the People's Republic of China*, edited by Jan Michiel Otto and Maurice V. Polak, 157–73. Boston: Kluwer Law International, 2000.

———. "Human Rights: Three Existential Forms (1991)." In *The Chinese Human Rights Reader: Documents and Commentary, 1900–2000*, edited by Steven C. Angle and Marina Svensson. Armonk, NY: M. E. Sharpe, 2001.

References

Li Buyun 李步云. *Fazhi Xinlinian—Li Buyun Fangtanlu* 法治新理念–李步云访谈录 [The New Ideas of the Rule of Law—Interview with Li Buyun]. Beijing: Renmin Chubanshe, 2015.

17. *Constitutionalism and China* (Beijing: Falü Chubanshe, 2006).

18. *Lun Xianfa* 论宪法 [On Constitutional Law] (Beijing: Sheke Wenxian Chubanshe, 2013).

19. *Lun Fali* 论法理 [On Jurisprudence] (Beijing: Sheke Wenxian Chubanshe, 2013).

20. *Lun Yixian Zhiguo* 论依宪治国 [On Rule by the Constitution] (Beijing: Shehui Kexue Chubanshe, 2013).

21. *Zhongguo Fazhi Zhilu* 中国法治之路 [The Road to the Rule of Law in China] (Hong Kong: Xianggang Chengshi Daxue Chubanshe, 2020).

22. See Pei Zhiyong, "Li Buyun."

———. *Maixiang Fazhi Xinshidai* 迈向法治新时代 [Toward a New Era of Rule of Law]. Beijing: Renmin Chubanshe, 2017.

———. *Wo De Zhixue Weiren* 我的治学为人 [My Research and My Life]. Beijing: Sheke Wenxian Chubanshe, 2010.

"Li Buyun" 李步云 [Li Buyun]. http://baike.baidu.com/item/%E6%9D%8E%E6%AD %A5%E4%BA%91/5250701 (accessed Oct. 2, 2016).

Pei Zhiyong 裴智勇. "Li Buyun: Gankai Diyiqiang De Faxuejia" 李步云：“敢开第一腔” 的法学家 [Li Buyun: The Legal Scholar Who "Dares to First Express His Ideas"]. *Renmin Ribao* 人民日报, Jan. 5, 2005.

Wang Yijin 王逸吟 and Yin Hong 殷泓. "Dang Lingdao Renmin Zhili Guojia De Jiben Fangzhen: Zhuanjia Xuezhe Huixiang He Chanshi 'Yifa Zhiguo' De Tichu, Queli He Wanshan" 党领导人民治理国家的基本方针：专家学者回想和阐释“依法治国”的提出, 确立和完善 [The Party's Leadership Policy of Governance: Experts and Scholars Recall and Explain the Proposal, Confirmation, and Perfection of "Rule by Law"]. *Guangming Ribao* 光明日报, Oct. 17, 2014.

Xiao Haijun 肖海军 and Liu Shiping 刘士平, eds. *Wei Yuan Huaxia Xianzhimeng* 为圆华 夏宪治梦 [To Realize China's Dream of Rule by Constitution]. Beijing: Sheke Wenxian Chubanshe, 2013.

31. Luo Haocai (罗豪才)

(1934–2018)

Administrative Law and Constitutional Law

Professor of law at Peking University, Luo Haocai was a scholar, a politician, and vice president of the Supreme People's Court (1995–2000). He was one of China's most influential scholars and practitioners of administrative law, as well as an expert in comparative constitutional law and human rights.

Educational Background

Luo was born in Singapore. Due to his participation in radical political activities, he was taken into custody by the British colonial authorities and was deported when he was seventeen. He came to China in 1952 and completed middle school and high school in Guangdong Province and Jiangsu Province. In 1956, he entered the Law Department of Peking University and graduated in 1960. Between 1984 and 1985, Luo spent a year at Columbia University as a visiting scholar. During that time, he had exchanges with Professor Walter Gellhorn and audited the classes of Professors Luis Henkin and Peter L. Strauss.[1] He also visited more than twenty law schools in the United States and Canada.

---

1. Zhou Qiang 周强, "Luo Haocai" 罗豪才 [Luo Haocai], in *20 Shiji Zhongguo Zhiming Kexuejia Xueshu Chengjiu Gailan: Faxuejuan* 20 世纪中国知名科学家学术成就概览: 法学卷 [Introduction to the Achievements of Famous Chinese Scientists in the

Career Highlights

Luo began his teaching career right after graduating from Peking University, where he worked from 1960 to 2018. At the beginning, he assisted Professors Lou Bangyan (楼邦彦) and Gong Xiangrui (龚祥瑞) in teaching foreign constitutional law. Later, he taught constitutional law and political systems of Western countries. In 1983, Luo served as executive chair of the Committee on Legal Education Exchange with China (CLEEC).[2]

During his long career of teaching constitutional law and administrative law, Luo held many academic and political positions. He was associate director of the Law Department (1985–1986) and vice president of Peking University (1986–1992). He became vice president and later president of the China Zhi Gong Party[3] (1992–1999). Luo held the positions of vice president and member of the Judicial Committee of the Supreme People's Court from 1995 to 2000 and was one of the vice presidents of the National Committee of the Chinese People's Political Consultative Conference. He became the first dean of the School of Government of Peking University in 2001. As vice president of the All-China Federation of Returned Overseas Chinese, he visited Chinese people in more than forty countries between 1993 and 1999. From 2007 to 2016, he was president of the China Society for Human Rights Studies. He participated in the legislative work of many administrative laws. In 2013, Luo received a Peking University lifetime achievement award: the Cai Yuanpei (蔡元培) Award.[4]

Twentieth Century: Law Volumes], vol. 3, edited by Jiang Ping et al. (Beijing: Kexue Chubanshe, 2014), 464.

2. For information regarding CLEEC, see footnote 1 in chapter 16 on Zhang Guohua.

3. The China Zhi Gong Party was created by overseas Chinese in San Francisco in 1925. It is one of the legally recognized democratic parties in China today.

4. Cai Yuanpei (蔡元培) (1868–1940) was president of Peking University from 1916 to 1927. The Cai Yuanpei Award is Peking University's highest honor. It has been given to ten high-achieving professors every five years since 2006. Please see http://baike .baidu.com/view/1974862.htm (accessed Feb. 19, 2017).

Research Areas and Publications

Luo's teaching and research focused on comparative constitutional law and administrative law. In 1983, Luo and his colleague published *The Constitutional Law and Political Systems of Capitalist Countries*,[5] which was one of the earliest books in the field. This book provides introductions to politics, constitutional laws, and judicial systems of Western countries and gained widespread attention. His 1993 publication, *China's Judicial Review System*,[6] was rather influential and thus earned him a social science and humanities award from the State Education Commission. His other award-winning publications include "The Core and Theoretical Model of Administrative Law" (2002),[7] "The Transformation of the Governance of Public Domain" (2005),[8] and *Soft Law Is Law* (2009).[9]

Luo's scholarship is known for his "balancing theory" of modern administrative law. In 1993, he and his colleagues first proposed balancing theory, which addresses the relationship between administrative power and citizens' rights in modern society. According to them, this conflicting yet mutually dependent relationship could be adjusted to protect citizens' rights and public interests. Administrative law not only granted the necessary powers to administrative agencies but also prevented them from abusing their powers and violating citizens' legal rights. There was a

---

5. Luo Haocai (罗豪才) and Wu Xieying (吴撷英), *Zibenzhuyi Guojia De Xianfa He Zhengzhi Zhidu* (资本主义国家的宪法和政治制度) [The Constitutional Law and Political Systems of the Capitalist Countries] (Beijing: Beijing Daxue Chubanshe, 1983).

6. Luo Haocai 罗豪才 et al., eds., *Zhongguo Sifa Shencha Zhidu* 中国司法审查制度 [China's Judicial Review System] (Beijing: Beijing Daxue Chubanshe, 1993).

7. "Xingzhengfa De Hexin Yu Lilun Moshi" 行政法的核心与理论模式 [The Core and Theoretical Model of Administrative Law], *Faxue* 法学 8 (2002): 3–6.

8. Luo Haocai 罗豪才 and Song Gongde 宋功德, "Gongyu Zhizhi De Zhuanxing: Dui Gonggong Zhili Yu Gongfa Guanxi De Yizhong Toushi" 公域之治的转型: 对公共治理与公法关系的一种透视 [The Transformation of the Governance of Public Domain: An Examination of Public Administration and Public Law Relations], *Zhongguo Faxue* 中国法学 5 (2005) 3–23.

9. Luo Haocai 罗豪才 and Song Gongde 宋功德, *Ruanfa Yifa—Gonggong Zhili Huhuan Ruanfa Zhizhi* 软法亦法–公共治理呼唤软法之治 [The Transformation of the Governance of Public Domain: Public Administration Calls for the Rule of Soft Law] (Beijing: Falü Chubanshe, 2009).

dynamic balance between private interests and public interests.[10] This theory has inspired many discussions and led to new and in-depth explorations in the field. Today, balancing theory has evolved into an important school of public law study and is recognized as an original theory of legal study in China.

"Soft law" is another topic that Luo was passionate about. He was one of the first scholars in China to explore this concept. He defined soft law as rules of conduct coming from nonlegislative bodies, such as the Communist Party and social organizations. Unlike "hard law," soft law has no strict legal authorities. It is implemented by cultural heritage, social media, and moral ethics. Like hard law, soft law is also an instrument of administration and governance. As early as 2005, Luo teamed up with his then PhD student Song Gongde (宋功德) to discuss soft law in an article published in *China Legal Science*.[11] When China's first Soft Law Research Center was launched at Peking University in 2005, Luo was named its honorary director. He published several books and articles on the topic. Soft law has become a hot topic in the field of administrative law in China.[12]

Because of his political, administrative, judicial, and social responsibilities, Luo's scholarship was not only reflected in his publications but also in his talks and speeches. His most influential speeches addressed China's concept of human rights. At the Second Beijing Human Rights Forum in 2009, Luo discussed the new Chinese model of human rights. He pointed out that the traditional concept of human rights reflected mostly Western values. He proposed that the new Chinese concept of human rights should emphasize the right to life, the right of development, and environmental rights.[13]

10. See Luo Haocai 罗豪才, Yuan Shuhong 袁曙宏, and Li Wendong 李文栋, "Xiandai Xingzhengfa De Lilun Jichu: Lun Xingzheng Jiguan Yu Xiangdui Yifang De Quanli Yiwu Pingheng" 现代行政法的理论基础：论行政机关与相对一方的权利义务平衡 [The Theoretical Foundation of Modern Administrative Law: On the Balance of Rights and Responsibilities between Administrative Agencies and the Opposing Party], *Zhongguo Faxue* 中国法学 [China Legal Science] 1 (1993).

11. Luo Haocai 罗豪才 and Song Gongde 宋功德, "Gongyu Zhizhi."

12. See Zhang Xiangyong 张向永 and Zhou Qiang 周强, "Luo Haocai: Haoqing Chizi Zhufahun" 罗豪才：豪情赤子铸法魂 [Luo Haocai: Seeking the Soul of Law], http://dangjian.people.com.cn/n/2015/0706/c117092-27261447.html (accessed Sept. 25, 2016).

13. Luo Haocai, "Zhongguo Zhubu Xingcheng."

Bibliography of English Publications by Professor Luo Haocai

Luo, Haocai. *The Core and Theoretical Models of Administrative Law.* n.p., 2005.
———. *On the Rule of Law and Human Rights.* Beijing: China Intercontinental, 2015.
Luo Haocai, Song Gongde, Ben Armour, and Tang Hailong. *Soft Law Governance: Towards an Integrated Approach.* Buffalo, New York: William S. Hein, 2013.
Xiao Weiyun, Luo Haocai, and Wu Xieying. 2001. "How Marxism Views the Human Rights Question." In *The Chinese Human Rights Reader: Documents and Commentary, 1900–2000,* edited by Stephen C. Angle and Marina Svensson, 281–88. Armonk, NY: M. E. Sharpe, 2001.

References

Cheng Hai 成海. "Luo Haocai: Cong 'Jiaoshujiang' Dao Quanguo Zhengxie Fuzhuxi" 罗豪才：从"教书匠"到全国政协副主席 [Luo Haocai: From Teacher to Vice President of the National Committee of the Chinese People's Political Consultative Conference]. *Zhonghua Yingcai* 中华英才 20 (1998).
Luo Haocai 罗豪才. *Weile Quanli Yu Quanli De Pingheng: Fazhi Zhongguo Jianshe Yu Ruanfa Zhizhi* 为了权利与权力的平衡：法治中国建设与软法之治 [For the Balance between Rights and Power: China's Construction with the Rule of Law and the Governance of Soft Law]. Beijing: Wuzhou Chuanbo Chubanshe, 2016.
———. "Zhongguo Xingzhengfa De Pingheng Lilun" 中国行政法的平衡理论 [The Balance Theory of China's Administrative Law]. *Fazhi Ribao* 法制日报, July 1, 2009.
———. "Zhongguo Zhubu Xingcheng Renquan Baozhang 'Zhongguo Moshi'" 中国逐步形成人权保障"中国模式" [China's Model of Human Rights Protection Has Been Gradually Developed]. http://news.sohu.com/20091102/n267903493.shtml (accessed Sept. 25, 2016).
"Luo Haocai" 罗豪才 [Luo Haocai]. http://www.baike.com/wiki/%E7%BD%97%E8%B1%AA%E6%89%8D (accessed Sept. 25, 2016).
Zhang Xiangyong 张向永 and Zhou Qiang 周强. "Luo Haocai: Haoqing Chizi Zhufahun" 罗豪才：豪情赤子铸法魂 [Luo Haocai: Seeking the Soul of Law]. http://dangjian.people.com.cn/n/2015/0706/c117092-27261447.html (accessed Sept. 25, 2016).

32. Ying Songnian (应松年)

(1936–)

Administrative Law

Professor of law at the China University of Political Science and Law, Ying Songnian is one of the pioneer scholars who started administrative law research in China after the Cultural Revolution. He coauthored China's first textbook on administrative law and participated in the drafting of all major administrative laws in China. According to Professor He Haibo, "In a sense, so far, contemporary Chinese administrative law study belongs to Ying Songnian era."[1]

Educational Background

Ying was born in Ningbo (宁波) City of Zhejiang Province. He graduated from the East China College of Political Science and Law (now the East China University of Political Science and Law) in 1960. Unlike many prominent scholars of his generation, whose legal training occurred overseas, in the old China, or by Soviet scholars, Ying was trained by Chinese scholars in the new China after 1949.

---

1. See He Haibo, "Ying Songnian," 531.

Career Highlights

As the 1957 Anti-Rightist Movement spread in China, many intellectuals were sent to remote areas for reeducation. Upon his graduation from college, Ying was sent to Yili (伊梨) Autonomous Prefecture in Xinjiang Province. He worked there from 1960 to 1981 and eventually became an officer in the education bureau of the local government. In 1981, during the reestablishment of the Northwestern College of Political Science and Law, Ying was invited to teach at the State Law Department. He worked there until 1983 and then was hired by the China University of Political Science and Law. He taught at the university from 1983 to 1995. Then he moved on to the National College of Administration, where he was director of the Law Department. He was also an adjunct professor at the China University of Political Science and Law, where he was granted a professorship with tenure in 2009. He has been teaching there since then.

Ying was a representative of the Beijing People's Congress and the National People's Congress. He is president of the Research Association of Administrative Law of the China Law Society. Ying is a part-time legal adviser to several provincial governments and the central government. He was named Outstanding Teacher of Beijing and was awarded an honorary doctor of laws degree from Nagoya University in 2000. At his seventieth birthday celebration event in 2006, he launched the Yin Songnian Administrative Law Scholarship Fund. He has visited many countries and conducted academic exchanges in Japan, South Korea, the United States, and Europe.

Research Areas and Publications

Ying is a self-taught administrative law scholar. During the twenty years of his life spent in Yili after graduating from college, he did not have a chance to conduct legal research or legal education. When he was hired to teach at the Northwestern College of Political Science and Law, he was a middle-aged government official. Therefore, he had to relearn the law and learn it fast. Since law schools in China had just started to reopen, many fields of legal study were understaffed or had no one to teach. Administrative law was one of the fields that few people had expertise in or were interested in teaching. Ying took to the challenge. He read every book on administrative law in the library of the Northwestern College of Political Science and Law. While he was offering an administrative law class, he was learning it. His effort bore fruit when he was selected to participate in writing China's first administrative law textbook[2] in 1983.

In 1984, now a professor at the China University of Political Science and Law, Ying wrote one of the earliest textbooks on administrative management.[3] This book explained for the first time the relationship between the study of law and the study of administrative management. It earned him a first prize book award in the field.

In 1985, with a few colleagues, Ying started the Research Association of Administrative Law of the China Law Society. In 1986, he worked with a legislator, Tao Xijin (陶希晋), to create a legislative research group on administrative law. Over the years, he has led this group to contribute to the drafting of many administrative laws. As a scholar and member of the legislature, Ying participated in drafting of, among others, the Administrative Litigation Law, the State Compensation Law, the Administrative Punishment Law, the Law on Legislation, the Administrative Licensing Law, and the Education Law.

In 1993, Ying teamed up with Professor Luo Haocai (罗豪才) to start China's first academic journal on administrative law,[4] which is published to this date. His articles, essays, speeches, and other short works have been published in *China's Exploration of Administrative Rule of Law* (1996)[5] and in two volumes with the same title, *A Collection of Essays by Ying*

2. Wang Mincan 王珉灿, ed., *Xingzhengfa Gaiyao* 行政法概要 [An Introduction to Administrative Law] (Beijing: Falü Chubanshe, 1983).

3. *Xingzheng Guanlixue* 行政管理学 [On Administrative Management] (Beijing: Beijing Shifan Xueyuan Chubanshe, 1986).

4. *Xingzheng Faxue Yanjiu* 行政法学研究 [Study on Administrative Law] (Beijing: Zhongguo Zhengfa Daxue Chubanshe, 1993–).

5. *Zhongguo Zouxiang Xingzheng Fazhi Tansuo* 中国走向行政法治探索 [China's Exploration of Administrative Rule of Law] (Beijing: Zhongguo Fangzheng Chubanshe, 1996).

Songnian, in 2006[6] and in 2015.[7] Since the 1980s, he has published more than three hundred articles and authored or edited dozens of books. His major publications include *General Introduction to Administrative Law* (1985),[8] *Administrative Act* (1993),[9] *Research on the Legislation of Administrative Procedure Law* (2001),[10] and *Toward a Government Rule by Law: Theoretical Research and Empirical Investigation of Administration by Law* (2001).[11]

Ying's most important work is *Contemporary Chinese Administrative Law*. As chief editor of this publication, he worked with more than forty authors to produce the first edition in 2005, which addressed the system and theories of China's administrative law study. It showcased the development of administrative law in China and has become an essential publication in the field. In 2018, he updated this book and produced a new version in eight volumes.[12] This theoretical and comprehensive publication has been called "an encyclopedia of contemporary Chinese administrative law."[13]

6. *Ying Songnian Wenji* 应松年文集 [A Collection of Essays by Ying Songnian] (Beijing: Zhongguo Fazhi Chubanshe, 2006).

7. *Ying Songnian Wenji* (2006–2015) 应松年文集 [*A Collection of Essays by Ying Songnian 2006–2015*] (Beijing: Zhongguo Fazhi Chubanshe, 2015).

8. Ying Songnian 应松年 and Zhu Weijiu 朱维究, eds., *Xingzhengfa Zonglun* 行政法总论 [General Introduction to Administrative Law] (Beijing: Gongren Chubanshe, 1985).

9. *Xingzheng Xingweifa: Zhongguo Xingzheng Fazhi Jianshe De Lilun Yu Shijian* 行政行为法：中国行政法制建设的理论与实践 [Administrative Act: The Theory and Practice of the Construction of the Administrative Law System in China] (Beijing: Renmin Chubanshe, 1994).

10. *Xingzheng Chengxu Lifa Yanjiu* 行政程序立法研究 [Research on the Legislation of Administrative Procedure Law] (Beijing: Zhongguo Fazhi Chubanshe, 2001).

11. Ying Songnian 应松年 and Yuan Shuhong 袁曙宏, eds., *Zouxiang Fazhi Zhengfu: Yifa Xingzheng Lilun Yanjiu Yu Shizheng Diaocha* 走向法治政府：依法行政理论研究与行政实证调查 [Toward a Government Rule by Law: Theoretical Research and Empirical Investigation of Administration by Law] (Beijing: Falü Chubashe, 2001).

12. *Dangdai Zhongguo Xingzhengfa* 当代中国行政法 [Contemporary Chinese Administrative Law] (Beijing: Zhongguo Fangzheng Chubanshe, 2005; Beijing: Renmin Chubanshe, 2018).

13. Wu Yian 吴屹桉, "Dangdai Zhongguo Xingzhengfa Xinban Bajuanben Chuban" 《当代中国行政法》新版八卷本出版 [The New Edition of Eight Volumes of Contemporary Chinese Administrative Law], http://www.cssn.cn/zx/bwyc/201806/t2018 0614_4367029.shtml (accessed July 11, 2020).

The core of his scholarship includes these principles: rule by law is the key of administration by law, and the spirit of law is the protection of people's rights.[14] Ying believes that a reasonable structure of powers (including legislature, administration, and judiciary), a scientific division of powers, strict procedures, and effective supervision are an interconnected and mutually complementary entity. Administrative law deals with the relationship of these elements. He hopes to establish the order of rule of law and protect people's interests through managing state officials and governing power.[15]

Ying emphasizes that one of the most important features of modern administration is governance by law. In a certain sense, the process of administrative management is also the process of formulating and implementing administrative laws. He stresses that the petition system should not be the main channel for administrative remedy; nor should it become a developmental direction in the future in China.

He has contributed to the development of administrative law study in China. His theoretical structure of administrative law embraces the elements of both common law and civil law systems. The general part of his administrative law study includes administrative organization law, administrative act, and administrative remedy. He is especially interested in administrative procedure. To support his effort to create administrative procedure law, he led legislative research and drafting work and published many works in this area.

Bibliography of English Publications by Professor Ying Songnian

Ying Songnian and Dong Hao. "Institutional and Jurisdictional Issues in Administrative Reconsideration." *Chinese Law and Government* 24, no. 3 (1991): 69–77.
———. "A Study of the Applicable Laws in Administrative Reconsideration." *Chinese Law and Government* 24, no. 3 (1991): 54–61.

14. See Gui Xiaoyan 桂晓燕, "Qingsong Bulao: Fang Woguo Xingzheng Faxue Xianqu Ying Songnian Jiaoshou" 青松不老: 访我国行政法学先驱应松年教授 [An Evergreen Pine: Interview with China's Administrative Law Pioneer—Professor Ying Songnian], in Ying Songnian, *Ying Songnian Wenji.*

15. He Haibo, "Ying Songnian," 535.

References

He Haibo 何海波. "Ying Songnian" 应松年 [Ying Songnian]. In *20 Shiji Zhongguo Zhiming Kexuejia Xueshu Chengjiu Gailan: Faxuejuan* 20 世纪中国知名科学家学术成就概览: 法学卷 [Introduction to the Achievements of Famous Chinese Scientists in the Twentieth Century: Law Volumes] vol. 3, edited by Jiang Ping, et al., 531–43. Beijing: Kexue Chubanshe, 2014.

———. *Yufa Tongxing, Ying Songnian Koushu* 与法同行，应松年口述 [Walking with the Law: An Oral Testament of Ying Songnian]. Beijing: Zhongguo Zhengfa Daxue Chubanshe, 2015.

Tao Yefeng 陶业峰 and Zhang Wei 张伟. "Ying Songnian" 应松年 [Ying Songnian]. In *Zhongguo Faxuejia Fangtanlu* 中国法学家访谈录 [Interviews with Chinese Jurists], edited by He Qinhua 何勤华, 140–48. Beijing: Beijing Daxue Chubanshe, 2013.

Wang Xinyou 王新友. "Ying Songnian: Yu Zhongguo Xingzhengfa Yitong Chengzhang" 应松年: 与中国行政法一同成长 [Ying Songnian: Growing Up with China's Administrative Law]. *Jiancha Ribao* 检察日报, Aug. 16, 2004.

Wei Peng 韦鹏. "Ying Songnian Zailushang, Yongyuan Buhuilao" 应松年在路上，永远不会老 [Ying Songnian Is on the Road and Never Getting Old]. *Falü Yu Shenghuo* 法律与生活 19 (2003).

33. Zheng Chengsi (郑成思)

(1944–2006)

Intellectual Property Law

Professor at the Law Institute of the Chinese Academy of Social Sciences, Zheng Chengsi was a pioneer and founding scholar of modern Chinese intellectual property law. He was given the honor of National Expert in intellectual property by the State Council in 1986. As a practitioner and promoter of intellectual property law in China, he was named to "the 50 Most Influential People in IP" in 2004, 2005, and 2006 by *Managing Intellectual Property* magazine of London.[1]

Educational Background

Zheng was born in Kunming (昆明) of Yunnan Province. He graduated from the Law Department of the Beijing College of Political Science and Law in 1967. From 1968 to 1975, Zheng was sent to a farm in Heilongjiang for reeducation and labor. Later he was assigned a job at a graphite mine. During this period, he taught himself English by reading and translating Mark Twain's *The Adventures of Tom Sawyer*. After the Cultural Revolution, Zheng came back to Beijing in 1979 and went to work at the International Law Department of the CASS Law Institute. In 1981, he passed the English exams and became a visiting scholar at the Faculty of

---

1. *Managing Intellectual Property* (London: Euromoney Publications, 1999–).

Law of the London School of Economics. In London, he met his mentor and good friend, Professor William R. Cornish, who gave him this advice: "Don't think you are nothing, and don't think you are everything."[2] This quote became a guiding motto for his future academic career. The following year, he published his first article in English, "Trademarks in China: The First Specific Law in the Field of Chinese Intellectual Property," in the *European Intellectual Property Review*.[3] He returned to China in 1983.

Career Highlights

After working at various jobs during the Cultural Revolution, Zheng returned to Beijing in 1975 and started his career at Beijing College of International Trade (now the University of International Business and Economics) and China International Publications Bureau from 1975 to 1979. Afterward, he went to work for the Law Institute of the Chinese Academy of Social Sciences. He was active in both academic and political spheres. Zheng was on the editorial board of several prestigious law journals, including the *European Intellectual Property Review*[4] and *China Legal Science*.[5] He served as director of the Intellectual Property Center of CASS.

Zheng was a member of the Ninth and Tenth National People's Congresses, an arbitrator of the China International Economic and Trade Arbitration Commission, and an arbitrator of the Arbitration Center of WIPO. Among many academic titles, he was vice chairman of the Chinese Intellectual Property Research Society and vice chairman of the Chinese Copyright Association. He was a member of the drafting group of China's first Copyright Law[6] and participated in the revisions of the Pat-

---

2. See Yang Xiaobo, "Zheng Chengsi," 626–27.

3. Zheng Chengsi, "Trademarks in China."

4. *European Intellectual Property Review* (Oxford, United Kingdom: ESC, Oct. 1978–).

5. For information about this journal, see footnote 3 in chapter 23 on Guo Daohui.

6. Zhonghua Renmin Gongheguo Zhuzuoquanfa 中华人民共和国著作权法 [The Copyright Law of the People's Republic of China) (promulgated by the Standing Committee of the National People's Congress, Sept. 7, 1990, effective June 1, 1991, amended in 2001, 2010, and 2020).

ent Law[7] and the Trademark Law.[8] He also participated in drafting other intellectual property legislation.

Zheng was an adviser to the International Copyright Society (IN-TERGU) and a member of the Executive Committee of the International Association for the Advancement of Teaching and Research in Intellectual Property (ATRIP). He was named one of "the 50 most influential people in IP."

Research Areas and Publications

Zheng is regarded by his peers as the top scholar in intellectual property law in China. When he began doing research in the field and publishing articles in the early 1980s, intellectual property was an unfamiliar topic in China. In 1982, he published his translation of Peter D. Rosenberg's *Patent Law Fundamentals*. He then produced China's first book on intellectual property in 1985.[9] His *Introduction to the International Agreement of Industrial Property*[10] was the only book addressing globalization and the regionalism of industrial property at the time in China. He wrote the first article on patent law after economic reforms took off in China.[11]

---

7. Zhonghua Renmin Gongheguo Zhuanlifa 中华人民共和国专利法 [The Patent Law of the People's Republic of China) (promulgated by the Standing Committee of the National People's Congress, Mar. 12, 1984, effective Apr. 1, 1985, amended in 1992, 2000, 2008, and 2020).

8. Zhonghua Renmin Gongheguo Shangbiafa 中华人民共和国商标法 [The Trademark Law of the People's Republic of China) (promulgated by the Standing Committee of the National People's Congress, Aug. 23, 1982, effective Mar. 1, 1983, amended in 1993, 2001, 2013, and 2019).

9. *Zhishi Chanquan Ruogan Wenti* 知识产权若干问题 [A Few Issues concerning Intellectual Property], (Lanzhou: Gansu Renmin Chubanshe, 1985).

10. *Gongye Chanquan Guoji Gongyue Gailun* 工业产权国际公约概论 [Introduction to the International Agreement of Industrial Property] (Beijing: Beijing Daxue Chubanshe, 1985).

11. "Shilun Woguo Jianli Zhuanli Zhidu De Biyaoxing" 试论我国建立专利制度的必要性 [On the Necessity for China to Establish a Patent System], *Faxue Yanjiu* 法学研究 6 (1980).

His article on the GATT was the first in China to address intellectual property issues.[12] In 1981, he published the first article on know-how.[13]

In his 1982 article "Copyright Law and the Free Circulations of Commodities"[14] and his 1986 article "On China's Complete Copyright Legislation,"[15] Zheng proposed many new ideas and provided practical advice. This included the idea that intellectual property was a form of commodity and should be used to gain profits through transfer, licensing, and other trade activities. His *Copyright Law* (1990)[16] and *On Intellectual Property* (1998)[17] became classic works in the field.

Through translations of foreign laws and sources, Zheng introduced new ideas, concepts, theories, and practice of intellectual property law to China. His own research addressed many important issues in the field. He promoted intellectual property as an independent discipline of study separate from the general studies of law. He explored the relationship between intellectual property and civil/business law. He pointed out that intellectual property was a special kind of civil right and defined the position of intellectual property in modern society.

As early as 1985, Zheng initiated discussions on the relationship between information property and intellectual property in the information age. His unique theoretical perspective on the topic was influential both in China and abroad. Based on his theory, Japan published the Strategic Outlines of Intellectual Property and the Basic Law of Intellectual Prop-

---

12. "Guanmao Zongxieding Yu Zhishi Chanquan" 关贸总协定与知识产权 [GATT and Intellectual Property], *Zhongguo Faxue* 中国法学 3 (1993).

13. "Cong Know-How De Yizhong Yifa Shuoqi" 从 Know-How 的一种译法说起 [Speaking from a Translation of Know-How], *Guoji Maoyi Wenti* 国际贸易问题 4 (1981).

14. "Banquanfa Yu Shangping De Ziyou Liutong" 版权法与商品的自由流通 [Copyright Law and the Free Circulation of Commodities], *Guowai Chuban Dongtai* 国外出版动态 6 (1982).

15. "Lun Woguo De Quanmian Banquan Lifa" (论我国的全面版权立法) [On China's Comprehensive Copyright Legislation], *Faxue Yanjiu* 法学研究 6 (1986).

16. *Banquanfa* 版权法 [Copyright Law] (Beijing: Zhongguo Renmin Daxue Chubanshe, 1990 [1st ed.], 1997 [2nd ed.]).

17. *Zhishi Chanquan Lun* 知识产权论 [On Intellectual Property] (Beijing: Falü Chubanshe, 1998).

erty in 2002, as well as put forward the basic national policy of "the Information Society Based on Intellectual Property Rights."[18]

In the 1990s, Zheng turned his focus to international trade and intellectual property, digital technology and intellectual property, and other topics. He followed the legislative process of the Agreement on Trade-Related Aspects of Intellectual Property Rights (TRIPS) closely. Within four months of the agreement being signed in 1994, Zheng published his translation of the document with Chinese and English side by side for comparison. He used TRIPS to help solve disputes during the U.S.-China intellectual property negotiations in 1994 and 1995.

Zheng believed that the intellectual property regime was not a perfect system. The key issue was to balance the rights of the property owners and the rest of people. The goal of intellectual property protection was to promote innovation rather than imitation and duplication. This was especially important in the information age.

Zheng published over thirty books in Chinese or English in China, England, the United States, and Australia. He authored or coauthored the most English-language legal books and articles among his generation of legal scholars.

Bibliography of English Publications by Professor Zheng Chengsi

Xue Hong and Zheng Chengsi. *Chinese Intellectual Property Law in the 21st Century.* Hong Kong: Sweet and Maxwell Asia, 2002.
———. *Software Protection in China: A Complete Guide.* Hong Kong: Sweet and Maxwell Asia, 1999.
Zheng Chengsi. "1992 Amendment of the Chinese Patent Law." *European Intellectual Property Review* 15, no. 1 (1993): 26–30.
———. "China: The Alternatives; Patent, Utility Model, or Design Registration." *European Intellectual Property Review* 9 (1987): 103–7.
———. *China's Intellectual Property and Technology Transfer Law.* Toronto: Carswell, 1987.

18. See Yang Xiaobo, "Zheng Chengsi," 630.

———. *Chinese Intellectual Property and Technology Transfer Law*. London: Sweet and Maxwell, 1987.

———. "The Chinese Patent Law of 1984." *European Intellectual Property Review* 6 (1984): 193–95.

———. *Copyright Law in China*. North Ryde, Australia: CCH Australia, 1991.

———. "The First Copyright Law of the People's Republic of China." *European Intellectual Property Review* 12, no. 10 (1990): 376–79.

———. "The First Unfair Competition Law of the PRC (China)." *European Intellectual Property Review* 16, no. 4 (1994): 181–82.

———. "The Future Chinese Copyright System and Its Context." *International Review of Industrial Property and Copyright Law* 15, no. 2 (1984): 141–68.

———. "GATT and Copyright Relations between the Mainland and Taiwan of China." *Social Science in China* 16, no. 1 (1995): 111–19.

———. "The Implementation of the Chinese Copyright Law." *Copyright World* 6 (1994): 38–41.

———. *Intellectual Property Enforcement in China: Leading Cases and Commentary*. Hong Kong: Sweet and Maxwell Asia, 1997.

———. "Intellectual Property and Information Property." *European Intellectual Property Review* 11 (1989): 327–29.

———. *Intellectual Property in the People's Republic of China*. London: Sweet and Maxwell / Stevens and Sons, 1988.

———. "Looking into the Revision of the Trademark and Copyright Laws from the Perspective of China's Accession to WTO." *European Intellectual Property Review* 24, no. 6 (2002): 313–23.

———. "The Protection of Computer Programs under the Chinese Copyright Law." *European Intellectual Property Review* 17, no. 7 (1995): 344–48.

———. "Trademarks in China: The First Specific Law in the Field of Chinese Intellectual Property." *European Intellectual Property Review* 4 (1982): 278–84.

———. "The TRIPS Agreement and Intellectual Protection in China." *Duke Journal of Comparative and International Law* 9 (1998): 219–519.

———. "TRIPS and the Amendment of Unfair Competition Laws in China." In *China's Participation in the WTO*, edited by Henry Gao and Donald Lewis, 231–40. London: Cameron May, 2005.

———. "TRIPS and Intellectual Property Protection in China." *European Intellectual Property Review* 19, no. 5 (1997): 243–46.

———. "Understanding the Protection of Neighboring Rights in China: The First Court Decision Regarding Performers' Rights." *Copyright World* 69, no. 4 (1997): 45–50.

Zheng Chengsi and Michael D. Pendleton. "China's First Court Decision on Copyright: Jiang v. Qiao and the Film 'Hospital Ward No. 16.'" *European Intellectual Property Review* 12, no. 6 (1990): 217–19.

———. *Chinese Intellectual Property and Technology Transfer Law*. London: Sweet and Maxwell, 1987.

———. *Copyright Law in China*. North Ryde, Australia: CCH International, 1991.

———. "A Response to United States Government Criticisms of the Chinese Copyright Law. (Includes 'Copyright Law of the People's Republic of China')." *European Intellectual Property Review* 13, no. 7 (1991): 257–66.

References

Shen Rengan 沈仁干. "Qianyan" 前言 [Preface]. In *Zheng Chengsi Banquan Wenji* 郑成思版权文集 [A Collection of Copyright Works by Zheng Chengsi], edited by Shen Rengan. Beijing: Zhongguo Renmin Daxue Chubanshe, 2008.

Yang Xiaobo 杨晓波. "Zheng Chengsi" 郑成思 [Zheng Chengsi]. In *20 Shiji Zhongguo Zhiming Kexuejia Xueshu Chengjiu Gailan: Faxuejuan* 20 世纪中国知名科学家学术成就概览: 法学卷 [Introduction to the Achievements of the Famous Chinese Scientists in the Twentieth Century: Law Volumes], vol. 3, edited by Jiang Ping 江平, et al. 625–37. Beijing: Kexue Chubanshe, 2014.

Zheng Chengsi 郑成思. *Zheng Chengsi Wenxuan* 郑成思文选 [Collected Works of Zheng Chengsi]. Beijing: Falü Chubanshe, 2003.

———. "Zheng Chengsi: Wode Zhishi Chanquan Yanjiu Zhilu" 郑成思：我的知识产权研究之路 [Zheng Chengsi: My Path to Intellectual Property Research]. http://www.law-walker.net/news.asp?id=35946&ctlgid=60 (accessed Dec. 26, 2020).

"Zheng Chengsi" 郑成思 [Zheng Chengsi]. http://baike.baidu.com/view/104028.htm (accessed Jan. 1, 2016).

Index

Harvard East Asian Monographs

(most recent titles)